**1986**

If the title of William Dicey's remarkable book calls to mind George Orwell's classic, that is because it, too, is about a dystopia, a country where things were not what they seemed and words did not mean what they meant; a country where apartheid meant separate development—not the assassinations, the exploitation, the forced removals and the rank racism that were, in fact, the very definition of its system of rule. This was a place so mired in doublespeak that one journalist felt compelled to attach an adjective to the word reform, lest his use be mistaken for the cynical spin that the government had attached to it. ... This book does not make for comfortable reading. But, then again, no book about South African history should. Read it!
– Jacob Dlamini

# 1986

William Dicey

**UMUZI**

Published in 2021 by Umuzi, an imprint of
Penguin Random House South Africa (Pty) Ltd
Company Reg No. 1953/000441/07
The Estuaries No. 4, Oxbow Crescent,
Century Avenue, Century City, 7441, South Africa
P O Box 1144, Cape Town, 8000, South Africa
www.penguinrandomhouse.co.za

First edition, first printing 2021
1 3 5 7 9 8 6 4 2

ISBN 978-1-4152-1052-9 (Print)
ISBN 978-1-4152-1065-9 (ePub)

Cover design by Michiel Botha
Cover images: AK-47 – Shutterstock; Winnie Mandela, P W Botha
and Gerrie Coetzee – Gallo Images; Casspir – Gideon Mendel
Image of dress shop window, Johannesburg, 1986 © Lesley Lawson
Text design by William Dicey
Set in Aldus 11/14

Printed and bound by Novus Print, South Africa

MIX
Paper from
responsible sources
FSC® C022948
www.fsc.org

*for* Hannah

# JANUARY

# Battle is on

**Staff Reporter**

ORGANISERS of tomorrow's Battle of the Bands concert at Greenpoint Stadium have sorted out their problems.

*The Argus*, 31 December 1985

ON 1 JANUARY 1986, in the early hours of the morning, a band of vigilantes invaded Moutse, a rural district adjacent to the self-governing homeland of KwaNdebele. Wielding axes and guns, they abducted several hundred men and boys from their villages and took them to a community hall in Siyabuswa, the capital of KwaNdebele. The floor of the hall was awash with soapy water and cooking oil. The vigilantes forced the villagers to strip naked and to exercise until they dropped from exhaustion. The vigilantes then flogged their captives with quirts and sjamboks as they flailed about in the slippery grime.

The torture lasted a full day and was personally overseen by Simon Skosana, the chief minister of KwaNdebele, and Piet Ntuli, the minister of the interior. The pair had recently formed the vigilante group, naming it Mbokodo, or 'the grindstone'. Its mandate was to take action against 'troublemakers'. Twenty people died on New Year's Day, and many were later treated for injuries at a nearby hospital. When Skosana was asked by a reporter whether he and Ntuli had been involved in the abduction and torture, he replied, 'That is a secret of the government.'

The raid was a direct result of a decision by Pretoria to incorporate Moutse into KwaNdebele. Pretoria wished to enlarge the homeland and so make it viable for independence. Moutse's 120 000 inhabitants, who stood to lose their South African citizenship, opposed the move. This angered the vigilantes. 'Why do you hate us?' they demanded of the villagers as they tortured them. 'Why don't you follow our leaders?'

By the mid-Eighties, forced removals had become politically costly for the South African government, and it had opted instead to redraw homeland boundaries. Still, its plans for Moutse and KwaNdebele made little sense. They ran contrary to Verwoerdian theory, which sought to group people by ethnicity (the inhabitants of Moutse were Sotho, while the homeland in which they now found themselves was Ndebele). And they contradicted President PW Botha's reformist rhetoric, in particular his recent promise that homelands that did not want independence would be permitted to remain part of South Africa (the vast majority of KwaNdebele's inhabitants opposed independence).

Witnesses reported that South African security forces were present at the raid and did nothing to stop it. Some even reported that army trucks had transported the vigilantes to Moutse. 'Wherever Mbokodo is,' said one resident, 'you will always see the Casspir behind them, you will always see the van behind them.'

KwaNdebele had become the country's tenth and final homeland in 1974. The state had purchased nineteen white-owned cattle farms and had installed a government, thereby transforming a tract of veld into a self-governing territory. In reality, KwaNdebele was a dumping ground for the unwanted: evicted farmworkers; people forcibly removed from 'black spots'; non-Tswanas expelled from Bophuthatswana; and refugees from overcrowded townships. Almost all of them landed up in 'closer settlements', Pretoria's terminology for vast rural shanty towns. When the American journalist Joseph Lelyveld visited Kwaggafontein in 1981 (many parts of KwaNdebele still bore the Afrikaans names of the original farms), he encountered 'a rash of closer settlements spotted over open veld'. On a return visit two years later, the area had become 'part of a nearly continuous resettlement belt'. A hillside he recalled from his first visit 'no longer looked like a hillside. What it had become was a slight swell in a sea of shanties.'

He observes that 'such sights can be seen in other countries, usually as a result of famines or wars. I don't know where else they have been achieved as a result of planning.' The plan, of course, was to rid South Africa of its black citizens. When this proved impractical, principally due to the labour requirements of a growing economy, the government sought instead to limit the number of blacks who stayed within the country's borders overnight. Apartheid regulations created a commuter class, people who worked in South Africa by day and returned to the homelands at night. In essence, the closer settlements of KwaNdebele were labour dormitories. Bus stops appeared before taps or toilets.

Early one morning in 1983, Lelyveld and photographer David Goldblatt made their way to Wolwekraal depot, a fenced-off clearing in the bush in which fifty-odd Putco buses were parked. The first bus of the day had departed at 1 a.m. to fetch drivers. The next bus was scheduled to depart at 2.45, arriving at Marabastad terminal in Pretoria three hours later. 'At that place and that hour,' remarks Lelyveld, 'the sight of a couple of whites on the bus was as much to be expected as that of a couple of commuting walruses.'

Lelyveld's account of the journey appears in his book *Move Your Shadow*.* He sets the scene with some background information. The bus company Putco started servicing the route between Pretoria and KwaNdebele in 1979, with two buses a day. Putco had to draw its own maps, as its buses 'came in right behind the bulldozers'. A year later, it was running 60 buses a day, and by 1984 over 250. The cost of this service was far beyond what menial labourers could afford to pay, and so a crucial aspect of Putco's business – more important even than diesel or

---

* The title comes from the golfing section of an English-Fanagalo phrase book: 'Have you caddied before? I don't want a useless boy … Move your shadow. Don't rattle the bag.'

maintenance – was negotiating subsidies. By 1984, the bus subsidy was Pretoria's largest single expenditure on KwaNdebele. It was larger than the homeland's GDP.

Lelyveld interviewed a number of passengers. They had common woes. Even with the subsidy, the bus fares ate up a quarter of their wages. They got back home long after dark, and still had to wash, eat, see that their children had food to take to school the next day. Many worked six days a week. Only on Sundays did they get to see their families in daylight. Lelyveld calculates that 23 000 people made the KwaNdebele–Pretoria run each day and that many of them travelled further each year than a circumnavigation of the globe. All this on hard wooden seats designed for short hauls.

Goldblatt's photographs appear in *The Transported of KwaNdebele*. His grainy black-and-white images reveal a journey at once mundane (to those who made it every day) and yet remarkable (to those seeing it for the first time). The opening photograph features five men caught in the light of Goldblatt's flash. They are standing on the verge of a dirt road, surrounded by inky blackness. The caption explains that it is 2.40 in the morning and that these men spend up to eight hours a day on buses. Goldblatt shows passengers boarding, yawning, wrapping themselves in blankets. By 3.15, the seating is full and new passengers have to stand. By 3.30, the standing passengers have all slumped to the floor. Everyone is asleep. Some passengers are using their bags or bits of foam to cushion their heads against the windows or against the seats in front of them. It's as if this one bus trip – the boredom, the hardship, the endurance – comes to represent all of apartheid. Goldblatt would later say: 'I wasn't on the scene at the riots and the focal points of political life … events themselves were for me much less interesting than the conditions that lead to events. I was looking obliquely at things.'

*The Transported of KwaNdebele* features an essay titled 'The

Bus Stop Republic' as well as the oral testimony of a number of commuters:

> With us people, we get up at two o'clock in the night. You must wash yourself, you are a woman, you are a man, you must wash yourself, you must straighten yourself out. The first bus is at three o'clock. ... Sometimes you still miss the bus. You lose it. It is gone, or maybe it is too full. The next bus is at half past three and then again at four ... It takes about twenty minutes to that bus stop. And you must *walk*. You can't walk slowly. It is thirty minutes to get there if you take it easy. If the seats are full, we must stand in the aisle, so tightly packed. You sleep, you stand, you sleep. You fall on the one in front of you, and he falls on the next one, and we fall, we fall, we fall.

~

On 3 January, British heavyweight Frank Bruno, who had agreed to fight Gerrie Coetzee in a world title eliminator, shrugged off calls by the Anti-Apartheid Movement for the fight to be cancelled. 'I am a boxer, not a politician,' he said. 'I am just out to make an honest crust.'

~

On 8 January, Oliver Tambo, president of the African National Congress, delivered his organisation's annual January 8 statement. Speaking in Lusaka, Zambia, Tambo summarised the situation back home:

> Realising that power is slipping out of its hands, the Botha regime ... adopted new and more brutal ways of governing our country ... These include the proclamation of martial

law, handing over administration of large areas of our country to the murderous army and police, the use of secret death squads, the assassination of our leaders, massacres, mass arrests, stringent control of the press, continuing external aggression and the murder of our people outside the country.

In his 1985 statement, Tambo had called for a 'people's war in our country', with a view to rendering South Africa 'ungovernable'. In his 1986 statement, he expressed satisfaction with progress on this front and reiterated his call: 'We must continue to make South Africa ungovernable and apartheid unworkable.' Tambo declared 1986 the Year of Umkhonto we Sizwe, the ANC's military wing. 'Let us turn every corner of our country into a battlefield!'

These annual statements set the tone for the coming year. Distributed as leaflets and broadcast over Radio Freedom, they were the ANC's way of coordinating resistance in the townships. Cyril Ramaphosa, a leading trade unionist at the time, was later asked whether Lusaka had issued orders. 'Ja,' he replied. 'Those were the days we would scrutinise the January 8 statements very closely and carefully to watch out for calls being made on us.'

~

On 12 January, President PW Botha turned seventy. He celebrated at a restaurant in Wilderness, in the southern Cape. There were ninety guests in attendance, most of them senior members of the National Party. A former minister, Alwyn Schlebusch, was master of ceremonies. He presented Botha with an inflatable boat fitted with an outboard engine. 'I hope you will be as good a pilot of this gift,' said Schlebusch, 'as you are of this country's affairs.'

~

On 19 January, Leabua Jonathan, the prime minister of Lesotho, was deposed by his own military. The coup was provoked by South Africa, which entirely surrounds the mountain kingdom, and which for weeks had been enforcing an economic blockade. Within days of the coup, Lesotho expelled sixty members of the ANC and goods once again flowed across the border.

Jonathan had ruled his country ever since independence in 1966. Initially, he'd been on friendly terms with the South African government. In 1967, his counterpart, John Vorster, had entertained him at the Mount Nelson Hotel in Cape Town. Vorster had used the occasion to promote his doctrine of 'mutual respect and non-interference in another's domestic affairs'. When right-wingers took Vorster to task for entertaining a black man, he argued that the meeting had been 'interstate not interpersonal'.

In 1970, Jonathan was defeated in a general election. A South African-trained paramilitary force helped him seize control of the state, and from this point forward he ruled with dictatorial powers. Over time, the youth league of Jonathan's Basuto National Party started to show increasing solidarity with ANC members based in the country. Jonathan followed their lead, gradually shifting from a client of Pretoria to a critic. In 1975, he hailed the independence of Mozambique and Angola. The following year, he condemned the Soweto massacre and refused to recognise Transkei's independence.

South Africa responded with a programme of economic and military destabilisation. Its first move was to establish a surrogate force. The Lesotho Liberation Army was ostensibly the armed wing of a local opposition party, but in fact was trained and funded by the South African Bureau of State Security. As a leader of the LLA explained at the time, they had opted to 'ride on the back of the devil to cross the river'. In 1979, the LLA embarked on a campaign of sabotage and terror, bombing economic installations and government offices. They slipped in and out of South Africa with impunity, and on one occasion even launched a mortar barrage from South African soil, targeting Lesotho's only petrol depot.

Not to be outdone, the South African Defence Force launched a brutal night-time raid on Maseru in December 1982. A heliborne commando force landed in the capital, which was then lit up with powerful searchlights mounted on the South African side of the Caledon River. Thirty ANC members were killed, along with twelve Lesotho nationals. Speaking at their funeral, Oliver Tambo warned white South Africans that they too 'would have to start burying their dead'. In the wake of the raid, Lesotho was forced to deport a number of ANC members. Its foreign minister announced that the country 'could no longer withstand South African military and economic pressure'.

And yet Jonathan remained obdurate. He refused to sign a bilateral 'security' pact and openly declared his support for the ANC. South Africa supplemented the sabotage and bombing with sporadic border closures. It also threatened to refuse entry to Basotho migrant workers, whose remittances accounted for over forty per cent of their country's GDP. In December 1985, a Vlakplaas death squad, led by Colonel Eugene de Kock of the South African Police, raided two homes in Maseru. They killed nine people, including two senior Umkhonto we Sizwe operatives.

On 1 January 1986, South Africa closed its borders with Lesotho and enforced a total economic blockade. Supplies of food, medicine and petrol quickly dwindled. South Africa demanded the right to vet Lesotho's refugees, but Jonathan refused. The population became restive. On 16 January, three days before the coup, General Justice Lekhanya led a delegation to negotiate with the South Africans. Then, the day before the coup, Jonathan announced that he was seeking assistance from Cuba. Lekhanya, who was staunchly anti-communist, used this as a pretext to seize power. Given how swiftly the ANC was expelled and the blockade lifted, it seems clear that Lekhanya had agreed in advance to South Africa's terms. Two months after the coup, the countries issued a joint statement. Their respective territories were not to be used for acts of terrorism against one another.

Three months after the coup, Dan O'Meara, writing for the Toronto-based *Southern Africa Report*, observed:

> The blockade against Lesotho has sharply undermined Pretoria's own propaganda offensive against sanctions. If it is admissible for South Africa to force political change in Lesotho through sanctions, presumably it is admissible to use sanctions to try to do the same in South Africa. Moreover, as the coup proved, sanctions work.

~

On 21 January, at the Wanderers Stadium in Johannesburg, the South African cricket team won the third and final 'unofficial test' against the touring 'rebel' Australians, thereby securing the series. Facing a first-innings deficit, South Africa needed a big score in their second innings. Forty-one-year-old Graeme Pollock was unbeaten on fifty when a ball reared up off a length and broke his finger. He left the field, only to return when his team was nine wickets down. Prodding and poking with one hand, he hung around long enough for Kevin McKenzie to complete his century at the other end.

The tour was controversial, as South Africa was banned from international cricket at the time. Ever since the Fifties, sport had been a target of anti-apartheid protest, with demonstrators rallying behind slogans such as 'No normal sport in an abnormal society'. A key moment came in 1968, when exiled cricketer Basil D'Oliveira was selected by England to tour South Africa, the country of his birth. Under apartheid, D'Oliveira had been classified as 'Coloured'. His selection prompted then prime minister John Vorster to say: 'The team, as it stands, is not the team of the MCC selection committee but of the political opponents of South Africa.' The Marylebone Cricket Club immediately cancelled the tour.

The D'Oliveira affair sparked a concerted effort to ban South Africa not only from international cricket, but from all international sport. In 1970, South Africa played its last official cricket test match for over two decades. That same year, it was expelled from the Olympic movement, having been barred from the two preceding Games. In 1977, the United Nations called on member states to cease all sporting contact with South Africa. Pretoria responded in two ways. First, it softened its ban on 'multi-racial' sport by introducing 'multi-national' sport. 'We will have a representative Zulu team,' minister Piet Koornhof told a puzzled world, 'and a South African representative Xhosa team, Coloured team, Indian team, etcetera.' The teams would be permitted to play against one another. Pretoria's second response was to organise 'unofficial' tours. Individual sportsmen, many of them either marginal players or former stars nearing retirement, were paid vast sums to represent their 'countries' in South Africa.

In all, there were seven rebel cricket tours. The first, in 1982, was an English outfit known as 'The Dirty Dozen'. A Labour politician accused the players of 'selling themselves for blood-covered Krugerrands'. Next was Sri Lanka, then the West Indies (twice), Australia (twice) and finally England again. The punishments meted out to the rebel cricketers by their home countries varied widely. The English and Australians received short bans (in the case of the Australians, their two-year bans included the two seasons they'd played in South Africa). The Sri Lankans and West Indians were banned for life. They were ostracised when they got home and, for some of them, the fallout from the tours wrecked not only their careers but their lives.

Australian prime minister Bob Hawke branded the rebels

'traitors' for giving 'aid and comfort to that regime in South Africa … which is so blatantly and desperately seeking international legitimacy'. Hawke wasn't, however, in a position to throw stones. As bowler Rodney Hogg put it: 'I thought that if it was okay for Hawke to trade with South Africa, it was okay for me to go and play cricket there.' When interviewed about the tour thirty years later, Hogg had no regrets: 'I was happy with the money on offer. My career was pretty much over by then. Fast bowlers don't last forever.' Hogg took the line that he was a professional sportsman and was simply doing his job. Many of the South African players felt the same way. One could say of them what a biographer later said of Ali Bacher, head of the South African Cricket Board at the time and the prime mover behind the rebel tours:

> In truth, he did not have a thorough understanding of the political problems bedevilling his country. He was not alone; the majority of white South Africans were living in a cocoon of ignorance or disinterest. Naively, they wondered why politics was being dragged into sport.

~

On 24 January, Anton Rupert, businessman and founder of the Rembrandt Group, sent a private letter to President PW Botha. Rupert was following up on a recent meeting between the two men. It was a myth that apartheid guaranteed 'the white man's survival', he wrote. 'As a matter of fact, it jeopardises his survival. Apartheid is seen by too many as a transgression against humanity.' Rupert's letter, which ran to six pages, was an impassioned plea for Botha to reject apartheid: 'It is crucifying us; it is destroying our language; it is degrading for a once heroic nation to be the lepers of the world.'

Rupert's letter came at a time of growing calls from business for the government to reform apartheid. The majority of these calls were pragmatic rather than moral. For decades, business had profited from cheap labour. Indeed, critics have observed that the provision of a cheap and controllable workforce was a more fundamental feature of apartheid than the prohibitions on mixed marriages or sex across the colour line. By the mid-Eighties, however, the costs of apartheid had begun to outweigh the benefits.

Ever since the Soweto uprising of 1976, companies had been operating in a siege economy. They were cut off from technical innovations and foreign markets, and labour relations were volatile. As the economy developed, several industries experienced a shortage of skilled employees. Industry bodies called for the abolition of job reservation and for the urbanisation of the black workforce. Foreign correspondent Patti Waldmeir observes that business fought much harder for economic change than for political change.

In September 1985, a few months before Rupert wrote his letter, another wealthy businessman had called for an end to apartheid. 'We must do away with a system that has been wrong for forty years,' said Louis Luyt in an interview. Luyt, a proud National Party supporter and long-time apologist for apartheid, had played a key role in the the government's secret propaganda war (which journalists had exposed in the Information Scandal of the late Seventies). Using government funds, Luyt had tried to buy the company that owned the *Rand Daily Mail* and the *Cape Times*. When this venture failed, he started *The Citizen*, an ostensibly independent newspaper over which the Department of Information exercised full editorial control. Luyt was surprisingly frank in the interview: 'Whether business likes it or not, it has benefitted from apartheid. It is only now that apartheid has turned against them that they are seeking its removal.'

Also in September 1985, Gavin Relly, the chairman of Anglo American, led a delegation of businessmen and journalists to

Lusaka to meet with the ANC. Rupert had agreed to join them, but pulled out when PW Botha warned publicly of 'disloyalty' and of legitimating 'terrorists'. The position in which big business found itself in the mid-Eighties is perhaps best summed up by political economist John Saul: 'The dominant classes, mounted on the tiger of racial capitalism, now find that they can neither ride it entirely comfortably, nor easily dismount.' Neither Rupert nor Relly nor Luyt was explicitly in favour of a universal franchise. Relly was on record for having said that one-person, one-vote was 'a formula for unadulterated chaos at this point in our history'. Luyt, in the same interview in which he called for the abolition of apartheid, warned: 'We are not going to give this country away. There is no point in exchanging a bad white government for a bad black government.'

In referring to the Afrikaner nation as 'the lepers of the world', Rupert was locating himself in an unusual tradition. In 1960, shortly after the massacre at Sharpeville, *Die Burger*, an Afrikaans daily, had taken stock of the country's international reputation. It concluded that South Africa was 'die muishond van die wêreld'. Ambrose Reeves, the Anglican Bishop of Johannesburg, provided a loose translation when he called the apartheid government 'the polecat of the Western World'. Reeves was deported the following year.

In 1975, diplomat Les de Villiers published *South Africa: A Skunk Among Nations*. The title of his book comes from *Die Burger*'s 'muishond' comment. While 'polecat' is a more accurate translation, 'skunk' captures the moral dimension. Prospective readers of De Villiers's book might have expected him to be critical of apartheid, but in fact the title is ironic. *Skunk* is a diatribe against hypocrisy and double standards. De Villiers lists the sins of other countries – the Soviet Union killing dissidents, Australia issuing visas based on race – as well as the fact that Arafat was invited to join the UN the same year Vorster was expelled. 'South Africa,' De Villiers concludes, 'is one of a crowd in our all too imperfect world society.' When the Info Scandal hit, it emerged that De Villiers worked for the Department of Information. He was head of covert operations in the US. Writing the book was part of his job; it was simply another way of influencing international opinion.

The muishond-skunk-leper labels weighed heavily on Afrikaners. They had once been the darlings of the world, and now they were pariahs. 'A hundred years ago, my ethnic group was one of the most loved and admired people,' observes columnist Max du Preez. 'The nations of the world could not get enough of this quaint tribe of simple, proud people who stood up to the mighty British Empire.' Kenneth Kaunda, then president of Zambia, told Du Preez that all Africans were proud of the way in which the Afrikaners had fought the British. 'But your people were misled by despots after that.'

In his inaugural address in 1994, President Nelson Mandela announced: 'Never, never and never again shall it be that this beautiful land will again experience the oppression of one by another and suffer the indignity of being the skunk of the world.'

~

On 26 January, Vincent Crapanzano, an American anthropologist, wrote the preface to a new edition of *Waiting: The Whites of South Africa* (his book had first appeared the previous year). Crapanzano observes in the preface that most white South Africans had little direct experience of the unrest sweeping their country: 'They may note a new sullenness in their workers or complain about the cheekiness of the clerks in the hypermarket … but, for the most part, they concern themselves with the details of their everyday lives.'

Anthropologists usually study the dominated. Crapanzano, however, was interested in 'the effect of domination on the dominating'. What was the psychological toll of apartheid on the whites? For several months, he lived in a small town in the Cape winelands and conducted interviews with the inhabitants. He didn't lack for informants: 'Self-description is, like rugby, a national pastime.'

Crapanzano found people trapped in a state of waiting. Liberals and conservatives alike were 'waiting for something, anything, to happen'. Whereas black South Africans had a sense that time was on their side, white South Africans viewed the future 'with bewilderment and anxiety'. Their waiting didn't have a particular focus; rather, it was premised on a vague dread that history would have its way with them.

~

On 27 January, Bishop Desmond Tutu returned from a three-week tour of the United States. He landed in Johannesburg and 'stepped into a gale-force domestic controversy', as one newspaper put it. While on tour, Tutu had, for the first time, publicly supported the ANC. He had also raised the spectre of the liberation movement attacking 'soft targets':

> Most white households still have their morning coffee brought to them by black servants. Supposing the ANC, or whoever is behind all this, were able to [reach] even just a quarter of those servants and say: 'Look, here is something that we want you to slip into their early morning coffee.'

Facing a barrage of journalists and television crews at Jan Smuts Airport, Tutu defended himself. Far from encouraging domestic workers to poison their employers, he said, he had in fact been highlighting the 'apocalyptic' prospects which faced the country if South Africans failed to resolve their problems peacefully.

~

23

On 31 January, in his opening speech to Parliament, President Botha offered to free Nelson Mandela if the Soviet Union agreed to release dissidents Andrei Sakharov and Natan Sharansky, and if Angola agreed to release Wynand du Toit, a Special Forces recce who had been captured while sabotaging an oil refinery in Cabinda.

Bishop Tutu asked the obvious question: 'What has Nelson's release to do with Sakharov?'

A year earlier to the day, also in a speech in Parliament, Botha had offered to release Mandela on condition that he 'rejected violence as a political instrument'. Botha had ended this earlier offer on a bold note: 'It is therefore not the South African government which now stands in the way of Mr Mandela's freedom. It is he himself.' Mandela, incarcerated in Pollsmoor, listened to Botha's speech on the radio. By his reckoning, it was the government's sixth conditional offer to release him. As early as 1973, his freedom had been dangled before him, so long as he agreed to live a quiet life in the self-governing territory of Transkei.

Mandela considered his options. He needed to reassure the ANC that he wasn't about to renounce the armed struggle, and yet he didn't wish to slam the door on a negotiated settlement. Ten days after Botha's 1985 speech, the United Democratic Front held a rally in Soweto's Jabulani Stadium to pay tribute to Tutu, who had recently won the Nobel Peace Prize. Mandela's daughter Zindzi, the only member of his family not silenced by a banning order, took to the podium to read his response: 'I am surprised at the conditions that the government wants to impose on me. I am not a violent man.' The crowd went berserk. It was the first time Mandela's words had been heard in public in over twenty years. 'Only free men can negotiate,' read Zindzi. 'Prisoners cannot enter into contracts.'

Mandela turned the tables on Botha, pointing out that it wasn't the liberation movement that had started the violence:

It was … only when all other forms of resistance were no longer open to us, that we turned to armed struggle. Let Botha show he is different to Malan, Strijdom and Verwoerd. Let him renounce violence. Let him say that he will dismantle apartheid.

Botha summoned Kobie Coetsee, his minister of justice. 'We have painted ourselves in a corner,' he said. 'Can you get us out?' In the years to come, Coetsee would play a pivotal role in setting up talks between the government and Mandela.

The Sakharov offer aside, Botha's 1986 speech was genuinely reformist. He spoke of political power-sharing and common citizenship in an undivided country. He promised that influx control, which included the hated pass-book system, would soon be abolished. 'We have outgrown the outdated concept of apartheid.'

Trying to make sense of Botha's politics can be tricky. In the early years of his reign, he was far more reformist than any of his predecessors had been. In 1979, he warned Afrikaners that they needed to 'adapt or die'. He told them that 'a system in which material welfare is limited to a few within a sea of poverty is not only indefensible, it is objectionable'. Botha introduced many reforms, but they tended to focus more on the symbols of apartheid than on its fundamental structure. Historian Leonard Thompson characterises Botha's administration as 'a complex attempt to adapt to changing circumstances without sacrificing Afrikaner power'. In his book *The Imperial Presidency*, Brian Pottinger includes 'A Note on Terminology':

*Reform*: undoubtedly the most overworked and misunderstood word in the lexicon. In this book 'reform' is used to refer to President PW Botha's programme of adaptive change to classical apartheid, but where the word is meant to imply something more profound it is qualified as 'fundamental reform'.

By the mid-Eighties, however, with the township rebellion in full swing, Botha was less a reformist than a bad-tempered bully. Or, rather, he alternated, seemingly at random, between reform and repression. 'I try to be a man of peace,' he would say in 1987, 'but if people tempt me I can be a Thunderbird.'

Botha's contradictions are easier to understand – if not condone – when viewed in the light of his 'total strategy'. Prior to becoming prime minister in 1978 (and state president in 1983), Botha had for over a decade been minister of defence. Under his leadership, a new class of securocrats emerged and the military came to have a major say in government. The securocrats, perceiving a 'total onslaught' by communist forces, studied counter-revolutionary tactics, particularly those employed in Vietnam, Algeria, Malaysia, Chile and El Salvador. 'We're using the same hearts-and-minds technique here,' explained a senior member of the security establishment. 'First we neutralise the enemy, then we win over the people so they will reject the ANC.' Botha's 'total strategy', in other words, called for both reform and repression.

~

On 31 January, the same day that President Botha announced his reforms in Parliament, journalist and activist Zubeida Jaffer was detained by the security police. She was three months pregnant at the time. 'I know just what I'm going to do to you,' said Captain Frans Mostert. 'I have prepared a chemical for you to drink if you do not want to cooperate. You know what that will do to your baby? It will kill it. It will burn your baby from your body.'

Jaffer did not cooperate. As she later told the Truth and Reconciliation Commission, 'If [my daughter] is brought into this world thinking that her mother gave information so that she could live, that is a heavy burden for a child to carry.' Jaffer's decision was stone-cold brave. Mostert had a reputation for sexually assaulting female detainees; there was no reason to think he was bluffing. Besides, Jaffer had been poisoned by the police once before.

In 1980, Jaffer had been detained for exposing police brutality on the Cape Flats. She was twenty-two at the time, just a few months into her first job as a reporter at the *Cape Times*. She had access to the coloured community and was thus able to report on events that remained undisclosed by the police. The *New Statesman* noted that her reports were 'far more detailed and authentic than a white journalist, however well intentioned, could have produced'. Jaffer had been apprehended early one morning at her parents' home by Spyker van Wyk, a security policeman with a reputation even more notorious than the one Mostert would later achieve. Jaffer describes Van Wyk in her memoir *Our Generation*: 'Beady black eyes, white mat face, black hair oiled down flat on either side of a path running down the middle of his head. Hitler without a moustache. In our living room.'

Van Wyk had refused to tell Jaffer why she was being detained. When she asked whether he was taking her to Pollsmoor, he replied, 'Pollsmoor Prison is a five-star hotel compared to where you are going.' He then threatened to break her nose.

Van Wyk got his nickname 'Spyker' (nail) for nailing a detainee's foreskin to a desk. According to the final report of the Truth Commission, 'Warrant Officer Hernus J P "Spyker" van Wyk is the individual most consistently associated with torture in the Western Cape over a thirty year period.' This was the man who had held Jaffer in solitary confinement in 1980, who had beaten her, tortured her and even poisoned her. During one particularly brutal beating, a black security policeman was urged to 'rape her, just rape her' as she lay crumpled up on the floor. 'And this man came up to me,' Jaffer testified, 'and he … and he … he didn't actually rape me, but he … the threat of it was … I felt I was going to die at that point.'

On her release from her first spell in detention, all that Jaffer was charged with was possession of Frantz Fanon's *The Wretched of the Earth* and two other banned books. Jaffer left the *Cape Times* to continue her activism. 'After that detention, I became obsessed with changing the apartheid system. I couldn't really think of anything else. I felt that I'd been in the belly of the beast and I'd been confronted with the darker side of our country, and I was completely drawn into the mission of wanting to bring an end to that.' She joined the Clothing Workers Union and became an organiser for the United Democratic Front.

The reason given for Jaffer's second detention, in January 1986, was the making of thousands of little black, green and gold flags. Winnie Mandela had approached the UDF structures in the Cape, telling them that the Commonwealth was about to send a group of 'eminent persons' to visit the country. The group was scheduled to meet with her husband in Pollsmoor and it seemed likely that he would be released either shortly before or shortly after their visit. It would fall to the Cape structures, said Mandela, to prepare the celebrations for this great day. Jaffer set about organising the production of kilometres of bunting in ANC colours. On the fifth night of sewing, the police surrounded the factory and arrested the seamstresses.

Two weeks later, Jaffer was detained in a street in Athlone, along with her husband Johnny Issel. The police used several vehicles for the arrest and a helicopter hovered overhead. While Jaffer's ANC bunting would certainly have piqued the interest of the security police, Issel was likely their main target. He was one of the leaders of the UDF in the western Cape and had spent the better part of the previous decade either under banning orders or in detention. Issel was a dedicated revolutionary: his sons (by his first marriage) were named Yasser and Fidel.

Jaffer was held incommunicado, without access to a doctor or a lawyer. (As it happened, her lawyer had also been detained.) When she was eventually allowed to see a state gynaecologist, 'he was more interested in me providing him with explanations of arms caches in Gugulethu than he was in providing me with details of my [pregnancy]'. Jaffer's cell was a great improvement on the one she'd been held in six years earlier. 'I was definitely enjoying the privileges that comrades had fought for and died for in police cells all over the country. How much pain and sadness did so many people suffer for this cell to be clean and this bed to be my sleeping place?'

After Jaffer's release in June 1986, Mostert continued to harass her. Days before she was due to give birth, he knocked on her door, shouting, 'Maak oop, Zubeida. Open up.' She watched his 'pink arm' pull the curtain aside and smelt his 'sour odour'. With her 'huge belly swaying from side to side', she marched across the road to a local shop and escaped through the back. Her brother was waiting in a car and took her to their parents' home. Three days after she gave birth to a healthy daughter, Mostert barged into the house, brushing her father aside. When Jaffer saw him enter her bedroom with his 'red face' and 'liquor-bloated body in a cream safari suit', she became hysterical. She screamed 'like a woman possessed' until he left the house. In her memoir, Jaffer reports that for herself and Issel the Eighties were 'ten years of ongoing harassment'. There were 'always cops sitting in cars outside our home. … They kept on crossing the threshold and barging in, week after week, month after month.'

Years later, the National Prosecuting Authority approached Jaffer to ask whether she wanted to prosecute Mostert (Van Wyk had died by then). Mostert hadn't given evidence before the Truth Commission, and so didn't qualify for immunity. Jaffer declined:

They had already taken ten years of my life. And I didn't want to give more of my life to them. I wanted to be free of them. In my mind they were just small men in the overall scheme of things; little cogs in the wheel. And what was important was to discard the apartheid system. The more I see the situation improving here, if I see African people confident and I see my daughter not being a second-class citizen, then that for me is my vengeance.

# FEBRUARY

# Price comparisons

USING a basic list of monthly grocery supplies an average housewife would compile to feed her family of four, the cost difference in 10 years is staggering. The list had the following items on it with a comparison of prices charged in 1976 and 1986:

|  | 1976 | 1986 |
|---|---|---|
| Milk (30ℓ) | R7.83 | R24.90 |
| Meat: | | |
| Rump (3 kg) | R7.90 | R31.14 |
| Topside (3 kg) | R5.98 | R23.34 |
| Sirloin (3 kg) | R6.41 | R23.94 |
| Mutton chops (3 kg) | R5.49 | R29.64 |
| Chicken (4kg) | R3.96 | R13.68 |
| Butter (4 kg) | R5.48 | R21.44 |
| Cheese (4 kg) | R6.66 | R19.96 |
| Eggs (4 doz) | R1.81 | R5.12 |
| Coffee (1 kg) | R2.16 | R42.76 |
| Tea (500g) | R1.27 | R5.78 |
| Sugar (2,5 kg) | 43c | R2.09 |
| Bread (15 loaves) | R2.60 | R10.50 |
| Cereal flakes (2 kg) | R1.27 | R5.16 |
| Rice (2 kg) | R1.53 | R3.88 |
| Vegetables (mixed, fresh) | R15 | R35.00 |
| Bacon (500g) | R1.18 | R4.30 |
| | | |
| Monthly Grocery Bill | R76.96 | R302.43 |

NOTE: GST payable on some items listed for 1986 has not been included.
● The same grocery list for 1966 would have cost R39.27.

*Weekend Argus*, 1 February 1986

ON 2 FEBRUARY, the *Sunday Times* reprinted an article from *Style* magazine. The article noted that many people were thinking of emigrating because of the 'disappearing rand' and predictions of a 'bloodbath'. It listed 101 reasons for staying, including the following:

Braais are not the same in Houston, Perth, Toronto or
    Birmingham
America is full of people who say 'Have a nice day'
    when they couldn't care less if you dropped dead
No gardeners, cooks, housemaids elsewhere
Biltong
You can't throw naartjies at the ref in England.

~

On 7 February, in a speech in Parliament, Frederik Van Zyl Slabbert, the leader of the opposition, announced that South Africa had been 'torn apart' the previous year. Parliament's response, he said, had been 'a grotesque ritual of irrelevance'. Slabbert's speech was brimming with contempt for the ruling party. He denounced President Botha's reforms as a sham and spoke of the frustration of being 'trapped in a ridiculous political debate, while outside our country is bleeding'. Slabbert ended his speech with a bombshell: he was resigning with immediate effect.

Slabbert had spent much of his time in Parliament exposing the contradictions between the promises of apartheid ideology and the reality of its implementation. But to little avail. He observed in an interview that not only had he been powerless to stop the government's abuses, but also that he had been used to lend it legitimacy. He was tired, he said, of being hauled out as 'exhibit A for the government's sense of a democracy'. Slabbert's resignation was explosive precisely because the legitimising had come to an end.

Max du Preez, a parliamentary reporter at the time, noted 'utter shock in the eyes of PW Botha and his men'. One of these was Chris Heunis, minister of constitutional development. He later said that Slabbert's resignation had plunged him into 'deep despair about the future of parliamentary politics'. Alex Boraine, a fellow member of Slabbert's Progressive Federal Party, resigned a week later. He reported that most of their colleagues 'were very angry at Van Zyl's move'. Helen Suzman, doyenne of the PFP, accused Slabbert of selfishness and betrayal. The ANC, meanwhile, was effusive in its praise. 'Never in the history of our country,' declared Thabo Mbeki, 'has a white establishment political leader confronted the iniquity of ... minority domination as Dr Slabbert has today.'

Both Slabbert and Boraine sensed that the centre of gravity in South African politics was moving from the white sphere to the black. Following their resignation as MPs, they devoted their energies to extra-parliamentary politics. In 1987, they launched Idasa, the Institute for a Democratic Alternative for South Africa. Their aim, said Boraine, was 'to put negotiation politics firmly on the agenda'. They organised several international meetings between groups of white South Africans and the ANC. The best known of these meetings took place in Dakar, Senegal, in 1987. It was widely covered in the press and helped give the ANC a human face. Before Dakar, the idea of the Afrikaner establishment talking to the ANC was unthinkable. Afterwards, it seemed inevitable. In a Festschrift compiled for Slabbert's seventieth birthday, several contributors honour him for the role he played in persuading South Africans that their best option was a negotiated settlement.

Slabbert's resignation struck a blow at the heart of apartheid ideology. Historian Hermann Giliomee observes that ideology was important to the Afrikaners. Without it, 'apartheid's gratuitous cruelty, its greed and unfair privileges could no longer be justified'. The Nationalists were impelled to negotiate, says Giliomee, not by sanctions or unrest, but by the collapse of their moral convictions.

Slabbert's resignation came at a time when many of the ideological underpinnings of apartheid were starting to give way. A few years earlier, the Afrikaner-Broederbond, a secret society that acted as an advance guard on government thinking, had done a U-turn on apartheid, arguing that the exclusion of blacks from decision-making didn't aid white survival, but in fact threatened it. There had long been rumblings from within the Dutch Reformed Church. Later in 1986, it would break with apartheid, announcing that membership was open to anyone, regardless of colour. It had erred biblically, said the church, in its support of separate development.

These and other reverses had their roots in 1976, the year of both the Soweto uprising and the 'independence' of Transkei. The Cillie Commission of Inquiry into the uprising identified apartheid as part of the problem. More damning still was the international community's refusal to recognise the sovereignty of the first homeland. From this point forward, grand apartheid had been doomed to fail.

Another ideological anchor that was working itself loose at around this time was the idea that the Afrikaners had of themselves as a set-upon people, consigned to hardship and poverty following their defeat in the Anglo–Boer War. One of the main aims of apartheid was economic advancement. So successful had it been, argues Patti Waldmeir, that by the Eighties it had 'rendered itself obsolete'. A sophisticated and verligte (liberal) middle class emerged – professionals and businessmen, newspaper editors, teachers and academics. Their concerns 'were no different from those of the middle classes around the world: security, standards, the preservation of income'. Missing from Waldmeir's list is status. What good is money if you don't feel good about yourself? The new Afrikaners were tired of being the polecats of the world. They wanted political reform. Perhaps not anything as radical as one person, one vote, but enough change to rid them of the nagging sense that they were on the wrong side of history. The mining magnate Harry Oppenheimer liked to say that apartheid was felled by two things: the influx of black South Africans into the cities and the Afrikaners not liking to be disliked.

Van Zyl Slabbert's resignation wasn't the only noteworthy event in Parliament that day. Speaking immediately before Slabbert, PW Botha was at his belligerent best, hissing and wagging his forefinger. The focus of his ire was Pik Botha, his foreign minister, who earlier in the week had said that he would be happy to serve under a black president. The talk at the time was that FW de Klerk, a known conservative, had complained to PW, hence the reprimand. PW confirmed this years later, telling an interviewer that FW had been far more alarmed than he himself had been at Pik's mention of a black president.

~

On 9 February, Halley's Comet reached its perihelion, the point in its orbit closest to the sun. It was visible from Earth for a few months either side of this date. Halley's, which visits Earth every seventy-five years or so, cares not a jot for human affairs and as such offers a bracing point of perspective. During the course of the comet's 1910 visit, four British colonies amalgamated to form the Union of South Africa. In 1986, Afrikaner nationalists held sway. What will its next visit in 2061 bring?

~

On 11 February, General Tienie Groenewald of the South African Defence Force met with Mangosuthu Buthelezi, chief minister of the self-governing homeland of KwaZulu and leader of Inkatha, a Zulu nationalist organisation. Groenewald told Buthelezi that approval had been granted 'at the highest political level' for the SADF to provide military training to two hundred Inkatha recruits. This covert arrangement was code-named Operation Marion (short for 'marionette', a puppet manipulated by strings).

Buthelezi had launched Inkatha in 1975. It was a revival of a cultural movement that had been active in the Twenties. Initially, the ANC had been in favour of Inkatha, viewing it as an ally in the struggle against apartheid. By 1979, however, the two organisations were squabbling. The ANC accused Buthelezi of treating KwaZulu and Natal as his personal fiefdoms and of repressing opposition. It also accused him of collaborating with Pretoria. He supported the bantustan policy, it said, which allowed a handful of well-placed blacks to benefit from apartheid, while causing the majority to lose. Buthelezi, in turn, argued that the ANC's strategy of violent destabilisation, or 'ungovernability', was intended not only to topple the South African government but also to eliminate black competitors. The comrades were causing mayhem in KwaZulu, he said. They were attacking tribal chiefs, local councillors, and functionaries of the homeland government.

Buthelezi hated apartheid, and yet he played along with it to fulfil his political ambitions. 'In one mode,' remarks Walter Felgate, one of Buthelezi's senior advisors in the 1980s, 'he could offer the genuine rhetoric of the revolutionary. In the other, he spoke as a despised collaborator.' Historian Shula Marks labels Buthelezi 'an ambitious ethnic entrepreneur' and KwaZulu a 'one-party mini-state'. Inkatha and the homeland government, she observes, were practically synonymous. Many white South Africans considered Buthelezi a future president; to his black detractors, he was 'Bothalezi'.

Whatever his personal motivations might have been, Buthelezi was a perfect fit for Pretoria and its time-honoured colonial strategy of divide and rule. As early as 1976, the state had deployed Zulu migrant workers against anti-apartheid activists. In 1982, the SADF had urged the government to 'exploit and encourage' the divisions between Inkatha and the ANC. The advantages, it had argued, were twofold: the two groups would weaken one another, and their enmity would support the logic of separate development. As Eugene de Kock later put it: 'The black-on-black violence – Inkatha versus the ANC – that we encouraged was a handy propaganda tool because the outside world could be told with great conviction that the barbaric natives, as might have been expected, started murdering each other at every opportunity.'

In November 1985, three months before his meeting with Groenewald, Buthelezi had asked the South African government for assistance in establishing a paramilitary force. He wished 'to take the struggle to the ANC', he explained. The State Security Council appointed three ministers to look into the matter. At the time, the SSC, which comprised the state president, senior ministers, generals and securocrats, was more powerful than the cabinet: it effectively ran the country. In early February 1986, the SSC authorised 'the creation of a paramilitary element' for KwaZulu. A few days later, Operation Marion was given the go-ahead.

Buthelezi's personal assistant, MZ Khumalo, selected 206 men. In April, they were transported to Camp Hippo on the Caprivi Strip in northern South West Africa. For six months, they were trained by the SADF's Special Forces division. Khumalo would later claim that the training was 'defensive' in nature. He told the Goldstone Commission that the idea was to create 'VIP protection units' to counter the threat posed to Buthelezi and his ministers by ANC hit squads. This was contradicted by one of the trainees. He told the commission that he and his colleagues had been trained to use automatic weapons, hand grenades and

RPG-7 rocket launchers. They had also been instructed in techniques of urban warfare, surveillance, abduction and interrogation. The commission found it 'unlikely', on the evidence before it, that the recruits had been trained 'solely' for the purpose of VIP protection.

The Caprivi trainees, as they came to be known, would play a key role in the internecine violence that wracked KwaZulu and Natal in the late Eighties and then spread to the East Rand in the early Nineties.

~

On 13 February, the United Nations Security Council adopted Resolution 581, which condemned 'racist South Africa' for acts of aggression against neighbouring countries. The resolution was passed 13–0, with two abstentions – the UK and the USA.

The South African government had long envisaged a 'constellation of states' centred on Pretoria. When this plan unravelled following the independence of Mozambique and Angola in 1975, and Zimbabwe in 1980, South Africa launched campaigns of destabilisation. These took many forms: direct military aggression; targeted attacks on liberation movements; the establishment and support of surrogate armed forces (such as Unita, Renamo and the Lesotho Liberation Army); and economic sabotage. The plan was to weaken logistical support for the ANC, as well as to promote the idea that 'black majority rule' was bound to fail.

Historian Leonard Thompson reports that 'South Africa's destabilising tactics between 1980 and 1989 led to the deaths of one million people, made a further three million homeless, and caused $35 billion worth of damage to the economies of neighbouring states'. Angola and Mozambique bore the brunt of this. Namibia endured, in the words of military historian Gavin Cawthra, 'one of the most intense and sustained military occupations in modern history'. Lesotho was the victim of a South

African-sponsored coup, while Botswana, Zimbabwe, Zambia and Swaziland each experienced an assortment of air strikes, bombings, assassinations, border blockades and propaganda campaigns. These countries – which eventually formed a coalition called the Frontline States – were cowed into submission and forced to sign non-aggression pacts. President Kenneth Kaunda of Zambia captures the spirit of the times:

> Yes, humble Swaziland agrees, humble Mozambique accepts, humble Zambia hosts meetings of unequal neighbours like South Africa and Angola. What else can we do? But we are not doing it with happy hearts. We do it out of fear, but that fear will end one day.

Although UN resolutions are routinely ignored, the Frontline States must have found at least some solace in the adoption of Resolution 581. A few years earlier, they had observed: 'South Africa can invade and occupy sovereign states, blow up vital installations, and massacre populations at no apparent cost to its relations with its main allies.'

~

On 15 February, in Alexandra township in Johannesburg, the police tear-gassed mourners at the funeral of schoolboy Michael Diradingwe. Alexandra erupted. For a week, bands of youths fought running battles with the police in the streets of the densely populated township. The conflict became known as the Six Day War.

Diradingwe had been shot by a security guard outside the Jazz Supermarket in London Street. He was not an activist, and his death was not political, but it took place in an atmosphere of heightened tension. There had been other shootings and the police had recently fired rubber bullets at a mass funeral. A civic leader later explained that people's anger had been 'at a very high level, and they couldn't hold it anymore'.

The community mobilised for the funeral, and a large crowd gathered for a night vigil. At two in the morning, the police fired tear gas at mourners in the Diradingwes' yard. Young people fought back with bottles and stones. They attacked the houses of local policemen and set fire to Jazz Supermarket. Hostilities abated during the funeral service itself, but, as the mourners made their way from the stadium to the cemetery, the police again fired tear gas.* There ensued, as one newspaper put it, 'a week of living hell'.

The youth formed into militias and directed their anger at councillors, officials and anyone else considered to be collaborating with the state. They roamed the township, ransacking municipal buildings, Putco buses and other visible symbols of apartheid. The police and the army arrived with their armoured Casspirs and Hippos. They 'careered around Alexandra', reported the *Weekly Mail*, 'mounted like cowboys on stagecoaches'. The fighting was 'a gross mismatch', according to American journalist William Finnegan:

> [W]hile the comrades threw stones and half-bricks, and used homemade catapults to launch crude missiles made out of nuts and bolts and old spark plugs, the security forces fired shotguns, tear gas, and high-powered rifles from inside their armoured vehicles.

The comrades had some tricks up their sleeves, however. At night they dug 'tank traps', three-foot-deep trenches that hampered the progress of armoured vehicles; they also rigged 'clothes

---

* Journalist Allister Sparks has written about the 'grim momentum' of the mid-Eighties, whereby each funeral would provide the bodies for the next funeral.

lines', strands of barbed wire strung across roads at the height of a soldier standing atop a Hippo. They made Molotov cocktails, using petrol siphoned from residents' cars.

Over the course of six days, between twenty-nine and forty-six residents died, most of them children (these are the respective figures of the government and the South African Council of Churches). Many atrocities were reported. Two days after the funeral, a schoolgirl witnessed a policeman jump down from a Casspir, walk up to her unarmed friend Jerry Mthembu, and shoot him in the stomach. 'As Jerry was shot he screamed. His intestines were hanging out and he held his stomach and jumped over [a] fence.' A man named Alfred Radebe tried to drag Jerry to safety and was shot in the leg. Radebe ducked into a shack, but a policeman charged in after him, saw his legs sticking out from under a bed, and shot him in his good leg.

Asked to comment on the Mthembu–Radebe incident, the police released a statement:

> The SA Police never have and never will condone or toler-
> ate violations of the law by any member of the force. The
> allegations should be made in affidavit form at any police
> station or through existing channels, so that they may be
> investigated and tested against other available evidence.

On the sixth day of the war, Dr Tim Wilson started his new job as head of the Alexandra Clinic. Four hours in, the police arrived and subpoenaed the clinic's records. They wanted the names of patients who had been treated for gunshot wounds. 'We discussed it in a gentlemanly way,' Wilson told a reporter, 'and agreed to take the issue to court and let the lawyers fight it out.' A decade earlier, he had been based in Soweto. He'd been on duty at the start of the student uprising and was the doctor to whom Hector Pieterson had been taken.

'At stake,' noted Wilson, 'is the principle of the confidentiality of the doctor-patient relationship. A major argument, too, against providing names is that the injured will be afraid to seek help.' There had been reports of injured children operating on one another, rather than visiting a clinic. A few days after the initial raid, the police returned to the clinic and seized the files of three hundred patients. Their subpoena hadn't yet been tested in court.

The Six Day War is something of a misnomer. It was but the first six days of a six-month-long insurrection that catapulted Alexandra to the forefront of the urban rebellion. A key feature of the conflict was the establishment of local committees at street, block and yard levels. These youthful organs of 'people's power' helped 'liberate' large areas of the township from state control. They renamed streets and schools, and set up people's courts to dispense revolutionary justice.

In March 1986, Zwelakhe Sisulu, the editor of *New Nation*, delivered a speech in which he stressed the distinction between ungovernability and people's power: 'In a situation of ungovernability, the government doesn't have control. But neither do the people ... In a situation of people's power, the people are starting to exercise control.'

The Alexandra Action Committee did much of the organising. It was following a script laid down by the ANC: 'We call on our communities in the black ghettos to replace the collapsing government stooge councils with people's committees in every block ... every black area must become a no-go area for ... those who wear the uniforms of apartheid.'

The ANC's call for 'committees in every block' was a rehash of its 'M-Plan', which dated from the 1950s. Though the 'M' had originally stood for Mandela, in Alexandra it became known as the Mayekiso Plan, in honour of Moses Mayekiso, the chairman of the Action Committee.

~

On 20 February, following a meeting in London, Dr Fritz Leutwiler announced that South Africa's foreign debt crisis had been resolved. Leutwiler, a prominent Swiss banker, was acting as mediator between Pretoria and thirty international banks.

Six months earlier, South Africa had unilaterally declared a standstill on debt totalling $13 billion, arguing that repayment should be delayed for four years. The banks threatened to seize assets, including trade goods and aircraft. Leutwiler held talks with a number of the banks. He proposed that repayment be frozen for a year, with a token sum payable in each of the subsequent four quarters. His proposal was on a 'take-it-or-leave-it' basis, to cut down on time-consuming negotiations. He knew the banks had to accept his offer if they wished to recoup their money.

The trouble had started in July 1985, when PW Botha instituted a partial state of emergency. Chase Manhattan Bank had called in its loans. This was bad news for Pretoria. Over the preceding few years, the government had found it increasingly difficult to raise money. It had resorted to high-interest, short-term loans, which the banks then rolled over from one year to the next. By 1985, two thirds of the country's debt could be demanded in full at short notice. If other banks were to follow Chase's lead, South Africa would be bankrupt.

It was in this climate of tightening credit that Botha delivered his ill-fated Rubicon speech. Several reformists in his cabinet had persuaded him to use his opening address at the National Party congress in Durban to ease international pressure. Foreign minister Pik Botha composed a draft speech which promised to unban the ANC and free Nelson Mandela. He flew to Vienna to relay the good news to South Africa's staunchest allies, the US, the UK and West Germany. According to journalist Allister Sparks, '[w]hat followed was like one of those whispering games played at children's parties', whereby a message is passed from child to child until it finally emerges 'hilariously distorted'.

Pik Botha told diplomats in Vienna to expect 'momentous announcements'. An American diplomat inflated this already buoyant message and then the press added its own layer of hype. *Time* magazine announced that PW Botha was about to make 'the most important statement since Dutch settlers arrived at the Cape of Good Hope 300 years ago'.

The speculation infuriated the president, and he decided to write his own speech. With the world watching expectantly, Botha gave a defiant and angry performance. 'I am not prepared to lead white South Africans and other minority groups on a road to abdication and suicide,' he declared. 'We have never given in to outside demands and we are not going to do so now. South Africa's problems will be solved by South Africans and not by foreigners.'

Careful listeners were surprised at how reformist the speech actually was. Buried in the bellicosity was a quiet commitment to 'shared citizenship' in 'a multicultural society' and a determination to press on with reforms. Botha repudiated a core concept of apartheid when he promised that black homelands that did not wish to become independent could remain part of South Africa. Most listeners thought it incongruous when he claimed that he was crossing the Rubicon of reform, but in fact he was – in word, if not in demeanour. FW de Klerk later noted that the substance of Botha's speech – 'if properly presented and marketed' – would have satisfied the international community. But the presentation was belligerent and the marketing over-blown. In De Klerk's estimation, it was 'probably the greatest communication disaster in South African history'.

De Klerk's speech in 1990 is often described as the Rubicon that Botha shrank from crossing. Some commentators, however, have argued that De Klerk never grasped the full consequences of his actions. Even after his celebrated speech, De Klerk insisted that he would never accept majority rule. Niël Barnard, head of the National Intelligence Service in the Eighties, says Botha understood that freeing Mandela and unbanning the ANC would inevitably lead to the end of white rule. De Klerk, he says, never understood this. Hence the terrible friction between De Klerk and Mandela.

The fallout from Botha's Rubicon speech was severe. Most of the creditor banks refused to roll over their loans and in a few short months South Africa owed $13 billion. The currency plunged, losing thirty-five per cent of its value in two weeks. Gerhard de Kock, the governor of the Reserve Bank, estimated that the speech had cost the economy more than a million rand per word (and it ran to several thousand words).

Investors rushed into gold, which propped up the local stock exchange. 'The share value,' remarked a broker, 'reflects what South Africans are thinking: that everything is okay. The rand reflects what the world thinks, and it's saying God Help You.'

~

On 24 February, *The Star* reported the results of a survey in which black, coloured and Indian South Africans had been asked who they would like to see as 'the head of state in a non-racial South Africa':

Nelson Mandela (17.7%)
Desmond Tutu (16.6%)
Allan Boesak (13.3%)
Frederik Van Zyl Slabbert (12.5%)
Oliver Tambo (10.1%)
Walter Sisulu (7.1%)
PW Botha (4.6%)
Mangosuthu Buthelezi (4.1%)
Allan Hendrickse (1.4%)
Saths Cooper (1.4%)
Amichand Rajbansi (0.7%).

The survey had been conducted by the Institute for Black Research. Its director observed that Mandela would likely have received a larger percentage of the vote 'if the survey had been done at a time when he was not portrayed as a dying man'.

~

On 25 February, the twenty-seventh Congress of the Communist Party of the Soviet Union commenced in Moscow. It was much anticipated, both at home and abroad, as it was the first congress to be presided over by Mikhail Gorbachev, the recently elected and notably reformist general secretary. Gorbachev didn't disappoint. He introduced two key concepts that would guide future Soviet policy: 'glasnost' (transparency) and 'perestroika' (restructuring). Gorbachev's reforms would play a key role in the demise of the communist empire and the end of the Cold War. They would prove important for South Africa, too – more important than any of Botha's reforms.

The Soviet economy was in crisis and could no longer afford imperial ambitions or an arms race. When Gorbachev met with US president Ronald Reagan in Reykjavík, Iceland, later in the year, he pushed for a peaceful resolution to all costly regional conflicts involving the superpowers. This decision had severe implications for the liberation movements of southern Africa. The likelihood of the ANC achieving a military victory had been slim enough as it was. Without Soviet funding and military materiel, its chances dropped to practically zero, and a negotiated settlement became its best option.

The implications for the South African government were equally severe. Their propaganda machine had long played on fears of Soviet imperialism. Indeed, their 'total strategy' was premised on it. Allister Sparks would later suggest that the waning of communism posed for the government 'a crisis no less severe than the death of Satan would for Christianity'.

Economist Sampie Terreblanche reports that Moscow pressured the ANC 'to seek a negotiated solution', while Washington exerted similar pressure on Pretoria. As a result, says Terreblanche, 'The year 1986 was the real turning point in South Africa's democratic transformation.'

~

On 27 February, *Beeld* reported that Eugène Terre'Blanche, leader of the AWB, defended the open-handed salute used by his members as an old German greeting meaning 'I come in peace'. The AWB, or Afrikaner-weerstandsbeweging (Afrikaner Resistance Movement), was a neo-Nazi paramilitary organisation. Its logo was a three-armed version of the swastika.

'How can I help it,' asked Terre'Blanche in reference to the salute, 'if Hitler also used it?'

~

On 28 February, in Lusaka, Oliver Tambo had two important meetings. The one was with George Bizos, a lawyer who was acting as go-between for the imprisoned Nelson Mandela. The other was with Malcolm Fraser and Olusegun Obasanjo, the co-chairmen of the Commonwealth Eminent Persons Group. The two meetings had similar agendas. Bizos was there to discuss Mandela's wish to enter into secret talks with the South African government, while the EPG wished to promote the idea of a negotiated settlement.

Three months earlier, in November 1985, Mandela had been admitted to hospital as he required surgery for an enlarged prostate. His wife flew down to Cape Town to join him. Kobie Coetsee, the minister of justice, was on the same flight. He stopped by Winnie Mandela's seat in economy class to wish her husband well. With characteristic chutzpah, Mandela followed

Coetsee back to business class and sat down next to him. By the time the aeroplane landed two hours later, Coetsee had decided to visit her husband in hospital.

In *Long Walk to Freedom*, Mandela characterises Coetsee's visit as 'an olive branch'. Though the two men didn't talk politics, Mandela sensed that the government was seeking 'some accommodation'. He was concerned, however, that the government might be trying to drive a wedge between the internal and external wings of the ANC. Mandela summoned Bizos and asked him to visit Lusaka and tell Tambo about Coetsee's visit. Bizos was to assure Tambo that Mandela was neither going soft nor was he overstepping his authority. Nothing would happen without Tambo's blessing. Bizos made two trips to Lusaka: the first, late in 1985, to apprise Tambo of the situation, and the second, early in 1986, to hear what the leadership had decided.

Once Mandela had recuperated from his operation, he was returned to Pollsmoor Prison, but not to the communal cell he'd been sharing with Walter Sisulu and others. He was now installed in a 'palatial' three-roomed cell of his own. 'I was not happy to be separated from my colleagues,' he writes in his autobiography, 'and I missed my garden and the sunny terrace on the third floor. But my solitude gave me a certain liberty, and I resolved to use it to do something I had been pondering for a long while: begin discussions with the government.'

In 1979, the government had sent a message to the ANC, via Mangosuthu Buthelezi, saying that it wished to talk. 'What has PW done,' responded Tambo, 'to suggest that he's worth seeing?' In 1983, the government again made overtures, but its preconditions for talking – in particular, the renunciation of violence – proved unworkable. In 1984, Professor HW van der Merwe, an expert in conflict resolution at the University of Cape Town, took it upon himself to travel to Lusaka. Once there, Thabo Mbeki asked him to help broker meetings between Afrikaners and the ANC. In 1985, Gavin Relly, the chairman of Anglo American, led a group of businessmen to Lusaka, and later that year Frederik Van Zyl Slabbert took the PFP executive to meet with the ANC. 'How infinitely more accomplished they were as politicians,' recalls Slabbert. 'We were novices and like putty in their hands.' By the end of the decade, over a hundred delegations from South Africa had made the pilgrimage to Lusaka.

Mark Gevisser, in his biography of Thabo Mbeki, reports that by 1985 the ANC, despite publicly advocating a 'people's war', had privately accepted the desirability of negotiations. And Niël Barnard observes that by 1986 even PW Botha 'had accepted, perhaps with reluctance, that a negotiated settlement was the best option to solve our political predicament'. Both sides recognised that they were in a stalemate. When American academic Samuel Huntington visited South Africa in February 1986, he found that the government was 'too weak to impose reform from above' and that the opposition was 'too weak to compel reform from below'.

It was in this climate that Mandela decided to embark on talks. Within a few weeks of his move to single quarters in Pollsmoor, he wrote to Kobie Coetsee 'to propose talks about talks'. He received no response. 'I wrote once more, and again there was no response.' Mandela was both perplexed and demoralised. He needed to find 'another opportunity to be heard'. That opportunity, he reports, came 'early in 1986' with the visit of the Eminent Persons Group.

The previous October, at their summit in the Bahamas, the Commonwealth heads of state had adopted an accord on southern Africa. Known as the Nassau Accord, it called on the South African government to undertake five steps: declare that apartheid would be dismantled; terminate the state of emergency; release Mandela and other political prisoners; unban the ANC and other political organisations; and initiate a process of dialogue. British Prime Minister Margaret Thatcher fought hard against the Accord, arguing that PW Botha and his government should be allowed to dismantle apartheid according to their own timetable. The rest of the Commonwealth were having none of this, but Thatcher stuck to her line. A split loomed. As a compromise solution, they established a seven-member Eminent Persons Group. The EPG was to assess the situation on the ground and report back within six months. It was also charged with encouraging the evolution of the Accord's fifth step: a process of dialogue.

The EPG consulted on a broad basis, speaking to the state president, senior government ministers, parliamentarians, leaders of both internal and external resistance movements, ambassadors, academics, journalists, businessmen, industrial and agricultural workers, squatters and refugees, priests, student activists, trade unionists, community organisers, civil rights campaigners and political prisoners. In addition, they travelled back and forth between Pretoria and Lusaka, engaging in 'proximity talks' between the government and the ANC.

'From the beginning,' notes the EPG in its final report, 'we recognised the essential significance in any political settlement of one man – Nelson Mandela. ... His name is emblazoned across the length and breadth of South Africa.' When the advance guard of the EPG visited in February 1986, Obasanjo alone was granted permission to meet with Mandela. He petitioned for the full group to meet the famous prisoner, and the government relented. A meeting was scheduled for 12 March. All concerned were looking forward to it. Mandela wished to put the ANC's case, and the government was keen to score a public relations coup. Two days before the meeting, Brigadier Fred Munro, the commander of Pollsmoor, visited Mandela's cell with a tailor. 'We want you to see these people on an equal footing,' he said. Mandela observes that the tailor 'must have been some kind of wizard, for the very next day I tried on a pinstriped suit that fitted me like a glove'. Munro was delighted: 'Mandela, you look like a prime minister now, not a prisoner.'

Kobie Coetsee was at hand to introduce the EPG to Mandela, who was waiting in a large armchair in the Pollsmoor guesthouse. 'They were completely taken aback,' recalls Coetsee. 'I could see the disbelief on their faces. ... I felt that I had trumped them; they expected this emaciated person, and there he was completely in control.' To a large extent, the EPG report confirms Coetsee's recollection:

> We were first struck by his physical authority – by his immaculate appearance, his apparent good health and his commanding presence. In his manner, he exuded authority and received the respect of all around him, including his gaolers.

But it wasn't Mandela's appearance alone that left its mark on the visitors:

> We found him unmarked by any trace of bitterness despite his long imprisonment. ... We all agreed that it was tragic that a man of his outstanding capabilities should continue to be denied the opportunity to help shape his country's future.

Coetsee, too, was impressed by Mandela's performance that day: 'I was so struck by his presence. It was absolutely remarkable – his alertness, his composure, his bearing, the way he met these people as though he had been a pinstriped leader all his life.'

Mandela was the perfect host. He chatted about cricket with the Australian Malcolm Fraser, and asked Lord Barber, who had escaped from a prisoner-of-war camp, whether he had any tips. Once the actual meeting got underway, Mandela laid the ground rules. 'I am not the head of the movement,' he said. 'The head of the movement is Oliver Tambo in Lusaka. You must go and see him. You can tell him what my views are, but they are my personal views alone.' These views included a commitment to a non-racial future and an endorsement of the EPG's draft terms for negotiation.

The EPG left the country the following day, satisfied that there was potential for a negotiated settlement: 'No serious person we met was interested in a fight to the finish; all favoured negotiations and peaceful solutions.' The major stumbling block, it felt, was the government and the ANC each waiting for the other to make the first move. The EPG took it upon itself to resolve this problem. Back in London, it drew up a 'Possible Negotiating Concept'. If the parties each agreed to it, then they could act simultaneously. The concept called for certain concessions as a prelude to negotiations. The ANC would have to suspend violence, while the government needed to release Mandela, unban his organisation, and remove the military from the townships.

~

On 28 February, in Stockholm, Olof Palme, the Swedish prime minister, was walking home from a cinema with his wife when a lone gunman shot him from behind at close range. Palme, who prided himself on living a 'normal' life, had dismissed his bodyguards earlier that evening. He was, according to an obituary, 'one of the most informal and unpompous' of leaders. When Oliver Tambo came to visit, they would retire to the kitchen, where the prime minister would fry sausages for the leader of the liberation movement.

The assassination of Olof Palme has haunted Sweden for over thirty years. The crime remains unsolved and the investigation is ongoing (at one point, a petty criminal was found guilty, but he was later acquitted). To date, investigators have questioned over 10 000 people and have generated files that take up 250 metres of shelf space. In the estimation of a leading criminologist, the investigation is 'the largest in global police history'.

The case has given rise to a number of conspiracy theories. Depending on one's villain of choice, Palme was gunned down by Kurdish separatists, by the Yugoslavian security service, by the CIA, by arms dealers with links to India, by a Chilean fascist, or by Swedish right-wing police officers. The most popular and abiding theory, however, points to the South African state.

A week before his assassination, Palme delivered the keynote speech at a three-day conference, the Swedish People's Parliament Against Apartheid. Addressing anti-apartheid activists as well as leaders of the ANC (Oliver Tambo and Thabo Mbeki were both present), Palme referred to apartheid as a 'despicable, doomed system' that couldn't be reformed, 'it can only be abolished'. In essence, his speech was a call for the intensification of sanctions: 'Pressure on the regime must increase. It must be made clear to the minority regime that it has no support ... If the world decides to abolish apartheid, apartheid will disappear.'

Palme, who had travelled widely as a young man, had a special hatred for colonialism and its consequences. He had entered politics as a Social Democrat, but a radical one. He supported the welfare state and was committed to the abolition of poverty, oppression and war. 'We must not sit around,' he once said, 'like characters in a Chekhov play waiting for something to happen. We must give people hope.' Many considered Palme 'the world's conscience'. For others, he was a scourge. He supported a number of Third World liberation movements and was openly critical of the imperial ambitions of both the US and the Soviet Union. His fiercest criticism, though, he reserved for authoritarian regimes such as those of Francisco Franco, Augusto Pinochet and Pieter Willem Botha.

Palme was a great friend of Oliver Tambo and was instrumental in steering his government toward significant financial support for the ANC. In 1976, by which time Palme had completed the first of his two stints as prime minister, Sweden overtook the Soviet Union as the ANC's most important donor. The money came at a vital time for the exiled organisation. It hadn't fired 'a single shot in anger' in fourteen years, as Joe Slovo put it, and morale was in decline. Cadres spent their days repeating the same training routines they'd undergone for years, or they just sat around. A senior official in the ANC told the Swedish aid agency that year that, but for its support, his organisation 'would perhaps have disintegrated due to discontent among cadres'.

Providing food for the ANC was not a task for the faint-hearted. In 1977, the organisation presented the Swedes with a grocery list. It required 34 975 kilograms of meat, 22 400 kilograms of fresh produce and 10 655 bags of mielie meal *per month* to feed 5 000 people in seven countries. By 1985, the ANC's cash budget was $10 million annually, with Sweden providing almost half of it. To be fair to the Soviets and other Eastern Bloc countries, much of their support took the form of goods and services: armaments, vehicles, clothing, air fares, and overseas training. In 1985, the Soviets were presented with a shopping list of their own. Among other items, it called for 60 cars, 6 buses, 240 tons of soap, 16 000 tubes of toothpaste and 4 000 brassieres.

The Swedish authorities knew that the South African government had reason to dislike Palme. Indeed, they had intelligence that certain elements in its security services had considered the possibility of killing their prime minister. The problem for the Swedes was that they had very little evidence: just the fragments of two .357 Magnum bullets and a few inconclusive eyewitness reports. Their initial investigations led nowhere. Their first big break, so far as the South African angle was concerned, came in 1996, ten years after the murder. Eugene de Kock was testifying at a hearing in Pretoria in mitigation of sentence. Almost in passing, he mentioned that South African agents had killed Palme because he 'strongly opposed the apartheid regime and Sweden made substantial contributions to the ANC'. The killing had been orchestrated, said De Kock, by apartheid spy Craig Williamson.

Williamson was a plausible candidate. In the 1970s, he had infiltrated the International University Exchange Fund, getting himself appointed deputy director. The IUEF was based in Stockholm and was a major funder of anti-apartheid groups. When Williamson's cover was blown in 1980, he returned to South Africa. Stationed at Special Branch headquarters, he took to harassing local activists. It wasn't long, however, before he branched out into state-sponsored violence abroad. In 1982, for instance, he planned both the bombing of the ANC offices in London and the assassination of anti-apartheid campaigner Ruth First in Maputo, Mozambique. In 1985, he left the security police and secretly joined Military Intelligence. His central task was the setting up of Longreach Ltd, ostensibly a privately owned security firm that specialised in intelligence gathering, but in fact a front company for covert government projects.

De Kock's revelation regarding Palme sparked others. Dirk Coetzee, his death squad predecessor, and former policeman Peter Casselton each confirmed Williamson's involvement. Coetzee named Rhodesian Selous Scout Anthony White as the actual killer, while Casselton fingered Swedish mercenary and occasional apartheid operative Bertil Wedin. Other names to surface were those of Roy Allen, a former member of the security police, and Athol Visser, a former operative for the Civil Cooperation Bureau, a military hit squad. Swedish investigators visited South Africa in 1996, but were unable to secure reliable evidence. The following year, however, they were given another lead.

In March 1997, a South African shipping agent named Nigel Barnett was arrested in Maputo for attempted arson. He had evidently become involved in a feud with a business acquaintance and paid a group of street kids to set fire to the man's boat. When the police searched Barnett's flat, they discovered that he was an agent for South African Military Intelligence. He had been living undetected in Maputo for fifteen years. During their investigation, the police found evidence suggesting that

Barnett may have been involved in Palme's assassination. They subjected him to a polygraph test, asking: 'Did you participate in the murder of Olof Palme?'; 'Did you kill Olof Palme?'; and 'Do you know for sure who killed Olof Palme?' Barnett responded in the negative to each of these questions. The polygraph operator registered the first and the third responses as 'deceptive indicative' (polygraph-speak for lying). The Mozambicans contacted the South African Truth and Reconciliation Commission, which was underway at the time. It so happened that a Swedish law-enforcement officer, Jan-Åke Kjellberg, had been seconded to one of the TRC's investigative units, and he travelled to Maputo to interview Barnett.

Between them, the Mozambican police and Kjellberg uncovered significant circumstantial evidence. Barnett's adoptive mother was Swedish. He spoke the language and visited the country often. He knew both Craig Williamson and Peter Casselton. At the time of his arrest, Barnett had in his possession a number of handguns, including a .357 Magnum revolver (apparently his favoured weapon). Also in his possession were: a number of bona fide and false identification documents and passports; press clippings relating to Palme's assassination; video cassettes containing documentaries about Palme's assassination; photographs of Stockholm street scenes; and a photograph of a Saab station wagon that had been converted into a camper van. This last item was noteworthy in light of an article a Swedish journalist had written soon after the assassination. She had reported that three South Africans were responsible for the deed, and that they had conducted the operation from a station wagon that had been converted into a camper.

A search of Barnett's safety-deposit box unearthed a ticket stub for a flight from Johannesburg to Stockholm in May 1986. There was nothing, however, to show that he'd been in the Swedish capital three months earlier. Also, his gun turned out not to be the murder weapon. Running thin on evidence, the Swedes closed the investigation into Barnett – 'perhaps prematurely', in the opinion of Jan Bondeson, author of *Blood on the Snow: The Killing of Olof Palme*. The mention of snow in Bondeson's title chimes with an odd discrepancy in one of Barnett's interviews. He admitted to several visits to Stockholm in the mid-Eighties, but none of them coincided with the assassination. He casually mentioned that during one of these visits there had been a light dusting of snow on the streets of Stockholm. The Swedish police checked weather data for each of his claimed visits, but not once had it snowed. There had been a light dusting, however, on the night Palme died.

Journalist Terry Bell, who has written about the Palme assassination, suggests that Barnett was probably not the killer, but rather the person who carried the gun into Sweden. This would account for the odd choice of weapon. A Smith and Wesson .357 Magnum is a bulky, conspicuous gun. It has a notably loud discharge and cannot be fitted with an effective silencer. Few assassins would favour it. In Bell's view, Williamson planned the assassination, Barnett facilitated it, and Allen pulled the trigger.

Bell presents an account of Barnett's life prior to his posting in Maputo. Born Leon van der Westhuizen in Queenstown in 1949, he was given up for adoption by his mother. After being taken in by Jeffrey Bacon and Aina Eriksson, his name was changed to Henry Bacon. He was conscripted in 1969 and joined the navy as a diver. He took to life in the armed services, and once his conscription ended he joined the British South Africa Police in Rhodesia. He gained acclaim in the bush war and was drafted into the BSAP Special Branch, a unit devoted to 'clandestine operations'. In 1979, he received a citation for 'gallantry ... while engaged in anti-terrorist operations'. Bacon fought to the bitter end. After Rhodesia's transition to democracy in 1980, he headed south. 'A highly trained spy and killer,' reports Bell, 'he was just what apartheid South Africa wanted at the time.'

Bacon joined Military Intelligence as an operative in their Directorate of Covert Collection, a unit dedicated to the destruction of the ANC. He officially changed his name to Nicho Esslin and was posted to Polaris Shipping in Durban, one of the security establishment's many front companies. Once in Durban, he changed his name again, this time to Nigel Barnett, and became a director of one of Polaris's subsidiaries. Henry Bacon had ceased to exit. All that remained of him was a ghostly trace in Barnett's official documentation. Barnett's date of birth, revealed in the first six digits of his identity number (500630) was one year, one month and one day later than Bacon's (490529). Nigel Barnett, with no military history and a career in logistics, was ideally placed to become MI's man in Maputo. Throughout the years of destabilisation, Barnett collected and forwarded information on ANC members – their houses, their vehicles, their visitors, their activities. He also undertook operations outside Mozambique. For these, he used yet another name, HW Otto, so as not to jeopardise his spying activities.

Several years later, in 2010, Tommy Lindström, who had been head of Swedish crime intelligence at the time of Palme's assassination, suggested that the South African state remained the number one suspect. To this day, the Swedish police keep a file on Van der Westhuizen/Bacon/Esslin/Barnett/Otto. He remains a person of 'particular interest'.

# MARCH

## Peppered by shotguns

Few signs on the Blue Route, Ou Kaapse Weg, N2 freeway and other roads on the West Coast have not been "killed" at least once.

Some of the bullet holes are about two centimetres in diameter. Other signs have been peppered by shotguns.

A favourite target is a route marker on Ou Kaapse Weg which has 28 bullet holes in it.

A city firearms dealer said most of the holes had probably been caused by ,38 or 9mm handguns — bullets which can kill up to 2km.

Residents in the Tokai area with property directly behind the signs reported no damage from bullets fired by sign shooters.

*Weekend Argus*, 1 March 1986

ON 1 MARCH, the South African writer, journalist and actor William 'Bloke' Modisane died in Dortmund, West Germany. He had been in exile for twenty-seven years. Modisane is best known for his memoir *Blame Me on History*, which examines the psychological effects of living under apartheid. It is also a requiem to Sophiatown, which had been Modisane's home for thirty years. 'Something in me died,' reads the opening line, 'a piece of me died, with the dying of Sophiatown …'

Modisane grew up in difficult circumstances. His father was murdered when he was young, and a sister died of malnutrition. His mother turned their home into a shebeen to provide for her surviving children. She decided that Bloke should be a doctor and worked fourteen hours a day to this end. Modisane explains:

> To be a doctor like Dr Xuma would be to be respected, to live in a big house with separate bedrooms, a room for sitting, another for eating, and a room to be alone, for reading or thinking, to shut out South Africa and not be black; a house in which children would not be sent out if someone wanted to take a bath, we would not have to undress in the dark or under blankets.

Modisane is referring to Dr AB Xuma, who lived nearby. He was the first black South African to become a medical doctor, and he was also president-general of the ANC.

Dr William Modisane, I love the sound of the title, the respectability and the security it would have given our family ... I was not particularly concerned with the groans and suffering of humanity, was not dedicated to wiping out malnutrition, malaria, or dysentery, I had no pretentions to such a morality, I wanted solely, desperately, none of these things – only to pull my family up from the mud level of black poverty.

Modisane was a bright child and quickly learnt how to game the system. Once, after a history exam, he quizzed his classmates about the adjectives they had used, before excitedly telling them: 'I described Dingaan as malicious, venomous, ferociously inhuman, beastly, godless; I should get a good mark.' He had discovered early that 'the white South African is hopelessly and fanatically susceptible to flattery'. Modisane used this insight to escape the excesses of police brutality. Apprehended on the streets of Johannesburg one night, he was questioned about his failure to carry the required pass. Modisane launched into an excruciating defence:

Yes, my baasie, I was very stupid tonight, I was nearly led into the ways of the devil. This kaffir meid, my baas, was trying to trick me into sleeping in her room, but I know it is against the law, my baasie; so I said to her: the law says I must not sleep on the property of the white master.

The policeman was satisfied. 'Jy's 'n goeie kaffir,' he said, 'a very good kaffir. Let me see your Pass – you must be careful, these kaffir women are bad, very bad.'

Modisane excelled at school, but his interests were more in the literary arena than the medical. He secured a job first at Vanguard, a left-leaning bookshop, and then at *Drum* magazine. *Drum* was enamoured of beauty queens and gangsters, yet it also employed the country's finest black writers, and was known for its investigative journalism into the abuses of apartheid. Modisane joined a team that included Henry Nxumalo, Can Themba, Todd Matshikiza, Nat Nakasa and Lewis Nkosi. Nkosi once characterised this golden generation as 'the new African cut adrift from the tribal reserve – urbanised, eager, fast-talking and brash'.

The biggest investigative story each year was undertaken by 'Mr Drum' (generally Nxumalo). 'Mr Drum Goes to Bethal' exposed the labour practices on potato farms in the eastern Transvaal, while 'Mr Drum Goes to Jail' unmasked the thuggery of prison guards at the Old Fort in Johannesburg. In 1956, Modisane was chosen to be Mr Drum. He was tasked with investigating the colour bar in white churches. While 'Mr Drum Goes to Church' was a less hazardous assignment than some of its predecessors, Modisane was nevertheless frogmarched out of several establishments. 'I was shocked into trauma,' he writes, 'by the unashamed godlessness of the white Christians, who emphasised … that they were essentially white and incidentally Christian.'

Modisane preferred the forthright approach of the Afrikaans-speaking congregations, who forcibly ejected him, to the hypocrisy of the English, who invited him in, led him to a segregated corner and gave him the cold shoulder:

All of us in South Africa, black and white, accommodate the discrimination mentality of the Afrikaner, we accept this as an honest fact; the Africans admire it as a document of honesty, however wrong it may be; but the English-speaking South African has inherited all the hypocritical diplomacy of the British … the African resents the insidiousness of his intolerance and his contemptible sense of superiority.

*Drum*'s editorial team decided that Modisane wasn't eliciting the desired reaction and roped in Can Temba to assist. Temba was more confrontational and was twice arrested in his first weekend on the story – at a Seventh-day Adventist church on the Saturday, and at a Dutch Reformed church on the Sunday. Modisane was overcome by 'a depressing sense of failure and inadequacy'. His colleague's blunt approach didn't work out well for their story, however. The headlines that Monday were about black reporters forcing their way into white churches 'and all the excitement, the urgency, the revelation of religious apartheid was usurped from *Drum*'.

The destruction of Sophiatown was a pivotal event in Modisane's life. Sophiatown was one of the few areas in Johannesburg with freehold rights for blacks. It was, writes Modisane, 'the most cosmopolitan of South Africa's black social igloos and perhaps the most perfect experiment in non-racial community living'. An epicentre of politics and jazz, Sophiatown was a hub for black culture. The Nationalists hated it. It stood for everything they believed was wrong with the country, and, besides, it was too close to white suburbia. They started to plan its destruction the moment they came into power. In 1955, the bulldozers moved in. Sophiatown was flattened and a white suburb called Triomf was built in its place.*

For Modisane, Sophiatown comprised 'a kaleidoscope of variable moods and passions, movingly beautiful one minute, the next, indescribably ugly and horrid'. He neither succumbs to a romanticised version of the past, nor does he shy away from 'the overcrowding, the congestion of hate ... the starvation, the frustrating life in the ghetto'. At times, these problems overwhelm him. Much of the time, however, he and his fellows 'took the ugliness of life in a slum and wove a kind of beauty;

---

* This new suburb was far from the 'triumph' its planners envisaged. Marlene van Niekerk's novel *Triomf* tells the story of a family of poor whites who live on the ruins of Sophiatown and subsist on a diet of Coca-Cola, white bread, polony and incest.

we established bonds of human relationship which set a pattern of communal living.'

Typically, the chroniclers of life under apartheid are made of stern stuff. People such as Phyllis Ntantala, Emma Mashinini and Sindiwe Magona survived the iniquities of the system and still had the energy and gumption to tell their stories. There's a fragility, however, to Bloke Modisane. What died in him with the dying of Sophiatown was hope, and he never recovered. At times, *Blame Me on History* reads like a breakdown in progress. Modisane is undone not only by the brutality and injustice of apartheid, but also by loneliness and isolation: 'I have felt too much, alone, and bled too deeply, alone, the being alone is unbearable.' He is obsessed with the idea that he doesn't fit in anywhere. His smattering of education 'situates' him above his people, but whites consider him uneducated. For academic Ron Nixon, the 'blocked anger' of Modisane's life-writing highlights 'the historical need for Biko and Black Consciousness'.

Modisane eventually left South Africa in 1959. 'I wanted a little peace,' he says, 'some amount of freedom and a little time to reconstruct my battered soul under an easier political climate where I could humanise myself.' Modisane was not alone. Exile was the fate of 'a dizzying number of black South African journalists', reports fellow journalist William Finnegan.

They live all over Africa, Europe, and America, teaching, writing, working in the outlawed liberation movements. Many fail to cope: Nat Nakasa threw himself out a window in New York; Can Themba drank himself to death in Swaziland.

Jon Qwelane, a reporter for *The Star*, told Finnegan:

Even the ones who are doing well seemed so homesick, so out of place. The chap I stayed with in Paris got out and played some old jazz records that he used to love as a kid in Alexandra, and you never saw such pain in a man's face.

~

On 2 March, *The Observer*, a Sunday newspaper in Britain, published an interview with Thabo Mbeki, publicity director for the ANC. 'We are talking not of overthrowing the government,' he said, 'but of turning so many people against it that it would be forced to ... talk.'

This chimes with something Mbeki had said in an earlier interview: 'There is nothing to stop us from placing a bomb in a cinema of three hundred white people. But we don't do it ... With a white population of almost five million, it makes political common sense to win over as many of them as possible, to neutralise as many as possible, and not drive them into the arms of Botha.'

~

On 3 March, in Gugulethu township in Cape Town, seven young men were shot dead by the police. The police claimed that the men, aged between twenty-two and thirty, were ANC guerrillas, and that the officers had fired in self-defence. But residents of the nearby DairyBelle hostel told a different story. One of the victims had been shot while trying to surrender, they said. His hands were in the air. Another, unarmed, was shot while lying on the ground. The killing of the Gugulethu Seven, as they came to be known, was subject to two different inquests.* In each, the

---

* A grim tradition developed in the Seventies and Eighties, whereby a group of activists killed (or charged) by the state would be collectively referred to by the name of a place or an organisation, followed by a number. Thus: the Upington Fourteen, the Pretoria Twelve,

presiding magistrate found that no one was criminally liable as the victims had died in 'a legitimate antiterrorist operation'.

In 2000, filmmaker Lindy Wilson released a documentary about the Gugulethu Seven. Her film tells the story of the TRC investigative unit assigned to the case. In essence, it is a detective story. The viewer knows at the outset who was shot and who did the shooting, but not how the incident unfolded, nor why.

Two members of the investigative unit had journalistic experience and two were in the police force. The Gugulethu Seven was their first case. All they had to go on initially was a statement by the mother of one of the victims. She alleged that 'the children' hadn't attacked the police, but rather that the police had fired on them in cold blood and had then planted weapons on their bodies.

'There were no clues in the statement,' says Zenzile Khoisan, a member of the unit (and the lead character in Wilson's film). 'It was all the raw pain of the mother.' Khoisan and his colleagues needed court records, inquest reports, post-mortem results. They visited Gugulethu police station and asked to see the archives. The occurrence book for March 1986 was missing. When Khoisan asked the station commander to open his safe, 'This man nearly blew a blood vessel, because, I mean, who are you to come and open up a safe … this man is part of a police tradition where you couldn't even get the name of a detainee.' Khoisan pulled out a copy of 'the act' (the Promotion of National Unity and Reconciliation Act of 1995) and read from Section 29.1: 'The commission may for the purpose of … an investigation … seize any article which is relevant to the subject matter of the

_____

the Mamelodi Ten, the KwaNdebele Nine, the Cosas Eight, the Gugulethu Seven, the Sharpeville Six, the Alex Five, the Cradock Four, the Delmas Four, the Motherwell Four, the Quarry Road Four, the Chesterville Four, the Katlehong Four, the Pebco Three, the Moroka Three, the Cosas Two.

investigation.' The station commander tried to appeal to a higher authority, but the unit wasn't swayed. 'When he opened that safe, I remember he had a heavy heart, you know, he turned around and it was like … it was almost like committing suicide as a policeman.' In the safe was a stack of files pertaining to the Gugulethu Seven. It was marked 'Geheim/Secret'.

The unit had another breakthrough at the headquarters of the Internal Stability Unit, better known as the riot police. Khoisan and his colleagues weren't having much luck finding useful documents, when a lowly black employee told them he'd seen people moving files into 'this other room over here'. The room was locked. A colonel told Khoisan that he didn't know where the key was. 'Kolonel,' said Khoisan, 'either you find the key or we do have a crowbar in the car.' A fax came through from TRC headquarters, and the colonel found the key. Inside the room were 'trunks filled with documents and papers and correspondence and dockets and occurrence books'. They seized everything: 'We had documents on the back seat, between our legs, in the boot and we had to make several trips, about five or six trips.'

The unit got to see the post-mortem results for the first time. 'Those seven young men sustained bullets,' says Khoisan. 'I mean, their bodies were riddled with bullets.' There were 'twelve, fifteen, sixteen' bullet wounds per body. All seven had been shot in the head. What had once looked like an operation gone wrong now looked like an execution.

The mothers of the Gugulethu Seven told their stories at the first hearing of the TRC in the Western Cape. Eunice Miya last saw her son Jabu at four-thirty in the morning, as she left to catch the five o'clock train. She was a domestic worker and needed to be at her place of employment by six. At around ten-thirty, her employer, who had been listening to the radio, came over to her and said, 'Eunice, I just heard from the news that there are Russians in Gugulethu who have been killed.' Miya assured her employer that her son wasn't involved in politics. That evening, she saw Jabu's body on television news. 'Oh no, Lord!' she said, 'I wish … I wish this news can just rewind.'

Mandla Mxinwa's mother went looking for her son in prisons and hospitals. She eventually found him in a morgue. Cynthia Ngewu, the mother of Christopher Piet, had heard that her son was dead and went straight to the morgue. That evening, she watched television news. 'I saw him in the TV lying down dead,' she testified. 'They busy pulling my child with a string … the police, they drag my child like that, it's just like a dog mos.' She was referring to footage in which the police attached a length of rope to her son's body and then pulled on it, rolling him over. The police claimed they were checking for an activated grenade. Ngewu saw it differently: 'Were their hands so clean that they couldn't even touch my son?'

Ngewu talked about her dissatisfaction with the inquests: 'Nobody spoke Xhosa or English, they only spoke Afrikaans and nobody was there to interpret for us. We didn't know what was going on. They would just talk and then they would say, "There is no case."' The post-mortem doctors told her that her son's body had twenty-five bullet wounds. Alex Boraine, deputy chair of the TRC, asked Ngewu what she thought had taken place that morning. 'When I'm just alone,' she replied,

I'm thinking to myself, was there any survivor out of all these killings? And why did the Boers kill everyone? Couldn't they just warn them? Not to leave even one to give witness. Now nobody knows the real-real story.

Wilson's account of the first TRC hearing closes with footage of Eunice Miya saying, 'My request is that these Boers must be put here, in front of us, in front of this commission, so that everybody here can see them.' The film then cuts to that very event. It is six months later, and nine police officers have been subpoenaed to appear at a special public hearing. 'For the first time in history,' says Khoisan, 'the entire command structure of a metropolitan police force was called to a public hearing to explain their actions.' One after another, the policemen take the stand – Odendal, Kleyn, Coetzee, Bothma, Grobbelaar. They all tell the same story: they received a tip-off that a police minibus was going to be attacked; five policemen hid in the bushes; the attackers arrived in a minibus of their own; one of them threw a grenade; all hell broke loose.

The police showed a video that they'd shot at the scene. The camera zooms in on a body with a grenade lying next to it. Then other bodies are shown. In each instance, there is a weapon nearby: an AK-47, a revolver, a Tokarev 7.62 mm pistol. 'Op die oomblik,' says the narrator, 'is daar 'n totaal van sewe swartes wat gedood is' – a total of seven blacks have been killed. The video then shows Christopher Piet's body being rolled over with a rope. This indignity was a step too far for the mothers. They had already been keening at the lingering close-ups of their dead sons. Now, several of them started wailing and screaming uncontrollably. They couldn't be consoled. Cynthia Ngewu threw a shoe at one of the policemen, and the hearing was adjourned.

The police video raised more questions than it provided answers. It opens with the words, 'It is now 7.40 on the 3rd of March, 1986.' This was just fifteen minutes after the first shot was fired, so how did the film crew get there so quickly? Stranger still was footage of an investigating officer inspecting a one-foot-deep hole in the ground. He explains that this was where the hand grenade thrown at the police had detonated. There is no damage to a vehicle parked three metres away, nor to a little white fence post just a metre away. The investigative unit consulted an explosives expert, who told them that a grenade of that type would have caused devastation within a fifteen-metre radius.

The police's version – that they had come under attack and had defended themselves – was looking increasingly unlikely. For one thing, they had fired far too many shots, particularly shots to the head from close range. Still, there was no conclusive evidence that they'd acted in poor faith, even if they had clearly been trigger-happy. The investigative unit continued its trawl through the mound of documents. Khoisan found correspondence from a Colonel Pieters to a Captain EA de Kock: 'Your vehicle was quite badly damaged ['taamlik beskadig'] during the operation and will be replaced as soon as possible.' Khoisan sat up. 'Is this the same man as "Prime Evil"?' he asked himself. Eugene de Kock, former head of the death squad at Vlakplaas, had recently been handed two life sentences plus 212 years. Khoisan established that it was indeed the same man. 'It is my firm belief,' he told TRC commissioner Mary Burton, 'that a death squad was involved.'

Rudolph Liebenberg, commander of the Cape Town security police's Terrorist Tracking Unit, was called to testify. He confirmed that Vlakplaas had been involved. Rian Bellingan, one of the men in the police video, had been a sergeant at Vlakplaas. And the minibus in which the activists had been transported to their deaths was registered to the security police in Pretoria. Gradually, the 'real-real story' started to emerge.

Towards the end of 1985, the security police in Cape Town had been struggling to cope with an escalation in armed attacks. They appealed to headquarters for assistance and were put in touch with Vlakplaas. De Kock decided to lure a group of activists into an ambush, and placed Bellingan in charge of the operation.* In early January 1986, Bellingan and his team travelled to

---

* It is somewhat surprising that De Kock opted for an ambush. Just a few months earlier, in October 1985, the government had been acutely embarrassed by an ambush known as the Trojan Horse Massacre. Children in Athlone had been throwing stones

Cape Town, where they were briefed by Liebenberg. Thereafter, Johannes Mbelo, a black policeman from Vlakplaas, infiltrated a group of activists. When the activists became suspicious, Mbelo was withdrawn and the askaris Jimmy Mbane and Shakes Maluleke were sent in (askaris were former freedom fighters who had been turned by the state). The two men supplied the group with weapons and repaired a faulty AK-47. Mbane reported back to Liebenberg that the activists were youths, and that only one of them had received any military training. Liebenberg told Mbane that it was his job to train them. For two months, Mbane instructed the activists in basic combat, while Maluleke provided political education. Together, the activists and the askaris planned an attack on a police minibus that each morning transported senior officers to Gugulethu police station.

At 3 a.m. on the morning of the ambush, the police held a briefing at Wingfield Naval Base. According to Mbelo, the words 'swept', 'eliminated' and 'taken out' were used. It was clear that the activists were to be killed. After the briefing, twenty-five heavily-armed policemen were deployed to the corner of NY1 and NY111 in Gugulethu. At 7.25 a.m., Jimmy Mbane, driving a Vlakplaas minibus, began dropping off the activists. Within minutes, they were all dead. Christopher Piet was the only one who had time to fire a shot. The TRC reports that the two askaris, Mbane and Maluleke, each received a R7 000 bonus for the operation. This was calculated at R1 000 per victim.

---

at government vehicles. Seven policemen armed with shotguns hid in wooden crates on the back of a South African Transport Services truck, which then drove slowly through a demonstration in Thornton Road. When a stone hit the windscreen, the truck stopped and the policemen appeared from the crates. They fired indiscriminately, killing three children and wounding many more. The incident was captured on film, and caused an international uproar. PW Botha responded by banning camera teams from unrest areas.

Only three people applied for amnesty: Bellingan, Mbane and Mbelo. As one of the requirements for amnesty was full disclosure, their testimonies included a wealth of new information. Bellingan admitted that the video team had been on standby at Wingfield. 'That video was made for the benefit of the members of the cabinet,' he said. 'For president PW Botha to be able to justify our police budget.' Mbane told the commission that he had pointed out the ambush spot to Bellingan and Liebenberg from a vehicle with tinted windows. When asked by the commissioners whether he wished to add anything to his testimony, he said, 'The only thing I can say is that I took other people's children and I trained them and led them to their death and I'm not happy about it.' Mbelo testified that weapons had indeed been planted on some of the bodies. 'The man I shot,' he said, 'he came running out of the bush with his hands up.' The man told Mbelo in Xhosa that he could take them to where the others were. Mbelo relayed the message to the white cop next to him. The cop said, 'Skiet die donner.' So Mbelo shot him. 'Jy skiet kak,' sneered the cop and took over. He pressed his R1 to the fallen man's stomach and pulled the trigger.

All three applicants received amnesty. 'This thing called reconciliation,' said Cynthia Ngewu, '… if I am understanding it correctly … if it means this perpetrator, this man who has killed Christopher Piet, if it means he becomes human again, this man, so that I, so that all of us, get our humanity back … then I agree, then I support it all.'

Wilson's film ends with Ngewu sitting in her living room. 'The spot where our children died, I would really love it if a monument could be erected there … It must be something so that coming from any direction a person should be able to see that this is where our children died.' In 2005, a monument to the Gugulethu Seven was unveiled on Human Rights Day. It is positioned precisely where Ngewu wished it to be. There is a separate statue for each of the fallen:

75

Christopher 'Rasta' Piet
Jabulani 'Jabu' Miya
Zandisile 'Semi' Mjobo
Mandla 'Baba' Mxinwa
Themba 'Tsepho' Molefi
Zabonke 'Walk Tall' Konile
Zola 'Mandela' Swelani

~

On 4 March, in Wembley Arena in London, Frank Bruno stopped Gerrie Coetzee in seventy-five seconds. It is unclear whether the bulk of South Africa's boxing fans were enthusiastic or not about a black Briton beating a white South African.

The Guyanese writer E R Braithwaite, who visited South Africa in 1974, provides one perspective. In his book '*Honorary White*', Braithwaite remarks that whenever he told black South Africans that he was from South America, they would ask him whether he knew Bob Foster, the American light heavyweight who had recently beaten South Africa's Pierre Fourie in the Rand Stadium in Johannesburg.* 'He's a great boxer,' they would say. 'A big champion. He beat the white man.'

Jacob Dlamini provides a contrary view. In his book *Native Nostalgia*, he says that he and his family supported Gerrie Coetzee. At the time, the Dlaminis lived in Katlehong, a township about ten kilometres from Coetzee's home town of Boksburg. 'He was one of ours and we cheered him on without reservation.' When Coetzee challenged Michael Dokes for the world heavyweight title in 1983, the Dlaminis followed the fight on Radio Zulu. When Coetzee stopped Dokes in the tenth

---

* Braithwaite explains that visiting 'Non-Whites' were designated 'Honorary Whites' to ensure that they escaped racial segregation and 'the many embarrassments which would otherwise attend them'.

round, his family 'was ecstatic. So were the other families on our street.'

*Native Nostalgia* is essentially an attempt to answer the question: 'What does it mean for a black South African to remember life under apartheid with fondness?' Dlamini is no apologist, however. He makes it clear that it is the life that is remembered with fondness, and not apartheid. Black support for Coetzee, he writes, 'may come as a surprise to those who would like to think that the world of apartheid was one of moral clarity'. In reality, the sports boycott wasn't that important to the people of Katlehong: 'What mattered was that [Coetzee] was one of us and we claimed him as such.'

~

On 7 March, President Botha lifted the partial state of emergency that had been in force in parts of the Witwatersrand and the eastern Cape for the previous eight months. He was taking this step, he told Parliament, as 'the situation has improved sufficiently'. Critics said Botha was responding more to international pressure than to any improvement in the security situation. Far from subsiding, unrest had escalated during the emergency.

The Eminent Persons Group remarked that martial law had been terminated only 'from a technical viewpoint'. In reality, South Africa was 'sliding even further into a permanent state of emergency in terms of the ordinary laws of the land'. Local lawyers had told the EPG that the existing array of state powers (coupled with the 'extraordinarily wide' definitions of words such as 'communism', 'terrorism' and 'treason') effectively rendered the country a police state. There had been no need for martial law, and the lawyers expressed surprise that it had been imposed in the first place. Most likely, they surmised, the government had been seeking to placate its conservative wing.

Whether the emergency had been necessary or not, the state

had taken full advantage of it. Almost 12 000 people had been detained without charge, and a further 25 000, the majority of them children, had been arrested for 'public violence'. Nearly 800 people had died in political unrest, with the security forces killing half of them. Botha had proclaimed the emergency, in July 1985, in response to an urban rebellion centred on the townships. The rebellion, which smouldered throughout the Eighties, burned fiercely for just over two years, from September 1984 until the end of 1986. Much of the political activity of the mid-Eighties only makes sense when viewed through the lens of this great uprising.

The trouble had started in 1983, when Pretoria proposed a new Tricameral Parliament. Indian South Africans and those classified as 'Coloured' would each get a chamber, and thus a limited say over their 'own affairs'. Black South Africans were excluded from the plan. They were expected to make do with the 'Koornhof Bills', named for the minister in charge of black affairs. This legislation introduced Black Local Authorities, a form of limited self-government in the townships. The BLAS were given the same powers as white municipalities, but, as journalist Brian Pottinger points out, they 'suffered terminally in three areas': legitimacy in the eyes of the public; funding; and administrative experience.

Pretoria presented these new measures as constitutional reforms, yet they were roundly rejected by the majority of South Africans. The UDF, a nationwide coalition of six hundred organisations – civic, community, church, trade union, youth, sport – was launched to oppose the measures. It urged voters to boycott elections for both the BLAS and the Tricameral Parliament. As a result, just eighteen per cent of eligible coloured voters turned out, and twelve per cent of Indians. The black turnout was even lower. Other organisations flocked to join the UDF, and it soon came to represent over two million people. Internal resistance, dormant for twenty years, was reactivated at a stroke.

Botha's plan had been to maintain white control by ceding political ground to 'moderate' blacks. But the territory he freed up was seized by radicals. Rather than easing pressure, his reforms had the opposite effect, triggering the most significant revolt in the country's history. It provided a textbook example of Alexis de Tocqueville's dictum: 'Experience teaches us that, generally speaking, the most perilous moment for a bad government is when it seeks to mend its ways.' Cabinet minister Gerrit Viljoen later called the Tricameral Parliament 'the greatest miscalculation in the history of the National Party'. Whites were divided by it (the Conservative Party split from the National Party), while blacks were united in opposition to it.

The great uprising started in the Vaal Triangle on 3 September 1984. While this happened to be the day the Tricameral Parliament took effect, the proximate cause was a decision by the BLAS to sharply increase rent and the cost of electricity. A protest march turned violent and led to rioting in Sharpeville and Sebokeng. Three councillors were hacked to death and their bodies burnt. The unrest soon engulfed neighbouring townships – Boipatong, Evaton, Tembisa, Bophelong – and spread from there. The BLAS were crippled by rent boycotts, and almost two hundred councillors resigned. In October, trade unions and youth organisations led mammoth stayaways, comprising 800 000 workers and 400 000 students.

It was the dawn of 'ungovernability' and the youth were the shock troops. They took it upon themselves to drum up support for mass meetings, rallies and demonstrations. They enforced strikes and stayaways, bus boycotts and consumer boycotts. They led attacks on 'puppets' working for local authorities, and on anyone else considered a 'collaborator', a 'sellout' or a 'quisling'. Many of their victims they burned. This practice morphed into a grisly new form of vigilante justice known as the necklace. A car tyre was forced over a victim's head and shoulders, filled with petrol, and set alight. Necklacing was reserved for the worst offenders – councillors, black policemen, and izimpimpi (informers).

Some of those who violated the consumer boycotts were also necklaced. More often, though, they were forced to consume what they had bought, whether this was raw chicken, cooking oil, soap powder or drain cleaner. An old woman died when youngsters forced her to drink a litre of Sta-Soft, a popular brand of fabric softener. Over time, the definition of 'collaborator' expanded to include anyone who rose above the crowd. Successful businessmen were deemed 'beneficiaries of the system' and were liable to have their shops looted, their cars burnt, or their homes destroyed.

A number of political commentators considered the urban rebellion to be a low-intensity civil war. Louis le Grange, the minister of law and order, saw it as 'war, plain and simple'. The state hit back hard, sending troops into the townships. 'For the majority of South Africans,' observes economist Francis Wilson, '1985 was a year of funerals.'

~

On 7 March, the Eminent Persons Group met with representatives of Women Against Apartheid. Trade unionist Emma Mashinini asked Malcolm Fraser, the former prime minister of Australia, why South African multinationals were allowed to operate in his country. She reminded him that when Pick n Pay had opened a store in Brisbane the previous year, the low prices had caused a stampede and a shopper had died. The only reason Pick n Pay was able to price itself so competitively in Australia, she said, was because it exploited black workers in South Africa.

Mashinini later published a memoir, *Strikes Have Followed Me All My Life*. She devotes much of it to the misery and deprivation of everyday life, especially as experienced by black women.

I resent being dominated by a man, and I resent being dominated by white people, be they man or woman. I don't know if that is being politicised. It is just trying to say, 'I am human. I exist. I am a complete person.'

Mashinini observes that '[s]ome of the jobs reserved for whites were so simple that we laughed to ourselves to see how superior they felt in performing them.' When she develops this line of thought, it reads like a theory for why an empire (or a regional superpower) might become decadent and fall:

In a society such as this, whites developed into very lazy people, because all the menial and hard tasks were landed on the backs of black people, and black women in particular gained from this and learned to develop resourcefulness, and talents and skills, and trained themselves to become truly competent.

~

On 15 March, a mass funeral was held for six of the Gugulethu Seven. It was a big day on the political calendar, and thirty thousand people attended. Rian Malan was one of them. In *My Traitor's Heart*, he remarks that journalists and cameramen were the only white civilians who dared venture into townships on days when protest action was imminent. Malan joined a contingent of local and foreign media huddled outside the gates of Gugulethu Stadium. People were streaming in. An old man stopped to accost them: 'We are not fooled! We know how you live, with your cars, your big houses, your swimming pools!' A marshal led the man away.

Inside, an army of young comrades was raising dust on the floor of the stadium. They were dancing the *toi*, a township war dance, running on the spot, their feet thundering in unison. They were cradling imaginary mortars, bazookas, and AK-47s in their arms and singing war songs about soldiers coming to free them.

A young boy was leading the comrades through a call-and-response routine.

In America such a boy would have been playing video games, but here he was already a soldier, smiting the sky with his tiny fists, puffing out his child's cheeks, and howling 'Harrrrrrrrrrrr,' in electrifying imitation of a machine gun.

In her documentary on the Gugulethu Seven, Lindy Wilson overlays footage of the funeral with the voice of an unidentified young man. *Our lifestyles were hectic*, he says, as a coffin is carried down a narrow lane between corrugated-iron shacks. *Some of us had to make many sacrifices – really. Losing your youth, playing, attending schools and so forth, being a child again, you lost it in the heat of the struggle, because you were now meddling in the national affairs, in the adult world.* Youths dressed in khaki fatigues and berets file past the camera. They are carrying coffins draped in the colours of the ANC, and their free hands are raised in fists. *We faced the apartheid regime, which was fully prepared to face us. … The townships were like a battleground. You could be maimed, you could be killed, you can be detained. You also had to prepare yourself for torture.* Clerics dressed in white lead a procession from the stadium. A police helicopter hovers overhead. *We were hoping that it won't take more than two years. Really, what is two years in service of the revolution when you can have a lifetime of liberation and freedom?* The procession is no longer a procession. It's now a huge mass of people, singing and ululating, dancing and bobbing in unison. They're like a river in full spate, gliding over whatever obstructs its path. Their combined voice drowns out all other sound, including the buzz of the helicopter. *Our experiences of poverty militarised us. When you send troops [into] the townships, really, we are going to force them, stones if needs be, guns if they were available.* The road is blocked by a line of Casspirs, with heavily armed soldiers standing before them. The crowd, still jogging, still bobbing, flows off to the right. *We were inspired by many things – poetry, oral histories, songs that we sung that Oliver Tambo must bring us guns so that we can liberate the country. We were no longer prepared to accept the second-class or third-class citizenship in a country of our birth.* Youths in yellow t-shirts and sunglasses lower a coffin into the ground. A woman's hand extends from under a blanket and drops a handful of earth. *Perhaps the best way to describe what we faced then is to quote the words, 'We were born in vinegar times and we were fed with lemons.'*

~

On 17 March, the State Security Council discussed the possible release from prison of Nelson Mandela. It considered nine options:

1. Unconditional release
2. Release subject to limitations
3. Release in exile (outside South Africa)
4. Release to the Transkei
5. Continued imprisonment with possible release at a later stage
6. Indeterminate/continued imprisonment
7. Indeterminate/continued imprisonment in household circumstances (luxury villa on Robben Island)

8. Conditional release: release on the condition that violence is abandoned
9. Release as a quid pro quo for something else (exchange for other prisoners).

The ssc discussed the pros and cons of each option. A perceived advantage of unconditional release, for instance, was that 'Mandela's martyr image will be damaged and may even disappear'. A disadvantage of the proposed villa on the Island was that 'it makes a joke of the SA legal system. Mandela is a criminal and not a political prisoner.'

The ssc endorsed option five, 'Continued imprisonment with possible release at a later stage.' It envisaged a number of advantages to this option:

The possibility that his health will deteriorate to such an extent that if he is released at a later stage, he will only be able to perform leadership functions for a short time

The position of Buthelezi and other TBVC [Transkei, Bophuthatswana, Venda, Ciskei] political leaders will not be threatened immediately

The government has time to break Mandela down psychologically, and to discredit him before release.

~

On 24 March, Fidel Castro cautioned the ANC against its policy of nationalisation. At a meeting in Havana, the Cuban president picked up a copy of the Freedom Charter – the ANC's Bible – and waved it at Oliver Tambo and Thabo Mbeki. Such a document, he said, would cost them dearly once they got into power. He gave the example of the Bacardi family that had fled the revolution and settled in Florida. As a consequence, Cuba no longer had the right to call its rum 'Bacardi', and thereby lost a significant proportion of its foreign income.

~

On 26 March, in Winterveld, a resettlement camp in the nominally independent homeland of Bophuthatswana, five thousand people gathered on a dusty soccer field to protest against the detention and torture of local youths. The crowd was mainly women and children, as most of the men were away in Pretoria, either working or seeking work. Policemen and soldiers arrived in trucks. They were dressed in riot gear and carried assault rifles. Colonel Andrew Molope of the Bophuthatswana Police addressed the residents with a loudhailer. He rebuked them, saying that they had not applied for permission to hold an open-air meeting. When a rumble of discontent started up, Molope warned the crowd that he would 'leave them lying all over the field like ants'.

A familiar sequence commenced: a stone, tear gas, more stones, a petrol bomb. True to his word, Molope ordered his men to open fire. Eleven people died and two hundred were wounded, some in the shooting and others in the beating that followed. Over a thousand people were arrested. By the time lawyer Peter Harris arrived on the scene, the field was deserted. Shoes were strewn everywhere, scraps of clothing hung from a barbed-wire fence, and 'dark patches of blood swarmed with blue flies'.

Bophuthatswana was the quintessential bantustan. It comprised seven distinct parcels of land spread across three South African provinces. Its geography alone demonstrated the folly of its existence. Bophuthatswana's president, Chief Lucas Mangope, was an articulate man, yet he was as intolerant of opposition as any of the bantustan puppets. Like Mangosuthu Buthelezi in KwaZulu, Mangope had declared war on the ANC. He was a key player in Pretoria's regional defence system. The SADF trained and armed his defence force. In return, Mangope took the fight to Umkhonto insurgents and local activists.

Mangope's fiefdom was prone to bloated administration, rampant embezzlement and monstrous infringements of human rights. As with all the homelands, there were regular struggles for power, involving coups, counter-coups and attempted assassinations. None of this entered the consciousness of white South Africans. To them, Bophuthatswana represented one thing and one thing alone: Sun City. The casino complex offered a release both from Calvinist morality (there was gambling, nudity, sex) and from cultural and sporting boycotts (Rod Stewart and Frank Sinatra performed; Jimmy Connors played Ivan Lendl). No one seemed to mind that the pleasure dome was situated within an archipelago of poverty.

Winterveld had no electricity or running water, and offered no local employment. Anyone who wished to work had to commute to far-off Pretoria. Seen from a functional point of view, the resettlement camp was a suburb of the city. Indeed, social scientists have described modern-day Pretoria as a 'three-lobed metro' consisting of the city itself, its north-western satellite (Winterveld) and its north-eastern satellite (the southern half of what had once been KwaNdebele). The two satellites, each of which is in a different province to the city itself, accommodate sixty per cent of the Tshwane Metropolitan area's working population.

The Winterveld massacre made international headlines, not least because a female French doctor was arrested and sjambokked. President Mangope ordered a commission of inquiry. Colonel Molope testified that the South African Police had trained him in 'methods of crowd control and the handling of unrest situations' and that he had followed best practice. 'I am certain,' he declared, 'there is not a single person in Winterveld who considers me a threat. I really work very well with the people.'

But Molope's actions belied his words. He always travelled with bodyguards and a police escort. He'd have known that he was a

86

marked man, having long been at the vanguard of the offensive against the youth. Molope had started out as a low-ranking policeman in South Africa. He transferred to Bophuthatswana in 1977, the year of nominal independence, and fast developed a reputation for brutality. Harris reports that Molope was 'a giant of a man who wore black reflective sunglasses and drove a black bullet-proof Mercedes-Benz with tinted windows'. Gliding through Bophuthatswana's bleak townships, he 'became the source of an almost mystical horror'.

Two months after the massacre, with the inquiry still in progress, Molope was promoted from colonel to brigadier. As he himself observed, the promotion was a public endorsement of the president's support. The families of the victims withdrew from the inquiry, and it devolved from a waste of time into a farce.

On a Saturday evening three months after the massacre, Brigadier Molope dismissed his bodyguards and drove to his girlfriend's house in Winterveld. Later that night, she answered a knock at the door. Two men with Kalashnikovs pushed their way in. Molope charged them, but they stopped him with several short bursts of automatic fire. They then emptied a few more bursts into his fallen body, just to be sure. The assassins walked out into the street, holding their weapons overhead. 'Ngenane ezindlini, singabe MK,' they told onlookers. 'Go into your houses, we are MK [Umkhonto we Sizwe].'

Molope was buried a week later. His coffin was enclosed in cement to prevent revenge pursuing him beyond the grave.

# APRIL

# 50 000 at festival

MORE than 50 000 people attended the Radio Thohoyandou music festival and ox braai at the Thohoyandou Independence Stadium on Saturday.

Housefull signs were up as early as 8am. People came from as far as Natal and Botswana. During the festival bottles were thrown after a power failure. This happened when Chico had just started performing.

But things calmed down when power was restored. The group that opened the festival, Rufaro, set the mood for the afternoon with their heavy African sounds.

The star of the afternoon was Yvonne Chaka Chaka. Others who performed were TZ Junior, The Juveniles, Pat Shange and Paul Ndlovu.

*Sowetan*, 1 April 1986

ON 1 APRIL, *Spitting Image*, a satirical puppet show on British television, released a song titled 'I've Never Met a Nice South African'. It appeared on the B-side of the show's chart-topping single 'The Chicken Song'.

The music video for 'I've Never Met a Nice South African' opens with PW Botha addressing a crowd of supporters:

My fellow South Africans, I feel it is time for me to tell you the facts as they really are:

1. Bananas are marsupials.
2. Cars run on gravy.
3. Salmon live in trees and eat pencils.
4. Reform in South Africa is on the way.

The crowd cheers after each 'fact', especially the last one. The action then cuts to a pub, where a patron is singing his life experience to an increasingly bored barman. Each verse comprises the same format: he has travelled the world from end to end, he has seen unicorns and the Yeti, he has met a Yorkshire miner who actually works, and he knows of a public swimming pool that isn't pissed in – 'but I've never met a nice South African'.

~

On 13 April, in Munsieville, a township near Krugersdorp, Winnie Mandela told a large crowd that 'the time for speeches and debate' had come to an end. 'We have no guns. We have only stones, boxes of matches and petrol. Together, hand in hand, with our matches and our necklaces we shall liberate this country.' Mandela's endorsement of necklacing caused an international outcry and was deeply embarrassing for the liberation movement.

It is not clear when the first necklacing took place. Hundreds of collaborators (and perceived collaborators) were killed in the urban rebellion of 1984–86. Many of them were burnt to death. In unconfirmed reports, a tyre was used in the burning of Sam Dlamini, the deputy mayor of Sharpeville, in September 1984. More substantial reports indicate that a tyre was used to burn Tamsanqa Kinikini, a councillor in KwaNobuhle, in March 1985. Kinikini was already dead, however, when the tyre was introduced.

The first indisputable necklacing – it was filmed by a Dutch news team – took place at Duduza on the East Rand in July 1985. A twenty-four-year-old activist named Maki Skhosana was attending the funeral of a group of fellow activists. They had died when the grenades they were trying to use exploded prematurely. A rumour went around that Skhosana was the girlfriend of 'Mike', the man who had supplied the booby-trapped grenades. A mob chased her, stoned her, beat her, ripped off most of her clothes, and then set her on fire with a petrol-filled tyre. The footage of the incident is difficult to watch. Skhosana is kneeling on the ground, swaying like a zombie, with fragments of smouldering material stuck to her skin and smoke rising from the top of her head. A jubilant crowd dances around her. They take turns in kicking her and pelting her with rocks. She topples over. A woman in a pleated skirt steps forward and kicks her repeatedly in the head to the rhythm of the onlookers' cries: 'Viva! Viva, Mandela!' and 'Mayife lenja (this dog must die)!'

It took many years for the story behind the booby-trapped grenades to emerge. Testifying before the TRC, members of the security police said that their sources in the townships had told them that certain activists linked to Cosas, the Congress of South African Students, were planning to attack the homes of black policemen. The activists were awaiting weapons from the ANC. The police decided to intervene, and launched Operation Zero Zero. A black policeman would infiltrate Cosas and supply the students with grenades of Soviet origin. The timing devices on the grenades would be set to zero seconds. The man chosen for the job was Joe Mamasela, a member of the death squad at Vlakplaas. He had become something of an expert at infiltrating groups of young activists, often presenting himself as an MK operative named Mike.

Mamasela befriended the students and offered them the grenades, as well as a limpet mine. He gave them a day of training and then informed them that the operation was to take place on the anniversary of the adoption of the Freedom Charter, 26 June. They were to attack the houses of the policemen with the grenades and destroy an electricity substation with the mine. Mamasela dispatched the students at midnight and watched from his car as they blew themselves to pieces. Eight students died and seven were seriously wounded. Mamasela was promoted to sergeant.

The TRC granted amnesty to thirteen security policemen for the East Rand grenade blasts. Mamasela didn't apply for amnesty. As a black man, he was a victim of apartheid, he said, not a perpetrator. The surviving students told the TRC that Skhosana knew nothing of the grenades. She had simply been in 'the wrong place at the wrong time'. Also testifying before the TRC was Skhosana's sister, Evelina Moloko: 'I approached her from the feet and I could identify the feet, I could identify her as my sister, but I could not see her face as there was a large rock on her face.'

Saturday, 20 July 1985, was a key day in South African history. It featured not only the first confirmed necklace killing, but also the funeral of the Cradock Four, a group of activists killed by the security police.* The funeral was a huge political event attended by thousands of people from all over the country. Nelson Mandela considered it 'the turning point' in the struggle. PW Botha must have been thinking along similar lines. That same night, he declared a state of emergency in thirty-six magisterial districts. Journalist Bridget Hilton-Barber remembers Botha's 'high-pitched, angry voice' as he spoke the words 'in light of the sit-hew-hayshun', before reading out the names of the districts: 'Aberdeen, Adelaide, Bedford, Cradock ...' The country erupted. So too did the incidence of necklace killings. Over the next few years, close to four hundred cases were reported. Three hundred of these took place in 1986.

Initially, the killing of Maki Skhosana wasn't seen as a new departure. Photojournalist Kevin Carter makes the point that it was the 'first' necklacing only because it was the first to be witnessed by people who dared not enter the townships. Youth activists had long favoured burning as a means of eliminating their opponents. After Kinikini's death in March 1985, his name became an eponym for torching a body – with or without a tyre. By August, the term 'Kentucky' was in vogue, with the victim being likened to fried chicken. Other terms included 'shisanyama' (burnt meat) and 'three cents' (the cost of a box of matches). Gradually, the use of a tyre caught on. Hung from the neck, it pinned the arms to the body, helping to immobilise the victim. The rubber burned more fiercely than petrol alone, and started to melt at four hundred degrees Celsius, making it difficult to extinguish the flames.

The moment the term 'necklace' entered the lexicon, it was

---

* Had it not been for the funeral of the Cradock Four, Maki Skhosana might well have lived. On each of the two weekends preceding her death, Bishop Tutu had attended funerals on the East Rand. At each of these funerals, he had saved someone from a mob. The day Skhosana died, he was away in Cradock.

universally adopted. Everyone recognised the potency of its imagery. The comrades used it as a warning, and state officials used it as anti-ANC propaganda. While other forms of protest, such as boycotts and firebombings, peaked at the same time, it was the necklace that became the emblem of the revolution. Just as the guillotine had cast a dark shadow over Paris during the French Revolution, so the necklace struck fear into the hearts of South Africans. It sent out a plume of black smoke that announced: 'This is the site of a public execution.' Its primary function was to rid the townships of collaborators and quislings. The ANC considered collaboration a 'disease' that was delaying the fall of apartheid. 'We could have long defeated the white oppressors,' announced the movement in one of its pamphlets, 'if it was not for the black traitors who are prepared to work for them.'

In June 1986, in Soweto, a reporter for the *New York Times* interviewed a youth in school uniform. He identified himself as Comrade Vusi and said he was proud to have taken part in necklacings. But was there not a better way, asked the reporter, of dealing with collaborators? 'No,' said Vusi. 'Say we take someone and tell them they must not inform on us. Then we let them go. They go straight to the system and identify us, and then we are all detained. It is better …' he began, allowing a fellow comrade to complete the sentence for him: 'just to get rid of them. Finished.' Both schoolboys smiled, whereupon the reporter asked whether it was necessary to use such a gruesome form of execution. 'Yes,' said Vusi. 'Then the others will know better than to inform. They will know not to delay the struggle.'

Also in June 1986, William Finnegan spoke to 'a chubby, pretty, soft-spoken' woman named Ruth, who lived in Alexandra. 'I think the necklace is a good thing,' said Ruth. She told Finnegan about a known impimpi who had been warned to stop. Later, the woman was spotted in a police Hippo, identifying activists. She was caught and set alight. 'It makes people think twice before they will collaborate,' said Ruth, 'even if they have no job and the system offers them money to inform. We are unarmed. They are armed. We must take and use the little weapons we have. Informers have been the system's greatest weapon for a very long time. Finally, now, we are stopping them.'

Winnie Mandela's call to liberate the country with matches and necklaces met with an outraged response from the white public. Necklacing was 'savage', 'barbaric', 'demonic'; it was 'loathsome and despicable'; the youth who engaged in it were 'uncivilised mobs', a 'Khmer Rouge element'. Responses such as these, observes political scientist Mahmood Mamdani, are 'less a critique on necklacing than a settler discourse on the lack of civilisation among natives'.

As for the white press, Finnegan reports that it

> made much more of the cruelty and horror of necklacing than it did of the cruelty and horror of soldiers shooting children in the back, when the latter was really a more horrific sort of murder, if one wanted to rank murder by degrees, as the law did. The press coverage seemed to play to white fears of the black mob, while ignoring black fears of the police and army.

The ANC had a tricky job responding to Winnie Mandela's speech. It needed to appease its international supporters without discouraging its foot soldiers. The campaign against izimpimpi and other collaborators was extremely successful, and was decimating the state's intelligence network. All a cadre had to do to dissuade a possible informer was rattle a box of matches.

Speaking on the same day Mandela delivered her speech, Oliver Tambo noted that, while he hadn't become 'used to' the practice of necklacing, he didn't condemn it. As the months passed and the issue cooled down, the ANC became bolder in its pronouncements. In September, its secretary-general, Alfred

Nzo, told the London *Sunday Times* that collaborators needed to be 'eliminated'. When asked whether this might be done by necklacing, he replied, 'Whatever the people decide to use to eliminate those enemy elements is their decision. If they decide to use "necklacing", we support it.' In December, MK chief of staff Chris Hani put out a statement on necklacing:

[T]he Black policeman, the Black special branch and the Black agent stay in the same township as we are, they have been the conduit through which information about our activities, about our plans has been passed to the enemy. This has made the process of organisation and mobilisation very difficult. So the necklace was a weapon devised by the oppressed themselves to remove this cancer from our society, the cancer of collaboration of the puppets. It is not a weapon of the ANC. It is a weapon of the masses themselves to cleanse the townships … I refuse to condemn our people when they mete out their own traditional forms of justice to those who collaborate. I understand their anger. Why should they be cool as icebergs, when they are being killed every day?

In contrast to the ANC's ambivalence, anti-apartheid clerics such as Bishop Desmond Tutu and Reverend Allan Boesak were horrified by necklacing. If the practice didn't stop, said Tutu, 'I will pack my bags, collect my family and leave this beautiful country.' He observed that there were 'many people around the world who support us. When they saw that woman burning on television, they must have said that maybe we are not ready for freedom.'

Tutu was not afraid of drawing a moral equivalence between the atrocities of the security forces and those of the comrades. Necklacing, he said, was just as dehumanising as police brutality. Tutu's views placed him in direct opposition to somebody like Thabo Mbeki, a vocal critic of anyone who tried to equate the crimes committed in support of apartheid with those committed in opposition to it.

When Winnie Madikizela-Mandela died in April 2018, the obituaries bore witness to her contested legacy. The white-aligned press praised her early role in the anti-apartheid struggle, but then quickly moved on to her later excesses. Andrew Donaldson, for instance, wrote:

> Imperious, aloof and a law unto herself, the renegade Madikizela-Mandela not only endorsed such brutal acts as the 'necklacing' of suspected police informers, but was revealed as having been personally responsible for the murder, torture, abduction and assault of a number of men, women and children through the infamous Mandela United Football Club.

The black press took a more sympathetic line. It observed that Madikizela-Mandela had risen to prominence at a time when the ANC had temporarily lost the ascendency in the domestic liberation struggle. Youth activists led the way and their leader was Winnie – rather than her imprisoned husband or the exiled Tambo. She was the embodiment of ungovernability; she was the Mother of the Nation. It was she who bore the brunt of arbitrary arrests, solitary confinement, torture, endless banning orders, and even banishment for eight years to a small town in the Orange Free State. If she'd made errors of judgment, it was because she'd been scarred by the struggle.

Shortly after the obituaries, the political commentators weighed in. Several of them noted that in the early 1990s the ANC effectively hung Winnie Mandela out to dry. Negotiations were on the horizon, and the organisation wanted to distance itself from the anarchy of the Eighties. 'Winnie had to "fall" for South Africa to rise', read the title of an article by William Gumede, while James Myburgh went with: 'How the necklace was hung around Winnie's neck.' In 1992, the ANC described necklacing as 'a barbaric and unacceptable method of execution' that it had 'never condoned'.

Myburgh argues that Mandela's Munsieville speech was 'completely consistent' with ANC objectives at the time. A month before her speech, the organisation had announced on Radio Freedom:

> We have managed to weaken the enemy using rudimentary weapons of war. With the usage of Molotov cocktails and necklaces, stones and knives, we have managed to drive the enemy to the extent where he has to impose a state of martial law.

And again, a month after Munsieville:

> Let us take all our weapons, both rudimentary and sophisticated, our necklaces, our grenades, our machine guns, our AK47s, our limpet mines and everything we can get – let us fight the vigilantes, the so-called 'fathers', together with the apartheid regime, together with the police and the army.

Any cadre listening to these broadcasts would have had little doubt that the necklace was one of the 'rudimentary' weapons the ANC was urging them to use.

As Myburgh points out, 'ANC propaganda was, metaphorically speaking, broadcast on two separate frequencies, for consumption by two different audiences, with two incompatible messages.' The one audience was the cadres on the ground, who needed to be urged to keep up the fight. The other audience was overseas supporters, donors and governments, who were crucial to the ANC's drive to isolate the South African state morally, politically and economically, but wanted to hear messages of moderation, non-violence and democratic values. Mandela's mistake, contends Myburgh, was not so much that she came out in favour of necklacing, but rather that she mixed up her audiences. She was directing her words to township dwellers, but also present in the crowd at Munsieville that day were foreign journalists and cameramen. Within hours, footage of her speech had been beamed around the world. It was propaganda heaven for Pretoria. When Oliver Tambo embarked on a world tour the following year, apartheid spy Craig Williamson ensured that wherever Tambo spoke, the local media received a video cassette containing footage of both Maki Skhosana's necklacing and Winnie Mandela's speech.

The person best positioned to support Mandela when the ANC abandoned her was her husband. A month after Munsieville, Winnie visited Nelson in Pollsmoor. Nelson's lawyer, Ismael Ayob, took notes: 'NM approved of WM's necklace speech. He said it was a good thing as there had not been one Black person who has attacked WM [since].' Nelson's comment remained secret for many years. When a researcher for Anthony Sampson's authorised biography uncovered it, Nelson threatened to pull the book if Sampson used it. Had Nelson acknowledged his comment – or had Winnie herself broadcast it – it would have done much to ease the pressure on her. Instead, writes Myburgh, 'she was left to bear history's opprobrium alone'.

~

On 14 April, the day after Winnie Mandela's speech, police in the self-governing homeland of Lebowa announced that they had discovered the scene of a massacre. The remains of thirty-two bodies had been buried in shallow graves in the hills around the neighbouring villages of Apel and GaNkoane in the Sekhukhuneland district. The victims had all been necklaced.

When the newspapers broke the story the following day, they reported that 'radicals' had eliminated 'collaborators with the system'. In the first few months of 1986, Lebowa had emerged as a new front line in the struggle against apartheid. Sekhukhuneland, in particular, was a hotbed of protest against Cedric Phatudi's government. Youths aligned to the UDF and to the Sekhukhuneland Youth Organisation led boycotts and stayaways, burned down government buildings, and called for the removal of tribal chiefs.

Within a day or two, it was revealed that the victims of the massacre were all elderly women. Teenaged boys had accused them of being witches and had condemned them to death by burning. The newspapers took to this new development with relish, dubbing the incident 'The Sekhukhuneland Witch Killings'. An employee at *The Star* told William Finnegan: 'The editors love witch burnings. They always send somebody out to these villages to photograph the gory remains and talk to the neighbours.'

A woman told a reporter for *The Star* that the day the comrades came for her mother they had been rolling tyres down the street and singing freedom songs. 'I would never forget those tyres dangling round her neck and the pall of thick black smoke I saw coming from the top of the mountain where she had been taken.' At least two of the victims were blind. The comrades carted one of them off in a wheelbarrow. Wessel Ebersohn, writing for *Leadership* magazine, considers the fate of another:

> Ramatsimela Sekonya did not know where she was being taken. She was eighty years old and blind, and went with her executioners willingly and without fear. She knew the village so well that, despite her blindness, she must have been aware that they were leading her up the dry and rocky hillside behind the mud houses. She would have felt the morning's first warmth on her skin and known that the sun was rising. She probably didn't know what they intended until the tyres were forced over her shoulders and they started pouring the petrol.

The Pedi people traditionally believed that misfortune and death (barring death from old age) were the work of external agents. These agents might be ancestors or they might be human beings with supernatural powers – that is, witches, and, to a lesser extent, sorcerers. There had long been witch-hunts in the northern Transvaal. For over a century, however, the accused had typically been banished rather than killed. In those rare cases that did involve killing, the victims had either been drowned or thrown down a ravine.

The incidence of killings increased dramatically after the Soweto uprising. Fourteen alleged sorcerers were burnt to death in Lebowa in late 1976 and early 1977. Gradually, the traditional practice of burning came to the fore again. By 1984, it had become the standard method for disposing of witches. They were burnt alive in their huts, thrown onto open fires, or doused with petrol and set alight.

The rural practice of burning made its way to the townships, where it morphed into necklacing. This urban innovation then travelled back to the rural areas. In an article titled 'The Ritual of the Necklace', Joanna Ball stresses the continuity between the earlier burnings and the later necklacings. She argues that the victims of these public executions – witches, sorcerers, collaborators, informers, shebeen owners, rapists and murderers – shared a common crime: they were all 'traitors to the social solidarity of the community'. They were all 'sell-outs'.

At the time of the Sekhukhuneland witch killings, the social dynamic in rural villages was precarious. The homelands of the northern Transvaal – in particular, KwaNdebele and Lebowa – had the country's highest rates of male absenteeism due to migrant labour (and many adult women were also away working). In 1985, over seventy per cent of the permanent population of Lebowa was under the age of twenty. These youngsters lived off their parents' remittances and their grandparents' pensions. Many grandmothers were in an untenable position. With their children away working, and often their husbands too, they became the de facto heads of households and were forced into the twin roles of disciplinarian and holder-of-purse-strings. The male youth found themselves beholden to elderly women and they bristled with resentment.

In February 1986, comrades from Apel and GaNkoane resolved to 'fight the chiefs', and marched on a neighbouring kraal. The chief's followers opened fire, killing one of them. The funeral became a focal point for youth mobilisation. Soon thereafter, a comrade was struck by lightning. The youth called a meeting to establish who was responsible for this new attack. In their customary way, they consulted an ngaka, or traditional healer, whose job it was to 'sniff out' witches. Three women were identified. The community wanted a second opinion, but the youth were impatient. They led the three women off to the hills and necklaced them.

It is unclear what sparked the massacre a few weeks later. It might have been anything, even a mild rebuke, so volatile was the situation by then. The youth took the law into their own hands, dispensing with tribal hierarchies and traditional practices. There was no need to waste money on another ngaka, they said: 'We all know who are the witches here.'

Researcher Edwin Ritchken investigated a witch killing in another part of Lebowa. His findings are consistent with what happened in Sekhukhuneland:

The youth had taken power and their way of showing it was by displaying, in the strongest and most public terms, that domineering wives, uncooperative neighbours, tight-fisted pensioners and a multitude of other relationships would no longer be tolerated.

Many of the villagers interviewed after the Apel and GaNkoane killings lamented the absence of the men: 'If only our menfolk were here our mothers and grandmothers would not have been taken away and killed so ruthlessly.'

For several months prior to the killings, the villages of Sekhukhuneland had been a no-go zone for the Lebowa police. When news of the killings leaked out, however, the police enlisted South African support and stormed in. The comrades fled for the hills, but were flushed out by helicopter. Several hundred youths were taken in for questioning and over a hundred were charged. The Lebowa police tried to pin the blame for the killings on veteran activist Peter Nchabeleng, head of the UDF in the northern Transvaal. They surrounded his house in Apel late one night and arrested him. 'Last time it was Robben Island,' they told him. 'This time we are going to kill you.' The next day Nchabeleng was dead. In the ensuing court case, the officer in charge of the arrest declared: 'A policeman may beat a person to death if he resists – but not intentionally.'

Nchabeleng had in fact been trying to stop the witch killings. He had warned the youth that their actions would cause the police to step in and would thus undermine UDF activity in the area.

A month after the events in Sekhukhuneland, a further thirty women were necklaced in Mapulaneng, in the east of Lebowa. Many of these killings were orchestrated by the Brooklyn Youth Organisation. Its members patrolled the streets at night, singing songs:

Informers, we will destroy you. Hayi! Hayi!
Witches, we will burn you. Hayi! Hayi!
Those who commit abortions, you will be destroyed.
    Hayi! Hayi!
Mrs Botha is barren – she gives birth to rats. Hayi! Hayi!
Mrs Mandela is fertile – she gives birth to comrades.
    Hayi!
Hayi! Hayi! Hayi! Hayi!

~

On 18 April, in Transkei, an explosion rocked the Wild Coast Sun casino complex. Two people died in the blast and several were injured. Eyewitnesses described how patrons abandoned their cash in slot machines and their chips on gaming tables and dashed for the exits. Others, however, remained in their seats. Historian Thula Simpson elaborates:

> In an extraordinary exhibit of human behaviour, many, seemingly mesmerised, continue playing on the machines even after repeated calls to evacuate the building are issued over the casino's loudspeakers. It takes a while for security personnel to prise them away from the machines and seal off the premises.

A week before the attack, MK operatives Pumzile Mayapi and Ndibulele Ndzamela had been ordered to bomb the casino by a regional commander who went by the code name China. Both men had been trained to handle explosives, Mayapi in Bulgaria and Ndzamela in East Germany. On the day of the operation, they entered the casino, each armed with a pistol and a limpet mine. They placed the mines next to one another, under the outflow pipe of a toilet in Pebbles restaurant.

Mayapi and Ndzamela were arrested eight months later in a joint operation by the Transkei police and the South African Special Branch. In 1989, the Umtata Supreme Court convicted the pair of murder and sabotage, and sentenced them to death. The following year, General Bantu Holomisa, the head of Transkei's government at the time, released the two. This was in line with the first general amnesty granted to political prisoners following the unbanning of the ANC.

In 1999, Mayapi and Ndzamela were granted 'on the spot' amnesty by the TRC. It was the first such granting of immediate amnesty in the commission's three-year history. The applicants had provided full disclosure and had demonstrated a political motive devoid of personal gain. Their sworn affidavits corroborated one another and their actions fell 'within the ambit of the political objectives of the African National Congress'. The Amnesty Committee supported their contention that the casino at the Wild Coast Sun was 'a symbol of apartheid and homeland corruption'.

~

On 19 April, the City of London Anti-Apartheid Group (commonly known as City Group) started a non-stop picket for the release of Nelson Mandela. Over a thousand demonstrators marched from Camden Town Hall to the South African embassy on Trafalgar Square. The crowd was boisterous, with much singing and chanting and waving of banners. It was also diverse. As one participant recalls, there were 'communists, anarchists, socialists, liberals, young people, old people'. Several hundred additional demonstrators were waiting for the marchers in Trafalgar Square. Many of them had peeled off from an earlier protest outside the US embassy (the US had bombed Libya that week).

The picket had three demands: the release of Nelson Mandela and all other political prisoners; the imposition of sanctions; and the closing of the South African embassy in London. A number of speakers addressed the crowd. 'Britain is up to its neck in apartheid,' announced Carol Brickley, one of the organisers of the picket. 'That's why we're here today. That's why we're making our protest. That's why we're going to stay.' And stay they did, night and day, for almost four years, through some of the coldest and wettest winters London had experienced in decades.

The picketers set up shop on the pavement outside South Africa House. They handed out leaflets and engaged passersby in conversation. They made impromptu speeches and sang freedom songs. On Fridays, they held mini-rallies. The picket quickly became a feature of the London landscape, and thus a highly visible protest against apartheid. It lasted 1408 days, finally coming to an end thirteen days after Mandela's release from prison. The extra days were due to the organisers' concern that the South African government might not have been acting in good faith.

City Group was founded by the exiled South African activist Norma Kitson, and the non-stop picket was her idea. Kitson had left South Africa in 1965, shortly after her husband David was sentenced to twenty years in prison for sabotage, furthering the aims of communism, and joining the High Command of Umkhonto we Sizwe. On his release in 1984, David joined Norma in England and remarried her. (They had divorced by mutual consent once it had become clear that he was going to spend a long time in prison.)

In 1985, City Group was expelled from the Anti-Apartheid Movement. The Kitsons had fallen foul of the ANC for showing solidarity with all the liberation movements of southern Africa – and not exclusively with the ANC and its ally Swapo, the South West Africa People's Organisation.

~

On 23 April, President Botha discussed the fate of Nelson Mandela in the House of Delegates, the Indian chamber of the Tricameral Parliament:

> Knowing that he is going to continue with violence because he's not prepared to say he would stop it, as a responsible head of state, I must now release him so that he can carry on with his violence, and then arrest him? What a nonsensical argument.

~

On 24 April, the *Sowetan* reported that South African Airways had trained five air hostesses for Bop Air. Bophuthatswana's new airline had acquired a forty-four-seater Hawker Siddeley and would soon introduce international flights from Mmabatho Airport.

A spokesperson for SAA said that none of the women they had interviewed for the Bop Air positions had been 'suitable' candidates for their own flights. When asked whether he meant suitable black candidates, he said:

> There is an unfortunate situation in South Africa. We sometimes talk about Indians, coloureds and blacks. I like to call black 'black' without making any distinctions. In these terms, we have already got black air hostesses.

When asked whether SAA had any black hostesses other than Indian and coloured hostesses, he said they did not.

~

On 26 April, during a rugby match at Loftus Versfeld Stadium in Pretoria, Burger Geldenhuys punched Andy Dalton, breaking his jaw in several places. Geldenhuys was playing for Northern Transvaal and Dalton was captain of the visiting New Zealand Cavaliers. As the forwards broke away from a lineout, Geldenhuys ran up behind the unsuspecting Dalton and caught him with a round-house right. Dalton dropped like a sack of mielie meal.

The Cavaliers were an 'unofficial' New Zealand team. The players had been invited to South Africa after the cancellation of an official tour by the All Blacks the previous year, in 1985. Two lawyers in New Zealand had raised a legal challenge and a judge had ruled that sporting contact with South Africa would place the New Zealand Rugby Union in breach of its own constitution, in particular of a clause that committed it to 'the fostering and encouragement of the game of rugby'. The ruling was not unexpected. Political tension had been ramping up for decades. In the early years of apartheid, New Zealand had acquiesced to South Africa's veto on racially mixed sport and had overlooked Maori players for selection. In the build-up to the All Blacks' 1960 visit, 150000 New Zealanders signed a petition in support of 'No Maoris, No Tour', but the tour went ahead anyway. Prior to the All Blacks' 1970 visit, Prime Minister John Vorster created a loophole for Maoris, conferring on them the status of 'Honorary Whites'. Vorster was likely expecting censure from the left, but in fact his problems came from the right. A splinter of traditionalists broke away from his party and formed the Herstigte Nasionale Party. The All Blacks visited again in 1976. Twenty-five African countries boycotted that year's Montreal Olympics in protest.

Matters came to a head in 1981. Despite New Zealand being a signatory to the 1977 Gleneagles Agreement, whereby member countries of the Commonwealth agreed 'vigorously to combat the evil of apartheid' by withholding sporting contact, Prime Minister Robert Muldoon welcomed the Springboks to his rugby-mad country. 'Politics should stay out of sport,' he declared. Thousands of New Zealanders disagreed with him. They took to the streets, blockading motorways and airports. They interrupted broadcasts, tore down fences and invaded playing fields. Two of the games were called off, and the Auckland test was disrupted when a low-flying Cessna dropped flour bombs onto the pitch.

It was against this background that the Cavaliers tour of 1986 took place. It was much anticipated. Upon the arrival of the visiting players, a South African Rugby Board official crowed that rugby had 'changed the face of South Africa' by driving Nelson Mandela from the front pages of the country's newspapers. The Cavaliers were virtually a full-strength All

Black team, comprising twenty-eight of the thirty players who had been selected for the official tour the previous year. They weren't, however, allowed to play in black. Instead, their kit was a dark blue adorned with yellow strips (a nod to Yellow Pages, the tour sponsor). Centre Warwick Taylor describes the confusion he and many of his teammates felt:

> I remember, just before the last Test, I had an All Black tracksuit with me and I put it on because that'd get me going. But that's when I realised we weren't All Blacks, we were there as individuals and we weren't representing New Zealand, we were representing ourselves and the country wasn't behind us. We were just young guys who wanted our chance to beat South Africa on their own turf.

There were rumours of secret payments, with figures ranging from £30 000 to £50 000 per player (the lower end of this scale was roughly five years' pay for the average New Zealander). On the opening day of the tour, *The Glasgow Herald* speculated on the source of the funds. So starved was the South African public of international competition, that each of the four 'tests' was likely to gross £350 000 at the gates. The other eight matches would also be money-spinners. Yellow Pages was stumping up £850 000. Its parent company, a large Afrikaans-owned conglomerate, would receive a ninety per cent tax rebate on this figure (as had been the arrangement earlier in the year, when they'd sponsored the Australian rebel cricketers). The 'bands of gold' on the Cavaliers' kit, suggested the *Herald*, were 'an apt embellishment'. The players claimed they were receiving £14 per day, as per their contracts. Rugby was an amateur code at the time, and the International Rugby Board allowed for a maximum per diem of £15.

The Springboks won the 'test' series 3–1, but the tour was a public-relations disaster. They wouldn't again face quality opposition until the fall of apartheid.* For New Zealand, there was an unexpected benefit. When the rebels got home, they were banned for two matches and the selectors were forced to pick an entirely new team. Known as the Baby Blacks, the youngsters introduced a new style of running rugby and helped New Zealand win the inaugural World Cup the following year. They ushered in a period of All Black dominance that has lasted thirty years and counting.

While Burger Geldenhuys was never officially sanctioned for his brutal assault, he wasn't selected for any of the 'test' matches. In the weeks that followed, Geldenhuys's punch occupied more space in the minds of white South Africans than another event that took place that same day, the nuclear disaster at Chernobyl.

~

On 30 April, just before midnight, a seventy-four-year-old Capetonian named Mildred Dow was woken by a loud bang. 'I thought a bus had gone through my lounge,' she told a reporter from the *Cape Times*. 'So I phoned the Flying Squad right away. But they said, "Don't worry. It was a bomb."'

The blast had been caused by a limpet mine left in a toilet block at Mowbray station. It seemed at first that right-wingers might have been responsible, as Dow lived next door to the

---

* The fact that the Springboks were denied quality opposition may, in a small way, have hastened the fall of apartheid. When sixty Afrikaners met with the ANC in Dakar in 1987, an ANC delegate observed: 'Amazing. Here's South Africa in economic crisis because of sanctions, increasingly isolated from the currents of global culture because of the cultural boycott, and all these guys want to talk about is the Springboks.'

offices of the Black Sash, a women's organisation that fought for social justice. It transpired, however, that Umkhonto we Sizwe was attacking 'soft' targets on the eve of May Day.

# MAY

## TONIGHT TOP 10 SINGLES

1 (1) *When The Going Gets Tough* — Billy Ocean

2 (3) *A Good Heart* — Feargal Sharkey

3 (5) *Walk Of Life* — Dire Straits

4 (2) *We Built This City* — Starship

5 (6) *Say You Say Me* — Lionel Richie

6 (11) *Trapped* — Colonel Abrahams

7 (4) *They Say It's Gonna Rain* — Hazel Dean

8 (13) *Hit That Perfect Beat* — Bronski Beat

9 (7) *West End Girls* — Pet Shop Boys

10 (15) *The Sun Always Shines on TV* — A-Ha

## TOP LOCALS

1 *Let's Get It On* — **Sipho Hotstix Mabuse**

2 *Bongani* — **Brenda & The Big Dudes**

3 *Suburban Hum* — **Jennifer Fergusson**

4 *If You're Ready* — **Jonathan Butler**

5 *Third World Child* — **Johnny Clegg**

6 *Don't Dance* — **Kalahari Surfers**

7 *Do The Lurch* — **Cherry Faced Lurchers**

8 *Pambere* — **Mapantsulas**

9 *Suburb In The South* — **Tribe After Tribe**

10 *Come To Me* — **Stimela.**

*The Argus*, 1 May 1986

ON 1 MAY, one and a half million workers stayed away from work. They were joined by hundreds of thousands of school pupils and students. It was the biggest stayaway in South African history. The workers were commemorating the hundredth anniversary of International Labour Day, and demanded that the government declare May Day a public holiday.

Cosatu, a trade-union federation, held rallies around the country. It had been launched five months earlier, and represented half a million workers. 'A giant has risen,' announced Cyril Ramaphosa, then general secretary of its largest affiliate, the National Union of Mineworkers. Cosatu president Elijah Barayi used the federation's launch to nail its colours to the mast: 'Cosatu gives Botha six months to get rid of passes. If that does not take place, we will burn the passes of the black man.' He also called on the homeland leaders to resign. Overnight, Cosatu had become a powerful new player in the struggle against apartheid.

Mangosuthu Buthelezi chose May Day to launch Inkatha's union Uwusa. Seventy thousand Inkatha members filled King's Park Stadium in Durban. Uwusa was created in direct opposition to Cosatu, and was covertly funded by the South African government. A coffin emblazoned with the words 'Cosatu is dead' was paraded around the stadium.

Buthelezi arrived by helicopter.

'Is it your wish,' he asked, 'that disinvestment and sanctions should now be imposed in South Africa?'

'No!' roared the crowd.

~

On 14 May, the *Cape Times* published an article titled 'Maps reveal violent wave'. A year earlier, the newspaper had run its first 'Unrest Map', a daily geographical breakdown of violence. The article was basically a progress report:

> The maps reveal a wave of violence across almost all parts of South Africa and bring home the extent to which insurrection has spread from the major industrial centres to tiny rural towns which seldom if ever featured in the news before.

Over the course of the previous twelve months, the names of several townships had become household words: KwaNobuhle, Duduza, Tumahole, Lawaaikamp.

The Unrest Maps used an alphabetical index to label events. The article noted that previously the index had seldom extended beyond the letter 'H' (i.e., ten events per day). Now it regularly ran to 'x' and 'Y'. The map accompanying the article ran to 'U'. The letters were dotted all over the country: an illegal gathering in Daveyton; a stoned vehicle in Mamelodi; a charred body in Soweto; a petrol-bombed shop in Enjindini; birdshot fired at stone-throwers in Duncan Village.

~

On 17 May, hundreds of vigilantes from Old Crossroads, an established squatter camp in Cape Town, attacked the more recent satellite camps of Nyanga Bush, Nyanga Extension and Portland Cement. For five days, they torched and looted, leaving forty people dead and thirty thousand homeless.

The vigilantes were known as the Witdoeke, a reference to the pieces of white cloth they tied around their heads and arms for identification. They were covertly (and sometimes not-so-covertly) supported by state security forces. 'The vigilantes moved among the Casspirs,' reported a resident. 'The police at no stage attempted to stop the vigilantes from burning our houses.' The police were on the scene throughout, yet not a single vigilante was arrested. Several witnesses saw white men in balaclavas setting fire to shacks. Once the satellite camps had been razed, soldiers encircled the site with barbed wire to keep residents out.

The history of Crossroads and the satellite camps is in many ways the history of black people in Cape Town. In the 1960s, American writer Allen Drury visited South Africa. In his book *A Very Strange Society*, he characterises Cape Town as a place 'where such charming people live and such terrible things are done'. In the 1980s, another American writer visited. Joseph Lelyveld observed that white Capetonians considered themselves more enlightened than their compatriots in the Transvaal – and yet influx control was more ruthlessly enforced in Cape Town than it was anywhere else in the country. In his book *Move Your Shadow*, Lelyveld points to an area of a few square kilometres around the airport, labelling it an 'astonishing exposition of the racial caste system in operation'. A foreign visitor on a tight schedule could 'fly in and absorb the whole bitter lesson in a couple of hours'.

Cape Town was the only metropolitan area in the country where blacks were a minority. The government had declared the Cape a 'coloured labour preference area', which meant that a black person could only get a job if no coloured person wanted it. The policy failed, however, to stem the flow of 'illegals', most of them migrants from the Xhosa homelands. Transkei and Ciskei were places of deprivation and squalor. They were overcrowded and offered almost no employment. Their rates of infant mortality were four times higher than that of the squatter camps of Cape Town. As one migrant put it: 'The countryside is pushing you into the cities to survive; the cities are pushing you into the countryside to die.'

The authorities fought a brutal campaign against the squatters. They bulldozed shanties in the dead of winter, confiscated building materials, conducted almost daily raids, and deported anyone whose papers weren't in order. But their efforts were largely in vain. Deportees placed on trains bound for the Transkei got off at nearby Worcester and headed straight back to Cape Town. Police buses carried squatters a thousand kilometres to the Ciskei border. After one such journey, the officer in charge reportedly said, 'They will be back in Cape Town before us.'

In February 1975, people evicted from Brown's Farm squatter camp were told to go to 'the crossroads' east of Nyanga, where Landsdowne Road met Klipfontein Road. The authorities considered this patch of land a transit camp, but its new residents, most of whom had been in the Cape for over a decade, saw it as a permanent home. The initial 'legals' were joined by thousands of 'illegals', and the Bantu Administration Board started issuing eviction notices. The months – and then years – that followed were characterised by raids and resistance, threats and reprieves, petitions and press releases. The residents faced down the government and eventually won the right to stay. In the process, Crossroads became the best-known squatter camp in the world.

In 1978, Piet Koornhof became the minister in charge of black affairs. He was more lenient than his predecessors had been (halting a demolition on his very first day in office), yet ultimately his policies proved more divisive. He promised accommodation for those who qualified, and deportation for those who did not. This pitted 'legals' against 'illegals' and undermined the solidarity of the community. Josette Cole alludes to Koornhof's style of management in the subtitle of her book *Crossroads: The Politics of Reform and Repression 1976–1986*.

The women of Crossroads had played a leading role in the initial resistance and had become a more powerful force than the men. Koornhof's policies ushered in power struggles, and a new grouping of men rose to ascendency. Under the leadership of Johnson Ngxobongwana, they extorted 'taxes' from the residents and used the money to buy 'community' cars and to pay themselves salaries. They responded brutally to anyone who challenged their authority. Cole reports that the men ran Crossroads 'like a mini-bantustan', entrenching the idea of violence as a valid response to internal opposition. Some years after the rise of Ngxobongwana, resident Regina Ntongana told the *Cape Times*: 'We, the women, are the foundations of Crossroads. Since the men took over, things have never been the same. The men are only concerned with their own benefits.'

Ngxobongwana's reign was complex and contradictory. When the state announced plans to move legal squatters to Khayelitsha, a sprawling new township ten kilometres down the line, and to deport illegal squatters to the homelands, Ngxobongwana responded: 'If the government says black people should go to the homelands, then why don't they go back to Holland? … We will not leave. We will die here.' The UDF mistook Ngxobongwana for a progressive leader and backed him. His methods became increasingly autocratic and he came to rely on a private militia known as 'Ngxobongwana's army'. Wearing bits of white cloth to identify themselves, they attacked his political opponents and terrorised residents.

In 1985, the militant youth mobilised against Ngxobongwana and his cronies. In February, twenty-two people died in a pitched battle. As the nationwide urban rebellion gathered pace, and the Cape Flats gradually turned into a war zone, the situation in Old Crossroads remained tense, with periodic skirmishes throughout the year. A number of residents chose to move away. 'We are being forced to go to Khayelitsha,' said one. 'It is not our intention, but we are running away from the fighting. It is exactly what the government wants us to do.'

As the year drew to a close, open conflict broke out in New Crossroads, a satellite camp south-west of Nyanga. The press dubbed the opposing factions 'comrades' and 'fathers'. 'The children are being very disrespectful to the fathers,' reported one of the latter. On New Year's Eve, the comrades hacked a councillor to death with pangas. On New Year's Day 1986, the 'fathers' launched a series of revenge attacks, killing four. 'Unless the maqabane [comrades] cool down,' said Sam Ndima, Ngxobongwana's deputy, 'the people of Old Crossroads will hunt them down and beat them again. ... The maqabane have to stop making petrol bombs and holding kangaroo courts. We will not allow them to beat and punish their own people.'

In March, the comrades killed seven Witdoeke (as members of Ngxobongwana's Army were now known) as well as two policemen. From this point forward, reports Cole, the objectives of the state and of the Old Crossroads leadership fused: both wanted to rid the area of 'militant comrades' (and, indeed, of all 'illegal' squatters). The state wished to upgrade this eyesore near the airport, and the local leadership had been promised they would benefit from any such upgrades. Some 'legal' residents would also benefit, but three-quarters of them would be packed off to Khayelitsha or the homelands.

Ever since late 1985, when hostilities had escalated, Ngxobongwana and Ndima had periodically threatened the satellite camps, saying that they harboured too many comrades. In April, Ndima invited the leaders of Nyanga Bush, Nyanga Extension and Portland Cement to a meeting. He told them that the commander of the Athlone police station had promised him four hundred firearms. His men would use these weapons, he said, to 'flatten' their settlements.

The destruction of the satellite camps in May gave rise to thousands of refugees. Many sought shelter in KTC, a satellite camp named for a trading store. When it became apparent that KTC was the next target of the Witdoeke, the Legal Resource Centre approached the Supreme Court for protection. The LRC provided compelling evidence of state participation in the May attack. The court duly granted an interdict restraining the police, the defence force and the leadership of Old Crossroads from 'participating in, assisting in, encouraging, permitting, or allowing any unlawful attack upon … the area known as KTC'.

The interdict was ignored. On the morning of 9 June 1986, hundreds of Witdoeke gathered outside the Development Board offices near Old Crossroads. They were armed with axes, pangas, metal bars and the wherewithal for starting fires. The crowd set off for KTC in groups of twenty to thirty. According to affidavits provided by clergymen, journalists and residents, the participation of the security forces was even more blatant in June than it had been in May.

The main thrust of the attack consisted of a large number of Witdoeke headed by a police Casspir. 'The Casspir was driving very slowly,' reported a witness, 'at walking speed.' The column advanced on the Zolani Centre, which was providing housing to hundreds of refugees and aid to many thousand more. A crowd of KTC residents gathered to protect the centre. The Casspir started firing tear gas and birdshot at them, making it impossible for the residents to defend either the centre or their homes. Over the course of the day, and the three days that followed, KTC was systematically destroyed. The structures burned easily. Where a township like Nyanga comprised 'matchbox' houses, and the established squatter camps corrugated-iron shanties, the structures in satellite camps were made mostly from sheets of plastic and cardboard, reinforced with sticks and bits of wood. The Witdoeke's favoured method for setting them alight was to throw fragments of burning tyre onto the roofs. The police used an incendiary device: it fired projectiles which 'would explode', explained a witness, 'and there would be flames'.

Some historians conflate the Crossroads attacks of 17–21 May and 9–12 June into a single twenty-seven-day war. All told, sixty people died and sixty thousand lost their homes. It was the most brutal forced removal in South African history – notwithstanding the fact that the government had suspended its policy of forced removals the previous year. Pretoria distanced itself from the entire episode, labelling it 'black-on-black violence'. A handful of progressive publications raised objections, but for the most part this became the accepted narrative. 'It is blacks fighting against blacks,' reported US president Ronald Reagan, 'because there is still a tribal situation involved there in that community.'

Pretoria's use of the phrase 'black-on-black violence' was cynical in the extreme.* The government had gone out of its way to exploit divisions in black communities with a view to encouraging right-wing vigilantism. It was a new twist in the age-old strategy of divide and rule. 'The government has always used blacks to eliminate blacks,' observed Winnie Mandela.

> They want the rest of the world to see us as barbarians who don't know what we are doing, barbarians who are fighting each other, not Pretoria. They want to reduce the people's struggle to tribal factions, to civil war among ourselves.

Vigilante groups started to emerge in townships throughout the country towards the end of 1985. 'They came to greatest prominence,' notes Brian Pottinger, 'in the period between the first and second states of emergency' – that is, between March and June of 1986. These groups tended to comprise older men who had a vested interest in the apartheid system: homeland

---

* Activists took issue with the very phrase 'black-on-black violence', noting that it carried racist suggestions of tribalism, savagery and internecine violence. Audrey Coleman asked whether people spoke of 'white-on-white violence' in Germany and France during the Second World War: 'No. They spoke about the resistance and the killing of collaborators.'

officials, black councillors and policemen, shopkeepers, shebeen- and taxi-owners, as well as the disaffected and the desperately poor, who could be coerced or paid to take up arms against the comrades. The groups went by a range of colourful names: the A-Team, the Green Berets, the Peacemakers, the Russians, the Witdoeke, African Persons' Concerned Committee, Amadoda, Amabutho and Mbokodo. Mabangalala was a generic term. Almost everyone who addresses the issue identifies Inkatha as the largest and most influential of the vigilante groups.

In his book *Mabangalala: The Rise of Right-Wing Vigilantes in South Africa*, human-rights lawyer Nicholas Haysom argues that 'in almost every case' of so-called black-on-black violence, the police aligned themselves with 'the more conservative of the feuding groups':

> the fathers against the youth, the community councillors against popular civic organisations, homeland vigilantes against dissidents, and any group that challenges the UDF. Alleged police patronage of vigilantes need go no further than to afford such vigilantes a licence to continue their operations or lethargy in curtailing them.

In some instances, says Haysom, the security forces actively supported the vigilantes since the police and the army were 'limited by potential publicity and hindered by legal considera- tions in their ability to perpetrate the deliberate terror needed to combat popular organisations'. Oliver Tambo observed that the vigilante groups were internal versions of Renamo, Unita and other surrogate forces operating outside the country.

Not all vigilante action was initiated or sponsored by the state. In many townships, there was a genuine backlash against the excesses of the comrades. Conservative groups objected to the imposition of boycotts without consultation, the sentencing of alleged collaborators by people's courts, and especially public executions, often by necklacing. Initially, at least, these groups stood for the restoration of law and order.

When President Botha addressed the House of Delegates in April 1986, he said, 'Since the lifting of the state of emergency, black-on-black violence has increased alarmingly.' He bemoaned the fact that the press often reported the number of people killed in unrest situations without stating who was doing the killing. The impression was created that the state was responsible, he said, when in fact more blacks were killed by 'other blacks' than by the security forces. Botha was, of course, himself creating a false impression. He was inviting his audience to assume that 'radicals' were killing 'moderates', when in fact, as he well knew, the profile of township violence had changed over the previous few months and the majority of killings were now perpetrated by right-wing vigilantes, many of them sponsored by the state.

From the government's point of view, vigilantes proved a highly effective weapon. It took the Witdoeke less than a month to achieve what a succession of ministers had failed to accomplish in a decade: the removal of the most resistant squatters in Cape Town. In the process, Crossroads, once symbol of left-wing resistance, came to be associated with right-wing oppression.

~

On 19 May, the SADF launched cross-border raids on Gaborone, Harare and Lusaka. The operation was conducted on the orders of General Magnus Malan, with the full support of PW Botha. The two men didn't bother to inform the State Security Council. The ostensible target of the raids was ANC bases in neighbouring capitals, yet it seemed clear that the true target was the Commonwealth's Eminent Persons Group. The ANC certainly thought so, characterising the raids as 'the regime's crystal clear response' to the EPG's proposal for negotiations. An official in the Department of Foreign Affairs later removed all doubt, describing the raids as 'a deliberate, pre-planned act designed to shipwreck and totally derail the EPG initiative'.

Four days prior to the raid, the members of the EPG had arrived in the country for a second, week-long visit. They had been invited back by Pik Botha, the minister of foreign affairs. He had responded encouragingly to their 'Possible Negotiating Concept', going so far as to dispatch an envoy to London. The EPG met with Pik Botha on 15 May, Nelson Mandela on the 16th, Oliver Tambo on the 17th, and representatives of Cosatu, the UDF and the Azanian People's Organisation on the 18th. The moderates – in government as well as in the liberation movements – were in favour of negotiations, while the hawks opposed this. It appeared as if the ANC was set to accept the EPG's terms. The government, notes journalist Allister Sparks, had arrived at a moment of truth:

> Did it really want to negotiate with [the ANC] or not? There could be no more ducking and diving, no more doublethink and doublespeak, no more stalling even. The EPG was here and an answer would have to be given.

PW Botha gave his answer in no uncertain terms: he dispatched the helicopter gunships. Viewed as attacks on ANC bases, the raids were a flop. In Lusaka, the bombs missed their target, hitting instead a United Nations camp for Angolan and Namibian refugees. In Harare, they hit the designated target, but this target turned out to be a deserted house. If, however, the raids are viewed as an attack on the Commonwealth initiative, then they were a resounding success. The EPG abandoned its mission and flew out of South Africa that same day.

The raids proved a disaster for Botha. He alienated several senior cabinet ministers and a number of important allies, including Margaret Thatcher. Brian Pottinger observes that the raids, along with Botha's Rubicon speech, 'set the country irrevocably on the road to political isolation'. When Patti Waldmeir interviewed Botha some years later, all he had to say on the subject of the raids was that if Reagan could bomb Libya then he could bomb Zambia.

Penguin published the EPG report, *Mission to South Africa*, just twenty-four days after the group had left the country. Unsurprisingly, the report is vigorous in its denunciation of white minority rule. The opening sentences read:

> None of us was prepared for the full reality of apartheid. As a contrivance of social engineering, it is awesome in its cruelty. It is achieved and sustained only through force, creating human misery and deprivation and blighting the lives of millions.

*Mission to South Africa* looks briefly at history, in particular the Natives Land Act of 1913, whereby 86.3 per cent of the land was given to whites and only 13.7 per cent to blacks. 'Thus, a predominantly black country becomes predominantly white, and the black becomes an alien in his own land.' For the most part, however, the report concerns itself with the contemporary, providing a snapshot of the political climate in 1986. It considers President Botha's reforms and concludes that they should be seen in the context of 'a determination not to give up white control'. In the EPG's view, all reforms – those already implemented as well as those promised – 'founder on group rights'. The EPG goes on to remark that, even if reforms went so far as to repeal all apartheid legislation, 'economic factors alone would militate against dramatic change for a long time'.

In its consultations with 'all sectors of South African society', the EPG was 'forcibly struck by the overwhelming desire in the country for a non-violent negotiated settlement'. Even the government seemed keen – until, of course, Botha launched his 'calculated assault on the peace process itself'. The EPG makes the point that negotiations would only be possible if the government was prepared to deal with 'leaders of the people's choosing rather than with puppets of its own creation'.

> Among the many striking figures whom we met in the course of our work, Nelson Mandela and Oliver Tambo stand out. Their reasonableness, absence of rancour and readiness to find negotiated solutions ... impressed us deeply. If the Government finds itself unable to talk with men like Mandela and Tambo, then the future of South Africa is bleak indeed.

It was not within the EPG mandate to make recommendations. The group went out of its way, however, to raise the spectre of sanctions. In its conclusion, it points to the fact that 'the Government of South Africa has itself used economic measures against its neighbours and that such measures are patently instruments of its own national policy'.

The report observes that the South African government 'has perfected a specialised political vocabulary which, while saying one thing, means quite another'. When the government spoke of 'a right of self-determination for minorities', what it really meant was 'separate residential, educational and health facilities'. Government ministers declared apartheid to be 'outmoded' or even 'dead', yet the idea of separate 'groups' and 'communities' was alive and well.

In his book *Endgame in South Africa?*, which was published in 1986, social scientist Robin Cohen remarks: '[I]t is now rare to hear any government spokesperson mention the word "apartheid".' In its stead, he writes, officials employ 'a considerable variety of newspeak' – including such opaque terms such as 'ethnic pluralism', 'multi-national development', 'co-operative co-existence' and 'consociational democracy'. (In July 1986, the minister of home affairs, Stoffel van der Merwe, confirmed

Cohen's observation: the government no longer used the word 'apartheid', he said, as it was now used so often in English in a pejorative sense – perhaps a thousand times more often.)

It would appear that the more brutal a policy was, the more it lent itself to newspeak. There weren't such things as forced removals. Rather, 'surplus people' were 'endorsed out' of urban areas. Or 'inappropriately situated' communities, many of them in 'black spots', were subject to 'developmental relocation'. The security forces had a newspeak all of their own. Opponents weren't killed. They were 'eliminated', or 'got rid of' (ontslae raak), or 'a plan was made'. Anyone who spoke out against apartheid was a 'Marxist', and a township child with a stone was an 'armed terrorist'. When the defence force established a death squad in April 1986, it was named the Civil Cooperation Bureau.

Some of the government's verbal gymnastics weren't so much newspeak as misspeak. The term 'communism' was wilfully misused. Its definition in the statutes was so broad as to encompass almost any opposition to the government. This included the activities of liberals, most of whom were avowedly anti-communist. Prime Minister John Vorster admitted as much: 'You don't have to be a communist to be banned under the Suppression of Communism Act.' National Party MPs became adept at twisting language. When MC Botha was caught out in 1983, he complained that he hadn't meant 'promise' in the 'ordinary sense of the word'.

Sindiwe Magona identifies a subtler form of government newspeak. In her memoir *To My Children's Children*, she points to 'the worlds of difference between a library and a library'. Black South Africans were prohibited from using public libraries, she notes. 'Instead, we were fobbed off with inadequate, silly, and insultingly inferior things: one-room structures furnished with whatever was being thrown out by royal whiteness.' The fact that such vastly different spaces could be identified by the same word, notes Magona, 'is precisely what the government banked on when its publications gave statistics on, for example, how many libraries (or hospitals, or schools, or housing units, or whatever) had been set aside for the exclusive use of each racial group'.

~

On 21 May, Louis Nel, the deputy minister of information, labelled the ANC a terrorist organisation. Speaking at an international press conference, he noted that MK used landmines, limpet mines, hand grenades and car bombs. One couldn't be sure of one's victims with these weapons, said Nel. In choosing to use them, the liberation movement showed that it wasn't a guerrilla outfit targeting security forces, but rather a terrorist organisation targeting civilians. 'In this regard,' said Nel, 'the ANC does not differ at all from the PLO, the IRA and the Red Brigade.'

Nel provided figures for the period 1976–86:

The ANC had detonated 12 landmines (the security
    forces had located and seized 30 undetonated mines)
The ANC had detonated 115 limpet mines (the security
    forces had seized 409 undetonated mines)
The ANC had detonated 113 hand grenades (the security
    forces had seized 1 273 unused grenades).

Nel's press conference came a month after a harangue on terrorism by P W Botha. The president told Parliament that Muammar Gaddafi, 'the mad dog of the Middle East', was sponsoring international terror. That very week, said Botha, the ANC, the PAC, Swapo and the Palestine Liberation Organisation would be attending a 'clandestine conference' in Tripoli with a view to 'making 1986 the decisive year in the defeat of Pretoria'.

~

On 22 May, the AWB disrupted a National Party rally in Pietersburg in the northern Transvaal. Pik Botha was due to address the
rally, but two hours before the scheduled start a thousand members of the far-right organisation broke into the hall and took
possession of it. They had arrived from all over the Transvaal.
Allister Sparks witnessed the scene: there were 'burly farmers'
with 'revolvers thrust into their belts' and women dressed like
Voortrekkers, in ankle-length dresses and kappies; derogatory
posters aimed at the minister read 'Pik Swart' (pitch-black); and
there were little swastika flags everywhere.

Some National Party supporters tried to reclaim the ground
they'd lost, but they were beaten back by brown-shirted storm
troopers. The hall resounded with chants of 'A-W-B! A-W-B!'
as Eugène Terre'Blanche was hoisted onto sturdy shoulders
and handed a loudhailer. Hands shot up in stiff-armed salutes.
Terre'Blanche announced that the meeting was cancelled. The
crowd went into a frenzy. 'Tonight,' he cried, 'the volk has won
a great victory in the fight to get back our fatherland.'

A police officer gave the crowd three minutes to disperse. They
jeered at him. Tear-gas canisters were fired into the packed hall.
Sparks writes that he had just got out ahead of the stampede when
a window shattered above him and a man tumbled out, hitting
a cement walkway with a thud. 'The bastards!' the man yelled,
blood pouring from his face. 'They're supposed to do this to the
kaffirs, not us.' This was the first time the state had used tear gas
on fellow Afrikaners.

Sparks discusses the disrupted rally in his book *The Mind of
South Africa*. He presents it as one of two signature events that
illustrate a 'sudden diversity within what had been the solid edi-
fice of Afrikaner Nationalism'. He argues that the breakaway of
the Conservative Party in 1983, in protest against the Tricameral
Parliament, weakened Afrikaner solidarity by demonstrating that
it was no longer 'an act of ethnic treason' to leave the National
Party. Schisms started to appear on both the right and the left.

Sparks's other signature event took place a year later, when sixty verligte Afrikaners flew to Dakar, Senegal, to meet with the ANC.

~

On 25 May, in Mitchells Plain on the outskirts of Cape Town, Moegsien Abrahams was beaten to death at a UDF meeting. Whispers went around that Abrahams and another attendee were police informers. Pandemonium broke out when the chairman of the meeting announced that 'two unwelcome guests at the back of the hall must please leave'. Abrahams was escorted to the stage for his own safety. Officials tried to sneak him out of the back door while 'Nkosi Sikelel' iAfrika' was being sung, but a group of youths had gone around the outside of the hall.* They pursued Abrahams and beat him with a half-brick and an iron bar.

Two days after the killing, Trevor Manuel, the regional secretary of the UDF, released a statement. He said that his organisation regretted 'the loss of life of Mr Moegsien Abrahams', but that

the UDF cannot and will not take responsibility, whether directly or indirectly, for his death. The blame rests four square on the shoulders of those responsible for the breeding of hatred and anger by their maintenance of apartheid.

~

---

* A list of the national anthems of South Africa (starting in 1795) reads like a condensed political history: 'God Save the King'; 'God Save the Queen'; 'God Save the King'; 'God Save the Queen'; 'Die Stem van Suid-Afrika'; 'Nkosi Sikelel' iAfrika'; 'National Anthem of South Africa' (a hybrid of 'Die Stem' and 'Nkosi').

On 28 May, in South West Africa, two armoured vehicles belonging to the SADF were involved in an incident on the road from Oshakati to Ondangwa. An Eland was towing a broken-down Buffel. As the Eland rounded a corner, the Buffel swung out wide and hit a landmine. Technically, a Buffel is a mine-resistant, ambush-protected armoured personnel carrier, and so the soldiers inside should have been safe. One of them, however, wasn't strapped to his seat, and he was thrown out. The Buffel keeled over and fell on top of him, pinning his legs to the road.

Blood was squirting from an artery in the soldier's right thigh. His colleagues tried to restrict the flow, but there wasn't enough space for them to manoeuvre. One of them noticed a small boy standing nearby and shouted, 'Hei, Vambo, kom hier!' The boy came over and lay flat on his stomach next to the trapped soldier, squeezing his hand into the gap between the tarmac and the side wall of the fallen Buffel. He felt around for the artery and pinched it closed. There was already a large pool of blood on the road. As they lay there, the bleeding soldier told the boy about his mother, father and girlfriend back home. The boy said not to worry; injured soldiers were sent home and he'd soon be eating his mother's food again. The boy lay next to the soldier for a long time, losing all feeling in his hand and arm. Eventually, a helicopter arrived. The Buffel was lifted and the soldier freed. Medics applied clamps and loaded him onto the helicopter. His army buddies later learnt that he died on the flight.

Bertie Cloete describes the incident in his book *Pionne* (pawns). He himself was the soldier who'd hailed the boy. Twenty years later, Cloete was involved in an airline catering business in Namibia. One evening, he related the story of the overturned Buffel to a group of business partners. One of them, a Namibian named Sakeus 'Sacky' Shanghala, asked a number of pertinent questions and then stunned the gathering by telling them that he was the boy who had pinched the artery closed. Cloete and Shanghala had been business partners for three years, yet, until that moment, they'd had no idea that they'd previously met in the war zone.

Shanghala was able to flesh out the story. He had been eight years old at the time. His parents, a pastor and a nurse, had been heavily involved in the struggle to liberate Namibia. They regularly treated injured Swapo fighters at their home. Young Sacky would 'quote unquote' steal medicines and 'verbande' (bandages) from the local hospital, stuff them into his school bag, and cycle home. That was the reason he was out on his BMX that day. He'd watched as the Buffel toppled over 'in slow motion'. He was supposed to avoid the South African forces, but his curiosity got the better of him.

Shanghala recalled that once the 'chopper' had flown off, he was forgotten in the commotion. He sat on the side of the road, trying to get feeling back in his arm. His Twin Niagara Falls T-shirt was soaked in blood. One of the soldiers noticed him and gave him a Tarzan energy bar, which he remembered as being 'like a fruit with a lot of sugar on top of it'. He'd eaten it immediately and disposed of the wrapper. If anyone at home discovered he had been 'taking food from the other guys', his parents would get into trouble. As it was, his mother gave him a 'mooi pakslae' when he got home. 'Never talk to the South Africans,' she'd said as she gave him a good hiding.

By the time Cloete and Shanghala met again, the latter had acquired two law degrees. In 2012, Shanghala became a member of Parliament, and in 2015 was appointed attorney general. At the time of writing, he is Namibia's minister of justice.

*Pionne* tells the story of Cloete's two years of military service. The book is both sad and funny, but the abiding emotion is anger. Cloete wrote it because of something that was said at a braai one afternoon. He was turning the meat when he heard one of his father's friends say, 'The children of today have all the opportunities.' Cloete exploded:

What a load of kak! You guys fucked it all up for us! You lived like lords. You turned the blacks into slaves and you lined up a job for every Afrikaner on the railways and in the post office. We fought your wars for you and all you gave us was a hospital pass. Do you realise that white males can't find work in this country anymore?

Towards the end of the book, Cloete wonders why the war went on for so long. Did those at the top really not know, as everybody else seemed to know, that apartheid was doomed? 'Or maybe, just maybe, they did know, but there were other objectives. State pensions that needed to kick in. Careers that needed to complete their arc. How many pawn lives were enough?'

At the time of the Buffel incident, the conflict – known variously as the South African Border War, the Angolan Bush War and the Namibian War of Independence – had already been on the go for almost twenty years. The South Africans had a number of overlapping objectives: they wanted to prevent Swapo from liberating South West Africa; they wanted to establish a 'cordon sanitaire' to keep the ANC at bay; and, like the Americans in Vietnam, they wanted to halt the spread of 'worldwide red aggression'. Niël Barnard, the head of South Africa's National Intelligence Service throughout the 1980s, summed up the conflict thus: 'Yes, we were able to win skirmishes and certain battles and had other short-term successes, but it stands to reason that in the long run South Africa had no hope of emerging victorious from a military conflict with the Soviet Union. It was a fairly simple equation.'

Cloete describes his time in the army as 'some of the best years of my life that I never want over again'. He recalls being home on leave, reading through recent copies of *Die Burger* to see what it had to say about the war. It was all lies and propaganda. 'Suddenly I long for the border. Everything's honest and straight up there. Right or wrong. Alive or dead.' A few days later, Cloete flew back north with presents for his mates: the latest cassette tapes by A-ha, Jennifer Rush and Pet Shop Boys, as well as chocolates such as Mars Bars and Inside Storys. 'I feel at home here amongst the makalani palms, the sjonas [salt pans], the boerbokke, the orange-red sunsets – far removed from the complicated questions and structures of the fatherland.'

The chocolates are a reminder of how young the troops were. When Cloete and his cohorts received their first pay cheques, for many it was the most money they had ever seen. Some Saturdays they got leave and headed into town: 'What do you buy with this money that's burning a hole in your pocket? Cigarettes and all those things you always wanted to buy as a child. As many Bar Ones and salt-and-vinegar chips as you want.'

~

On 31 May, the far right celebrated the twenty-fifth anniversary of Republic Day at the Voortrekker Monument outside Pretoria. It was the first time the Conservative Party, the Herstigte Nasionale Party, the AWB and the Afrikaner Volkswag had held a joint rally. Eugène Terre'Blanche, whose AWB had been disrupting National Party rallies across the country, was the star of the show. 'We are not conservatives,' he thundered. 'We are freedom fighters.'

Ten thousand people showed up for the rally. This was far short of the hundred thousand the organisers had been expecting. A spokesperson for the Conservative Party blamed the poor attendance on the day's sporting events. The Springbok rugby team beat the New Zealand Cavaliers in the final 'test', and Bruce Fordyce won the Comrades Marathon from Bob de la Motte and Hoseah Tjale.

# JUNE

# Our 10 beauty spotters

**By DOREEN LEVIN**

THOUSANDS of Sunday Times and Rapport readers proved they could spot a winner when they correctly forecast that Sandy McCormack would become Miss South Africa 1986, that Nancy Riach and Marie-Louise le Roux would be her princesses, and that Meryl Stoltenkamp and Roberta Alessandri would make up the first five.

And the first 10 to get it right have each won a beautiful Tissot watch.

They are Mr C Barry of Windhoek; Mr J Booyens of Boksburg North; Miss L H Cooper of Clarens; Mrs E Harrison of Montana, Pretoria; Machel Lewis of Blinkpan; Priscilla Louw of Carletonville; Alice Mossner of Welkom; Mrs M Nel of Waterkloof; Mrs A Strydom of Pietersburg; and Mr W J van Zyl of Bethlehem.

*Sunday Times*, 1 June 1986

ON 1 JUNE, in New York, freedom fighter Seretse Choabe screamed at Professor Pieter de Lange: 'I'll shoot you, you Broederbonder!' They were attending a conference on education in South Africa sponsored by the Ford Foundation. Choabe was a senior official in the ANC and De Lange was chairman of the Broederbond.

Thabo Mbeki looked across at Mac Maharaj. Something had to be done. The ANC didn't want to look like a bunch of crazed revolutionaries hell-bent on wiping out Afrikaners. Maharaj invited the gathering to view Choabe's outburst as an expression of black frustration: 'If you want to understand what apartheid is about, and how it affects us, then listen to the raw anger of Seretse.'

The trouble had started when De Lange observed that there was ongoing debate between enlightened and conservative factions within the Broederbond – verligtes and verkramptes – over how they might accommodate black political aspirations. Choabe leapt to his feet. What happened in white circles was 'completely irrelevant', he yelled. 'We don't have the patience to wait while they end their debate.'

The Broederbond had always been a few steps ahead of the National Party. It had originally devised the concept of separate development, and for many years had operated as a think tank for government policy. Now it was plotting apartheid's demise. De Lange, who was elected chairman in 1983, immediately began ridding the organisation of conservative hardliners. In a discussion document titled 'Basic Political Conditions for the Survival of the Afrikaner', he reversed the logic of apartheid, claiming that 'the exclusion of effective black participation in the political process is a threat to white survival … the biggest risk which we run today is to take no risk at all'. Early in 1986, the majority of the Broederbond's fifteen thousand members voted for full citizenship for black South Africans – although this was not as progressive as it might sound. Some political analysts have observed that the Broederbonders weren't yet thinking of unbanning the ANC, but rather of striking a deal with 'moderate blacks' such as Mangosuthu Buthelezi.

De Lange and Mbeki talked for three hours one evening after the conference proceedings, and then met up again the following day for lunch. They had a chuckle when De Lange's Western-made lighter failed and Mbeki helped him out with one made in North Korea. De Lange was up against a formidable opponent. Mbeki, with his ever-present pipe, was a picture of urbanity and charm. Yet he was a master at beguiling adversaries and steering situations in his favour. When a delegation of verligte Afrikaners visited Dakar the following year, a journalist covering the event noticed a sign warning of pickpockets. 'Maybe someone should have warned the Afrikaners to beware of pipe-smoking ANC members bearing gifts of charm and charisma. Many of them were the victims, in the nicest possible way, of an emotional mugging.'

De Lange and Mbeki spent much of the time talking about PW Botha's reforms. The ANC considered these to be little more than window dressing. The previous year, Mandela had told a visitor to Pollsmoor: 'It is not my ambition to marry a white woman or swim in a white pool. It is political equality that we want.' De Lange tried to convince Mbeki that the removal of segregation was significant. It allayed Afrikaner fears and so opened the way to dialogue:

We can remove the Group Areas Act tomorrow and it's not going to make any difference, because your people don't have the money to move into the expensive white suburbs. So from your point of view it will be a meaningless change, but for us Afrikaners it will mean we will wake up one day and realise that nothing has changed, that we are still all right, we've not perished as a people.

Mbeki remained sceptical of De Lange's commitment to fundamental change. On De Lange's return to South Africa, however, he resigned as principal of Rand Afrikaans University and devoted himself to national reconciliation. 'There is a tremendous need,' he said, 'for more contact.'

~

On 2 June, the government's Bureau of Information published a booklet titled *Talking with the ANC*. Louis Nel, the deputy minister of information, stated in a press release that the aim of the booklet was to 'properly inform' South Africans 'on the nature of the ANC'.

The booklet presents statements made by leaders of the liberation movement on a range of topics, including violence, the economy and multi-party democracy. These statements are then juxtaposed with statements made by state officials. The booklet includes excerpts from both Nelson Mandela's Rivonia Trial speech of 1964 and Winnie Mandela's necklacing speech of 1986. There are also numerous excerpts from Radio Freedom broadcasts:

[O]ur people must begin to identify collaborators and enemy agents and kill them. The puppets in the Tricameral Parliament and the Bantustans must be destroyed.

*Talking with the ANC* is not a subtle document. It casts the liberation movement in a radical and violent light, while presenting the government as the voice of order and reason. ANC spokesperson Tim Ngubane is quoted as saying: 'We want to make the death of a collaborator so grotesque that people will never think of it.' President Botha is quoted as saying: 'It is my deepest wish that senseless violence be abandoned now.'

Academic Riedwaan Moosage identifies the booklet as a prime example of the state's 'discursive war' – in particular, its propensity to differentiate between 'supposedly primitive and civilised' behaviours. Brian Pottinger comments that *Talking with the ANC* 'had nothing to do with its title: it was really about not talking with the ANC'. By quoting selectively and ignoring context, the state was able to 'distort the debate'. No one could correct this distortion as it was illegal to quote members of the ANC.

Four days after the Bureau released its booklet, the *Weekly Mail* published an eight-inch photograph on its front page. The title of the accompanying article read: 'The first legal photo of Nelson Mandela in 22 years'. The subtitle read: '(Courtesy of the Minister of Information)'. The article explained that nobody knew what Mandela looked like, as it had been illegal to photograph him or reprint photographs of him since 1964 – 'Until this week, that is.'

The Department of Prisons had granted permission to the Department of Information to reprint an old photograph of Mandela in *Talking with the ANC*. Lawyers for the *Weekly Mail* chose to interpret this permission in the broadest possible sense, arguing that it pertained to the actual photograph, and not to the Department, the Bureau, or the booklet.

Using a tactic they called 'the all-clear flag', the newspaper's editors included this argument in the article itself. The idea, explains academic Bryan Trabold, was to 'bluff their way' past the security policemen whose job it was to read the newspaper the evening before publication. 'Given that the average security policeman had only a vague sense of the numerous and ever-changing media restrictions, and given the extremely hierarchical nature of South African society ... an impressive-sounding legal justification [carried] considerable weight.'

Three months later, the Bureau quietly re-issued *Talking with the ANC*, this time omitting Mandela's portrait. The *Weekly Mail* noticed the omission, and again reprinted the photo. Thanks to the photo, it reported, the booklet had been 'a surprise hit in the townships'.

~

On 3 June, *The Star* illustrated the onset of cold weather with a front-page photograph of two smiling girls wearing ski caps and woollen gloves. *The Star* Africa edition, which was aimed at black readers, went with a different photograph: a group of men, women and children standing around a fire in the rain. Their shacks had been destroyed by state-sponsored vigilantes.

~

On 6 June, on a gravel road south-west of Pretoria, George Henry Burt shot and killed Constable Jacob Buti Ndimande. Burt's motive for killing the policeman is not known. The story made the news not so much because of the killing, but because of the cover-up. Burt roped in a friend, and together they necklaced Ndimande's body. The press had a field day, with headlines such as 'White man faces necklace charge' and 'White guilty of necklace murder'.

William Finnegan drove around KwaNdebele a month after Ndimande's death. He met a priest who kept a record of political murders in the area. 'I can usually tell by the wounds who did the killing,' said the priest. 'R-1 rifles are the army. So are rifle-butt beatings. Pistols and sjamboks are Mbokodo. Burned is the comrades.' But things weren't so clear-cut any more. The priest had recently come across sixteen necklace killings that he didn't believe were perpetrated by the comrades. His story corresponded with 'a grisly new wrinkle' Finnegan had heard about: 'necklacings by vigilantes and security forces, which were subsequently blamed on the resistance'.

The ANC voiced its concern. In September 1986, Oliver Tambo accused vigilantes of 'sometimes necklacing anti-apartheid activists and then blaming it on the ANC'. In December, Chris Hani warned: '[O]ur people must be careful, in the sense that the enemy would employ provocateurs to use the necklace.'

~

On 7 June, George Matanzima, the prime minister of Transkei, announced that the Transkei Police had been ordered to necklace people who were caught necklacing others. Perpetrators would be 'doused in petrol to die the same way as their victims'. Matanzima made the announcement at a school function for the handing over of uniforms to drum majorettes. Matanzima's brother Kaiser, who had recently retired as president of Transkei, had introduced drum majorettes into schools as a way of dissuading children from getting involved in political protest.

~

On 10 June, George De'Ath, a freelance cameraman working for Britain's ITN, along with his sound man Andile Fosi, were attacked by Witdoek vigilantes while covering the violence in KTC squatter camp. Fosi had mistakenly addressed the vigilantes as 'qabane' (comrades). The vigilantes responded by slashing at the two newsmen with pangas.

De'Ath, who had been born in South Africa, had covered many of the world's hotspots, including the Rhodesian Bush War and the conflict in Beirut. He died in Groote Schuur Hospital a few days after the attack – the first journalist to be killed since the start of the urban rebellion in September 1984.

~

On 11 June, David Dalling, an opposition MP, read into the parliamentary record the affidavits of a number of victims of police brutality. Parliament was the only place in the country where freedom of speech was not curtailed, and the press were permitted to print anything that was said there.

The previous week, in a debate concerning the Public Safety Amendment Bill, Dalling had referred to abuses by the police. He had argued that the bill amounted to 'an official Government-approved licence to beat up and kill – that is exactly what it is – a licence to organise vigilante groups and a licence to terrorise entire communities, as they have done in Crossroads'. The minister of law and order took exception to Dalling's comments, and accused him of 'berekende onwaarhede' (calculated untruths). He called on Dalling to provide Parliament with 'the examples and the facts', adding, 'I challenge the honourable member to do so.'

Seven days later, Dalling once again stood before the House: 'Sir, I would like to avail myself of the opportunity which the honourable the minister has afforded me by issuing that challenge. I call as my first witness ...' Dalling did not, however, call on flesh-and-blood witnesses. Instead, he read the affidavits of people who had been beaten, tortured or shot by the police. Some of the affidavits were long and detailed. Many of them were shocking. One complainant, a minor, explained that, while watching the riots in Alexandra, he had been hit by a stray bullet. When the police came past and found him lying on the ground with a bullet wound, they shot him three more times, once in each leg, and once in an arm.

Dalling held up a stack of documents: 'I just want to tell those honourable members here who say that they do not condone excesses that I have approximately 150 affidavits right here – documents and statements emanating from Port Elizabeth, East London, Alexandra, Soweto and every corner of South Africa.' Dalling invited the MPs to read the affidavits:

> I am very keen that honourable members of this house should be aware of what is going on in this country because when the Nuremberg trials are held in this country – and it will happen – I do not want any members in this house to say, 'I did not know.'

~

On or about 11 June, Harry Oppenheimer and Cyril Ramaphosa, two of the most powerful men in the South African mining industry, met for the first time. They had been invited to speak at the *Weekly Mail*'s first-anniversary celebration, which was held at the Market Theatre in Johannesburg. Oppenheimer had been chairman of Anglo American and De Beers, while Ramaphosa was general secretary of the National Union of Mineworkers.

Ramaphosa's biographer, Anthony Butler, remarks that his subject had been invited to this supposedly genteel affair as 'the darling of the media'. It was a tense time for Ramaphosa, with NUM and De Beers locked in wage negotiations. Also, it was his first opportunity to tell Oppenheimer what he thought about the conditions on South African mines. Ramaphosa went on the attack:

> The mining industry ... is the industry which provided the furnace in which race discrimination was baked. ... Today it relies absolutely on the exploitative migrant labour system and on police oppression to operate. It pays black workers the lowest wages of any major mining company in the world, with the exception of India.

Oppenheimer was dismissive in his response:

> I differ a little bit from Cyril Ramaphosa in thinking this ought to be fun. I think it should be rather a cheerful occasion. ... The fact that Mr Cyril Ramaphosa is here to talk as he did talk tonight – a most touching and moving speech, made all the more touching by the neglect of facts – the fact that we are both here to talk together is something which gives me very great pleasure.

Ramaphosa managed to get the last word. While Oppenheimer loved diamonds, he said, 'I love diamond diggers.'

~

On 12 June, at a joint sitting of the Tricameral Parliament, President Botha announced: 'I have decided to introduce a state of emergency throughout the entire country.' The government, he said, had 'information at its disposal concerning what is being planned for the coming days by radicals and revolutionary elements'. Botha was referring to 16 June, the tenth anniversary of the Soweto uprising. There was a widespread belief that 'the revolution' would start that day.

The emergency was neither debated in Parliament nor discussed in cabinet. Not even the State Security Council had reached consensus. It was very much Botha's emergency – and just about every country that mattered condemned it, including South Africa's most important allies, the United States, the United Kingdom and West Germany. Local reaction was fierce. Colin Eglin, the leader of the opposition, labelled the new emergency 'the most severe clampdown on civil liberty ... in the history of South Africa'. He told Parliament that the country was now 'a police state'. Journalist Ken Owen observed that certain of the emergency regulations pushed the country 'across the line that separates authoritarian from totalitarian societies'. Only the Afrikaans press welcomed martial law. It had been imposed, remarked *Beeld*, 'chiefly to protect Black moderates from Black radicals'.

Botha announced the emergency during an afternoon sitting, noting that it applied 'with effect from today'. He failed to tell the parliamentarians that it had been in place since midnight, and that thousands of activists had already been detained. The following day, the *Sowetan* published a list of two thousand suspected detainees. The issue was duly banned, with the security police raiding vendors and news stands, and seizing all copies. Also banned was that day's issue of the *Weekly Mail*, which reported on its front page that the government was steering the country 'down a road to nowhere'. This phrase was deemed 'subversive' for undermining public confidence in the idea that martial law would come to an end one day.

The emergency regulations granted the security forces far-reaching powers. The lowliest member of the police, the military and the prison service was permitted to arrest suspects without a warrant and to detain them without trial. In addition, all state officials were indemnified in advance against any criminal or civil proceedings that might arise from actions they took under martial law. The new emergency was far uglier than the mini-emergency that had been lifted in March.

The immediate goal of the crackdown was to neutralise any possibility of violent insurrection on 16 June. When this date came and went, and the number of detentions continued to climb, passing first ten thousand and then twenty thousand, it became clear that there was a greater goal at work: the state was trying to break the back of the urban rebellion. It detained every known activist, including just about the entire leadership of the UDF, as well as anyone it could link to the 'alternative structures' that now governed the townships.

The restrictions on the press were harsher than they had

ever been. The state was anxious to prevent the outside world from knowing the full extent of the repression – as well as the full extent of the opposition to apartheid. The emergency regulations prohibited the filming or photographing of the security forces in action, and indeed of 'any public disturbance, disorder, riot, public violence, strike or boycott'. Media coverage of unrest was limited to items released by the Bureau of Information. 'There is not press censorship,' announced Louis Nel, the deputy minister of information, 'but there is a limit to what may be published.'

A week after Botha declared the emergency, a front-page report in *The Star* announced: 'Something happened at the University of the Witwatersrand residence in Soweto in the early hours of Sunday morning.' The rest of the report was blank. The *Sowetan* took to leaving its 'Comment' section blank, or printing just two words: 'No Comment'. Two weeks into the emergency, the *Sowetan* advised its readers that 'the police interpret the blank spaces we have left in the newspaper over the past few days as being "subversive". We will now fill the spaces with the most innocuous of writings.' These writings took the form of mock-serious articles – about potatoes, for instance, or minor spats in homeland houses of assembly.

Patti Waldmeir suggests that South Africa 'entered its darkest hour' on 12 June 1986. Many people who lived through this era recall that the outlook was bleakest the day Botha announced his nationwide emergency. Some years later, journalist Shaun Johnson, in an attempt to gain perspective on the appalling violence of the early Nineties, remarked:

But there is another way of looking at our catalogue of catastrophes: simply close your eyes and think back to 1986 – then compare that with our situation today. We are all uncertain, yes, but then we were terribly uncertain.

The 'terrible uncertainty' of 1986 had to do with whether the political violence would ever abate. Previously, after eruptions such as Sharpeville and Soweto, things had settled down again. By mid-1986, however, the urban rebellion had been on the go for almost two years and was showing no sign of letting up. A graph of political deaths over time would exhibit a sharp spike in 1960 (around 100 died in the greater Sharpeville uprising), another spike in 1976 (around 800 died in the greater Soweto uprising), and then a huge bulge starting in September 1984, climbing throughout 1985, and peaking in 1986. There were approximately 170 political deaths in 1984, 880 in 1985 and 1 300 in 1986. People living through this period would not have known that 1986 represented a peak – to them, it would have felt like exponential growth.*

The state of emergency achieved its objective. By the second half of 1987, the urban rebellion had been quashed. The townships were calm, if tense, and the ANC had been expelled from neighbouring states. In his memoir, former president FW de Klerk admits that the emergency constituted 'a serious restriction of normal civil rights'. Nonetheless, he claims that its 'draconian' measures were justified. The number of unrest-related incidents declined dramatically, from almost 3 000 per month in mid-1986 to fewer than 300 a year later. 'In the end,' writes de Klerk,

> the most important effect of the State of Emergency was to force revolutionaries to adopt more realistic perceptions of the balance of power between them and the government. During the anarchic months before June 1986, many of them believed that the tide of internal unrest was irresistible and

---

* 1986 was a local peak. There was a bigger bulge (and a higher peak) to come in the early Nineties, when the violence in KwaZulu-Natal and the East Rand kicked in.

that further action would soon lead to the revolutionary destruction of the government. By 1988 these perceptions had changed dramatically. The more realistic leaders of the ANC and the internal uprising realised that there could be no quick or easy victory. They also began to accept that a prolonged struggle between them and the government would be so bitter and destructive that there would be little left for anyone to inherit.

This change in perception, says De Klerk, 'was an indispensable pre-condition for the beginning of genuine negotiations'. De Klerk could, of course, be accused of tailoring his argument with the benefit of hindsight. Yet by 1987, even as dedicated a revolutionary as Joe Slovo would say, 'I believe the transition in South Africa is going to come through negotiation.'

~

On 12 June, the writer Elsa Joubert emerged from the quiet of the Archives onto a noisy Cape Town street. Joubert was 'ru ge-konfronteer' (roughly confronted) by the screams of newspaper boys selling a late edition of *The Argus*. Everyone seemed to be buying a copy, so she did too. The headline announced that the government had declared a state of emergency.

Joubert, who is best known for *Die swerfjare van Poppie Nongena*, a widely translated novelisation of the life of a domestic worker, walked to the bus stop in a daze. She read in snatches and looked at the photographs. There were Casspirs on the streets of Nyanga and Gugulethu. A bread truck had been overturned and set alight. Schools and clinics were on fire. An impimpi had been necklaced.

Everyone on the bus was reading the newspaper. 'Ons is almal betrokke,' she thought.

We're all involved. We all feel the weight of the times hanging around our necks like lead. How can we claim not to know? The newspapers scream of atrocities from every corner of the country.

A story about an old man caught Joubert's eye. It was brief, just a single paragraph, but she was transfixed. As the bus wound its way up the flank of Table Mountain, she imagined the scene. An old man is living on his own in a shack in Crossroads. Government officials arrive. They tell him they're going to take him to a better place, a place with houses and soup kitchens. The old man dismantles his shack and packs his materials – corrugated iron, cardboard, planks – in a neat pile. He places his bucket and his cup on top of the pile. He sits down on his blanket. Nobody comes. Night falls. Early the next morning, four boys approach. They're wearing white scarves on their heads. They circle him, circle him, in the grey light of dawn. One grabs at the lapel of his jacket and the material rips. They continue to circle him. 'So you're an impimpi, hey? We told people not to go. We told people to stay and resist. But you still want to go, hey?' The old man starts trembling. 'Are you cold, old man? Don't worry, we'll warm you.' They set fire to his cardboard and planks. 'Sit closer, old man.' They force him into the fire. His clothes catch alight and he burns to death.

The bus jerked to a halt, and Joubert was startled out of her reverie. It was her stop. She climbed out and stared at the placid waters of the Molteno Dam. She climbed the steps to her home, where her children were waiting for her.

'Ons elkeen beleef ons eie armsalige klein vuurproef.' We each experience our own wretched little acid test. Joubert's came that afternoon. She was busy typing up her notes from the Archive when the telephone rang.

'Madam!' screamed Lucy, a domestic worker who had last worked for her ten years earlier. In the background, Joubert could hear shouting and the smashing of furniture. 'Madam! The Witdoeke are killing us and the police are helping them. Can I come with the children?'

Trying to buy time, Joubert asked, 'Which children, Lucy?'

'The children, Madam knows them.'

The children would have been grown by then – Archie in his twenties, the girls a year or two younger.

'Madam, they're looking for the children! They want to kill them!'

Joubert fell silent as she pictured a black mob coming down her street with burning logs in their hands. They streamed onto her property and set fire to her house.

'Don't worry, Madam …'

'Lucy, listen …'

Lucy screamed. It sounded as if someone was dragging her from the phone. 'No, it's not the boere!' Lucy yelled. 'I wasn't talking to the boere!'

Joubert was mortified. She tried to call Lucy's neighbour, the only number she had for Lucy, but the line was dead. 'What kind of person am I that I didn't immediately say, "Come", with open arms, with an open heart?'

When Joubert's husband Klaas got home, she told him what had happened. He would talk to Lucy, said Klaas, if she rang again. He needed to know how many children, and how old. His first responsibility was to his family. Lucy was UDF, he said, she was radical, militant. There was a chance violence would accompany her.

There was a knock at the door. Joubert answered. Two members of the PFP, a man and a woman, were collecting tinned food for Crossroads. Joubert questioned them about conditions there, but they didn't know much. The man was a police reservist. He told her it was nonsense that the police were helping the Witdoeke.

Joubert spent the rest of the afternoon thinking up excuses to justify her hesitation. To no avail: the reproach sat like a lump in her breast. It only got worse when Klaas, a compassionate man, removed his old revolvers from the cupboard and started to clean them.

~

On 14 June, Robert McBride parked a Ford Cortina filled with explosives outside Magoo's Bar, a popular nightspot on Durban's beachfront. The car exploded fifteen minutes later, blowing a crater in the road and killing three people. A further seventy people were injured, many of them by shards of flying glass.

McBride, aged twenty-two at the time, was the commander of an MK Special Operations unit. A week before the bombing, he had travelled to Gaborone, Botswana, to meet with Aboobaker Ismail, a member of Special Operations command. They had discussed the feasibility of an attack on Durban's Marine Parade. McBride had told Ismail that he and his colleague Gordon Webster had done reconnaissance and had found that certain nightspots were frequented by off-duty soldiers and policemen. There was a high probability, though, that civilians would get hurt.

Ismail reminded McBride that the ANC had changed its policy on civilian casualties at its conference in Kabwe the previous year. Shortly before the conference, the SADF had launched a cross-border raid on Gaborone, attacking ANC offices and killing twelve people, including women and children. The ANC resolved that henceforth it would be less concerned about civilians caught in the crossfire. 'The distinction between "soft" and "hard" targets,' said Oliver Tambo, 'is going to disappear.'

June 14 seemed an auspicious day for the Durban operation. It was both the first anniversary of the raid on Gaborone and the last Saturday – that is, the last busy night – before 16 June, the biggest day on the political calendar.

On the evening of the chosen day, McBride drove slowly

down Marine Parade in a blue Cortina. As he approached the Parade Hotel, he flashed his lights. His girlfriend, Greta Apelgren, pulled out of a parking space, allowing McBride to take it. The car bomb was now within striking distance of a number of crowded nightspots: Magoo's Bar, Why Not Bar, Garfunkel's Restaurant and the Easy Beat Bar in the Empress Hotel. McBride reached between the seats and pulled a cord. It was rigged to the safety pin of a limpet mine, which was nestled in sixty kilograms of explosives. With the mine now activated, McBride and his comrade Matthew Lecordier climbed out of the Cortina. They walked down Marine Parade and got into Apelgren's Mazda.

McBride and Apelgren were arrested a month later at a house in Johannesburg and Lecordier was picked up soon thereafter. The police and the press were quick to label them cowards. It was the standard response to bombers. In McBride's case, the label didn't fit. Six weeks before the Magoo's bombing, he had led a daring raid on Edendale Hospital. His friend, Gordon Webster, had been shot by the police and was in the intensive-care unit, under police guard.

McBride headed up a raiding party consisting of himself, his father Derrick, Lecordier and Antonio du Preez. Apelgren and another member of the unit were across town, detonating grenades to divert attention. The raiding party set off for the hospital in a bakkie. They parked outside the grounds and cut a hole in the fence. McBride and his father went in, while the other two stayed with the vehicle. McBride concealed an AK-47 under a white doctor's coat, while his father carried a Makarov pistol under a priest's cassock. Once inside the hospital, they started to converse as if they were doctors. McBride recalls that they fast ran out of medical terms and ended up saying 'x-ray' a lot.

McBride waited on the stairs while his father scouted the second floor. 'Abort, civilians,' he said on his return. He'd also aroused the interest of a policeman. But his son wanted to have a look. As he stepped onto the second floor, he came face-to-face with the policeman. He fired a burst from his Kalashnikov and the policeman ran off. McBride told his father to keep an eye on the passage and pushed through the swing doors of the intensive-care unit. A policeman guarding Webster fired a shot. McBride returned fire and the policeman retreated to an adjoining room.

Ripping the drip and transfusion pipes from Webster's body, McBride tried to get him out of bed. Webster had recently undergone surgery, though, and couldn't stand up. McBride placed him on a laundry trolley and handed him the rifle. He then pushed the trolley out into the passage. People were dashing this way and that. Webster fired a salvo at the ceiling and the passage cleared. The two men proceeded to shoot their way out of the hospital, wounding four policemen.

Webster fell off the trolley as they made their way down the stairs, losing his blanket as he did so. He was now naked, though still holding the Kalashnikov. The McBrides dragged him down the final flight and found another trolley at the bottom. As they wheeled him out to the hole in the fence, they heard shouts of 'Amandla!' and 'Viva ANC!' The nurses and cleaning staff had gathered at the windows. They were ululating and singing freedom songs. Du Preez and Lecordier loaded Webster onto the bakkie, while the McBrides jumped into the cab. The intensive-care patient, still naked, was on the back of a speeding bakkie on a winter's night with part of the drip still attached to him. Du Preez and Lecordier did what they could to warm him with their jackets.

McBride was sentenced to death for the Magoo's bombing. In 1992, he was pardoned and released along with over a hundred other political prisoners. He applied to the TRC for amnesty. McBride testified that a few weeks before the attack, Magoo's had denied him entry because he was coloured. This raised concerns about his motives. These concerns were heightened when the commission found that his reconnaissance 'was of a highly amateurish nature', and that there was little to corroborate his claim that the bar was 'infested with security personnel'. The ANC came to his rescue, saying that it had ordered the attack, and he was duly granted amnesty.

McBride's subsequent career has never strayed far from controversy.

~

On 14 June, in Central America, Manuel Noriega, the military leader of Panama, impounded a shipment of illegal arms destined for South Africa. Hennie van Vuuren gives the backstory to this event in his book *Apartheid Guns and Money*.

The SADF had wanted 160 Soviet-built Gaskin missiles, along with 20 launchers, for their semi-covert war in Angola. They had instructed Armscor, the state-owned arms procurement agency, to source the weapons. Officials in Armscor's secret office in the South African embassy in Paris approached an Egyptian arms dealer, who passed on the order to a French arms dealer. The French dealer sourced the weapons from an East German company. The East Germans insisted on a Peruvian end-user certificate, in part to conceal the fact that they were trading with South Africa, and in part to piggy-back the deal with a shipment of arms to Peruvian leftists.

South Africa agreed to the arrangement and paid $21 million via a bank in Luxembourg. In due course, the *Pia Vesta* set sail from Rostok on the Baltic coast with two shipments of arms. In the meantime, the French dealer had approached an American dealer. They hatched a plan whereby the Peruvian weapons would be rerouted to the US-backed Contras in Nicaragua. When the *Pia* docked in Peru, the Peruvian weapons were offloaded, but then surreptitiously reloaded. The *Pia* headed north for Panama. The plan was for the Peruvian weapons to be offloaded there, while the South African shipment would continue on to Durban. But Noriega reneged on the deal, and impounded both shipments.

The SADF had been swindled out of millions of dollars and had very little recourse. They could hardly admit to contravening an international arms embargo and they certainly didn't want it known that they were doing business with the Eastern Bloc, the very communists they were supposedly fighting in Angola.

Van Vuuren reports that the SADF and Armscor would have felt the sting of embarrassment and reputational damage more keenly than the financial loss. He reveals that by the mid-Eighties the Special Defence Account, a secret slush fund the state used to buy weapons, was worth over R500 billion (at current rates of exchange). To provide perspective, this is six hundred times as much money as was spent on the Information Scandal, the covert campaign that had toppled the Vorster government in the late Seventies.

~

On 14 June, in New York City, forty thousand people converged on Central Park's Great Lawn to protest against apartheid. They marched from all over Manhattan: Harlem, the Upper West Side, Chelsea, Greenwich Village, the Lower East Side. A number of people addressed the rally, including ANC leaders, entertainer and activist Harry Belafonte, politician and activist Jesse Jackson, former tennis champion Arthur Ashe, and Mpho Tutu, daughter of Nobel laureate Desmond Tutu.

Several speakers criticised President Reagan's policies of 'quiet diplomacy' and 'constructive engagement', and called on him to impose strict economic penalties. 'Divestment and sanctions are pivotal,' said Belafonte. 'We believe the United States and Great Britain hold the key to whether South Africa will become a massive pool of blood.'

Tutu warned that her country was 'a blink away from Armageddon'.

~

On 15 June, Frederik Van Zyl Slabbert, the former leader of the opposition, attended a music concert on Île de Gorée, a small island off Dakar, Senegal. The concert was the finale of a week-long series of discussions and festivities in support of the South African liberation struggle. Slabbert was accompanied by two writers, Breyten Breytenbach and James Baldwin, each of whom were living in exile in France.

The concert featured musicians from all over Africa, including the South Africans Miriam Makeba and Johnny Clegg. The night was warm and fragrant, reports Breytenbach, the old slave island 'drenched in history and replete with symbolism'. The trees were festooned with coloured balls and the stars were 'swinging low'. Breytenbach and Slabbert had 'a devil of a time' keeping Baldwin on his chair – he was 'utterly drunk'. Later that night, on the ferry back to the mainland, Baldwin almost pitched overboard. He was like 'a waif, a wisp of the wind', reports Breytenbach, 'always at the point of falling down, but miraculously never doing so'.

Earlier in the week, the three had visited the Slave House Museum. Slabbert found the experience traumatic: 'Not so much the small oppressive dungeon-like cells or even the weighing room where you had to weigh at least sixty kilos for export, but that last final opening to the sea through which the slaves had to go to be shipped out.' This was a reference to the Door of No Return, through which thousands, if not millions, of enslaved Africans passed en route to the Americas. Baldwin told Slabbert that his grandfather had been one of those slaves. 'Yes, they sent my grandaddy through that hole and thought that was it. And here I am right back on the spot where he left, having a ball!'

Baldwin's was one of the most distinctive and humane voices of the American civil-rights movement. Much of what he had to say is applicable to any racist society:

> I'm terrified at the moral apathy, the death of the heart, which is happening in my country. These people have deluded themselves for so long that they really don't think I'm human. I base this on their conduct, not on what they say ... they have become moral monsters.

Breytenbach, like Baldwin, was as much an activist as a writer. He was raised within the Afrikaner establishment, but became fiercely critical of it. In the early Seventies, for instance, he gave a speech at the University of Cape Town's annual Summer School:

> We are a bastard people with a bastard language ... And like all bastards – uncertain of their identity – we began to adhere to the concept of *purity*. That is apartheid. *Apartheid is the law of the bastard.*

Breytenbach seemed determined to cause as much offence as possible. The Afrikaners, he said, were a fusing of 'all those noses and arseholes and arteries and ovaries of assorted nations':

> Nederlanders, Engelschen, Franschen, Hoogduitzers (of many regions), Savoyaards, Italiaanen, Hungaaren, Maleyers, Malabaaren, Cingaleezen, Javaanen, Macassaaren, Benjaanen, Ambioneezen, Bandaneezen, Boegineezen, Bubineezen, Chineezen, Madagascaaren, Angoleezen ...

In 1975, Breytenbach was arrested, convicted of treason, and imprisoned for seven years. After his release, he became involved with France Libertés, a foundation run by Danielle Mitterrand, wife of the French president. The foundation worked extensively throughout West Africa.

Four years after Breytenbach's release from prison, and four months after Slabbert's resignation from Parliament, the two dissident Afrikaners sat down under a Senegalese baobab and started 'dreaming of bringing together the ANC and a significant number of South African leaders and persons of influence'. A year later, a planeload of reform-minded Afrikaners touched down in Dakar. They were met by a dozen senior members of the ANC. It was a heady week for the Afrikaners. President Abdou Diouf of Senegal dubbed them the 'New Voortrekkers'. The leader of the ANC delegation announced: 'My name is Thabo Mbeki. I'm an Afrikaner.' There was a lot of talking – not all of it easy – and there was a lot of drinking and jollity. In Burkina Faso, the Afrikaners were serenaded by President Thomas Sankara and his cabinet. They responded with an impromptu rendition of the Afrikaans folk song 'Sarie Marais'.

Allister Sparks, who was covering the talks, describes an excursion to Gorée Island. At one point, Sparks was standing on the upper-level balcony of the Slave House, enjoying the view out over 'the shimmering Atlantic'. This was where the traders had lived in spacious quarters, while the slaves were crammed into dungeons below. Standing next to Sparks was a young Afrikaner theology student. He seemed to be struggling for breath. When Sparks asked him whether he was all right, he choked out the words, 'Robben Island'. Many delegates had already commented on the geographic parallels between Dakar's slave island and Cape Town's prison island. But the theology student had something else in mind:

They'll build a museum like this on Robben Island one day and people will come and look at it and wonder how we could have lived with such evil. These slave-owners were Christians, too. Yet they lived in all this comfort with all that evil just below them, and they did not see it. How, *how*, can we be so blind?

~

On 15 June, in Soweto, hundreds of roneoed flyers were distributed throughout the township. It was the eve of the tenth anniversary of the Soweto uprising and the flyer, purporting to be from the 'Office of the State President', urged residents not to take part in the planned stayaway.

> I want to talk to all you black bastards today and you better listen bloody well to what I have to say. I will not speak again. I will just fuck you up from the one side to the other.
>
> What shit is this 'stay-away' story of yours? This is now the third time and I am sick of all this bullshit.

The flyer, written in Afrikaans, carried on in this vein for a few short, threatening paragraphs, before signing off: 'Now fuck off back to work.'

Brian Pottinger remarks that the flyer achieved 'remarkable market penetration'. It was the source of much amusement in Soweto and took 'pride of place' in many households. Part of the attraction, observes Pottinger, was the clarity of communication: there was no bureaucratese here, no doublespeak.

~

On 16 June, two million people stayed away from work. The streets of cities and towns were deserted. It wasn't only black South Africans who stayed away. Thousands of anxious white parents kept their children home from school.

William Finnegan searched the radio for breaking news.

162

He finally heard the words 'special report' and turned up the volume: 'We'll be investigating the controversy surrounding weight loss in jockeys.'

~

On 16 June, Brian Sokutu, a freelance journalist from Port Elizabeth, was detained. He was held for a thousand days without charge. He was eventually released in 1989, when over a hundred detainees embarked on a hunger strike.

~

On 20 June, the headline of the *Weekly Mail* read:

> Our lawyers tell us we can say almost nothing critical about the Emergency. But we'll try.

The previous week's edition had been banned for containing a 'subversive statement'. Now, the co-editors, Irwin Manoim and Anton Harber, watched as the newspaper's attorneys read through proofs of that week's edition. One of the attorneys, Manoim later explained, was 'red-lining everything, left, right and centre, and Anton was having a screaming match with him'. Manoim's background was in design, and he saw an opportunity:

> I suddenly realised here's a visual metaphor. Let him do it. Let him do it. We're going to end up saying nothing anyway. So we just let him go ahead and wreck the paper and everything he put a red line through with a ballpoint pen we got a guy to follow after him putting tape on the pages.

At the bottom of the front page of the 20 June edition was a story about Pik Botha telling a US television audience that the South African press remained free. The story was heavily redacted. On page two was an article titled 'Journalist ██████'. The text of the article, itself redacted, made it clear that the blanked-out word in the title was 'detained'.

~

On 22 June, Argentina played England in the quarter-final of the FIFA World Cup. It was the first time the two countries had met on a football pitch since the Falklands War of 1982. Diego Maradona, the Argentine captain, scored two of the most famous goals of all time: the 'Hand of God', in which he punched the ball into the net (later saying it had been scored 'a little with the head of Maradona and a little with the hand of God') and 'The Goal of the Century', a solo effort in which he dribbled through most of the English team.

South Africans didn't get to watch the match. Football was considered a 'black sport' and wasn't generally televised. In place of the World Cup, the state television service broadcast local rugby matches and tennis at Wimbledon.

In 1986, there were eight South Africans in the men's singles draw at Wimbledon, and five in the women's. Not one of them, however, was expected to do well. Local fans had to pin their hopes on the 'South African-born' players Kevin Curren and Johan Kriek, each of whom had become naturalised American citizens. They were seeded eleventh and sixteenth respectively, but the tournament didn't go well for them. Curren, who had reached the final the previous year, lost in the first round, and Kriek in the second.

These losses would have pleased columnist Jon Qwelane. Writing in *The Star*, he described how he and his friends were rooting against the white South Africans in the Wimbledon draw. Sporting isolation was a sore point for whites, he explained, and it enraged them when blacks took pleasure in their discomfort.

~

On 26 June, Zwelakhe Sisulu was abducted at gunpoint from his home in Dube, Soweto. Four white men, two of them wearing balaclavas, burst in, grabbed him, and made off in an unmarked vehicle. Sisulu was one of the best-known black journalists at the time, in part because of his editorship of *New Nation*, and in part because he was the son of struggle icons Walter and Albertina Sisulu.

William Finnegan, who was in *The Star* newsroom the following day, writes that Sisulu's abduction was filed along with all the other detentions that couldn't be reported due to the emergency regulations. But Jon Qwelane wasn't satisfied. He phoned Sisulu's wife Zodwa to find out the details surrounding the incident. When Qwelane put down the phone, he announced: 'This is no ordinary detention. They never identified themselves as cops. So he is completely at their mercy. I'm going to write it up as a crime story, a kidnapping.'

The story ran on the front page. Louis le Grange, the minister of law and order, was furious, but there was little he could do. The police were besieged with requests for information, and were forced to disclose that there hadn't been a 'kidnapping'. Rather, the police themselves had forcibly taken Sisulu from his home. He became, remarks Finnegan, 'the first – and, for a long while, the only – person whom Pretoria officially admitted having detained under the state of emergency'.

Sisulu was released in August, but then detained again in December. He spent the next two years in solitary confinement. In 1987, an American journalist asked Stoffel Botha, the minister of home affairs, why Sisulu was being detained. 'He must be in jail,' said the minister, 'because he is not conducive to the state of affairs we want at this time.'

Sisulu was finally released late in 1988. He had been in detention for over seven hundred of the thousand-odd days his newspaper had been in existence. He was forbidden from working as an editor or journalist, and was to report to Orlando police station daily.

~

On 27 June, the *Weekly Mail* reported that a British group named Trolleys Against Apartheid had launched a campaign to spray South African fruit with human blood. The organisation's members, fourteen of whom had already donated the first tranche of blood, would leave a calling card in supermarkets: 'This product has been defiled by human blood. Please do not buy it. The sale of South African goods is morally unacceptable.'

~

On 28 June, Moses Mayekiso was detained at Jan Smuts Airport in Johannesburg. Mayekiso was secretary-general of Mawu, the Metal and Allied Workers' Union. He had flown in from Stockholm, where he'd been meeting with European metalworkers.

Mayekiso had departed South Africa just days before PW Botha had declared the state of emergency. In the intervening weeks, three thousand anti-apartheid activists, including a number of trade unionists, had been detained without trial. It had seemed clear that if Mayekiso returned to South Africa he too would be detained. His friends in Sweden and the UK had urged him to stay in Europe, but Mayekiso felt that he would be deserting his comrades back home; Mawu had not sent him abroad to go into exile.

After his arrest, Mayekiso spent seven months in solitary

confinement. It emerged that the state was interested not so much in his trade-union activities as his community activism. In addition to his role at Mawu, Mayekiso was chairman of the Alexandra Action Committee. He was eventually charged with treason, subversion and sedition, and was joined in the dock by four other activists – Obed Bapela, Richard Mdakane, Paul Tshabalala and his own younger brother, Mzwanele Mayekiso. Collectively, they became known as the Alex Five. The state alleged that, during the Six Day War of February 1986 and its aftermath, the accused had plotted to render Alexandra ungovernable and to usurp the legitimate functions of the state. If convicted, they faced the death penalty. More worrying still for the liberation movement was the fact that a guilty verdict could set a legal precedent whereby any protest or anti-government activity – even if it was non-violent – might be declared treasonable.

Moses Mayekiso was an obvious target. He represented the growing links between militant trade unionism and unrest in the townships. The state was terrified of the organisational skills that unionists were bringing to the urban rebellion. Mayekiso, for his part, emphasised that 'one could not separate community issues from factory issues. An issue like higher rents was directly linked to the fact that people were earning low wages.'

Two South African exiles in London, Terry and Barbara Bell, started a campaigning body called Friends of Moses Mayekiso. They signed up thousands of individuals, as well as religious groups, human-rights organisations, and trade unions. They raised funds both to support the families of the Alex Five and to assist smaller campaigns in California, Australia and Brazil. Mayekiso's plight captured the attention of workers worldwide and became a rallying point for the international anti-apartheid movement. For his second Christmas behind bars, the International Metalworkers' Federation, acting on behalf of fourteen million workers in seventy countries, placed a full-page advertisement in the South African *Weekly Mail*. It read, 'Merry Xmas Moses.'

The trial of the Alex Five dragged on for over a year. The state had prepared a 160-page indictment, and called many witnesses. Several were shopkeepers whose businesses had been crippled by boycotts. They described how street committees had wrested control of Alexandra from the state, and how these committees had set up alternative institutions such as schools and courts. Even the most hostile of the witnesses admitted under cross-examination that life under 'people's power' had been preferable to life under the previous dispensation: tensions had eased, and there had been less crime. The state seemed undeterred by these setbacks. As a newsletter distributed by the Friends of Moses Mayekiso put it: 'The prosecution was interested only in establishing that … the normal running of the apartheid state had been upset in this small and squalid corner of black South Africa.'

In essence, the trial came down to the question of whether or not the accused were justified in setting up alternative structures to address parlous living conditions. Alexandra – a black freehold township like Sophiatown and District Six – had once been destined for the bulldozers, but somehow it had managed to survive. The authorities had abandoned it, allowing it to decay into a slum. Its roads were rutted tracks streaming with water from defective drains. People shared taps and were forced to use bucket toilets. Very few homes were electrified – indeed, it was known as The Dark City. Each hectare housed 1 250 people, a population density twenty-five times that of the neighbouring white suburb of Sandton.

During the course of the Alex Five trial, Judge Pieter van der Walt conducted an in loco inspection of Alexandra. It was the first time he had been into a township and he was appalled by what he saw. In his final judgment, he said the Action Committee had responded in a positive and constructive way to the problems their community faced. What the prosecution had alleged were treasonable acts were, in fact, instances of people taking responsibility for their own affairs. He found the accused not guilty on all charges.

In 1994, Moses Mayekiso became a member of Parliament. He resigned two years later, saying he couldn't bear the thought of yet another committee meeting about yet another development project that had failed owing to lack of know-how at grassroots level.

~

On 29 June, in Britain, BBC television news headlined three stories: Richard Branson had broken the record for a trans-Atlantic crossing in his power boat, Virgin Atlantic Challenger; there had been violence in South Africa after a Zulu rally; and Argentina had beaten West Germany in the World Cup final.

The South African story centred on an Inkatha rally held in Soweto and addressed by Mangosuthu Buthelezi. Twenty thousand men brandishing spears and clubs ('impis', according to the BBC) had poured into Jabulani Stadium. Many had been bussed in from KwaZulu, reported the BBC correspondent, 'to reinforce the chief's supporters here and prevent disruption from his sworn enemies, the radical comrades'.

Buthelezi used the occasion to reiterate his opposition to sanctions. He also raised the spectre of 'black-on-black' violence:

I am here because I know that if we do not do something about the high toll of deaths of blacks at the hands of blacks we are on the verge of a civil-war situation which will never be stopped, even if liberation is achieved tomorrow.

The rally was a clear act of provocation. The comrades showed up afterwards and thirty-four people were injured in the ensuing violence. One of them died.

Two months after the rally, the wife of Winnington Sabelo, a member of the KwaZulu legislative council, was killed when a hand grenade was tossed into their home. 'The black civil war I warned about has now materialised,' said Buthelezi. 'I cannot see what can break the spiral of this violence.'

# JULY

## Martial Arts

MARTIAL arts senseis in Tembisa could not believe it when their charges in both karate and judo performed badly against the visiting Pretoria teams at Tembisa's Technical Centre on Saturday.

**Soshanguve Mkhari Spurs (2) 2**

**Soshanguve Las Vegas (0) 0**

SOSHANGUCE Mkhari Spurs blasted Soshanguve Las Vegas 2-0 in a Mainstay elimination game at Soshanguve Stadium on Sunday.

Amos "Heel Extension" Mkhari scored the first goal after collecting a corner-kick shot by Jacob Maluleke. The 2-0 victory came via Smutha Makuwa who passed to Mkhari. The latter in turn passed to Ben Thintha who shook the net to give Spurs a 2-0 win.

*Sowetan*, 1 July 1986

ON 1 JULY, the pass laws were formally repealed with the signing of the Abolition of Influx Control Act. For two hundred years, these laws and their forerunners had placed a limit on the number of black South Africans allowed in the country's cities and towns.

Some months earlier, in April, a White Paper on urbanisation had accepted 'the permanence of black people' in urban areas. The government had announced that blacks were no longer required to carry the hated pass book – also known as the dompas (dumb pass) – and that all prisoners held under the pass laws would be released.

Over the course of the previous seventy years, more than eighteen million people had been arrested for pass-law offences – this amounted to one arrest for every minute of daylight. And yet even this Herculean effort failed to stem the tide of black urbanisation. Jonny Steinberg records that greater Johannesburg's black population almost doubled between 1976 and 1986, with 'illegal' newcomers packing themselves into single rooms or into shacks in strangers' backyards.

The abolition of influx control elicited mixed reaction. The *Financial Mail* called it 'the most fundamental change since 1948', and opposition MP Helen Suzman considered it 'the most important' of Botha's reforms. Black leaders were less enthusiastic. They were happy to see the back of the pass laws, yet they anticipated little actual change. The country was in recession, jobs were scarce, and townships were full to bursting. Working men wouldn't be able to find accommodation for their families, and so the migrant labour system would effectively remain in place. And nothing had changed for the six million citizens of the nominally independent states: they were considered 'aliens' and still required special permits to work in South Africa. Also, the government had announced that it was replacing influx control with 'orderly urbanisation'. This policy called for the vigorous enforcement of existing laws governing squatting, trespassing and segregated living. It seemed unlikely that the 'freedom of movement' promised by the government would materialise.

Bishop Tutu took a confrontational line. '[B]lacks are no longer interested in ad hoc adjustments to apartheid,' he said. 'We are interested now in political power ... You don't reform a Frankenstein. You destroy it.'

PW Botha had introduced many piecemeal reforms over the previous five years: the recognition of black trade unions; the granting of ninety-nine-year leaseholds; the repeal of job reservation; the relaxing of restrictions on interracial sport; amendments to the Immorality and Mixed Marriages acts; and the relaxing of social segregation (which entailed the opening to all races of certain public amenities, including post offices, libraries, trains and beaches, as well as the granting of permission for select hotels, restaurants, theatres and cinemas to open their doors). Critics argued that these reforms were cosmetic. Botha was chipping away at petty apartheid, they said, in the hope of keeping the lid on the revolution, while grand apartheid remained largely intact.

~

On 3 July, anti-apartheid activist Bridget Hilton-Barber was detained by the security police at her place of work, the *Grocott's Mail* offices in Grahamstown. She was in her early twenties, having recently obtained a degree in journalism. She joined five other detainees in the back of a police van. 'I was the only whitey; the rest were coloured and black student activists. I felt terrible because I knew they had reason to be far more scared than me.'

Hilton-Barber evokes the political atmosphere of Grahamstown in the early Eighties in her memoir *Student Comrade Prisoner Spy*. The surveillance and harassment of '82 and '83 usher in the mass action of '84 and '85 – the boycotts and stayaways and general ungovernability. Repression shifts up a gear under emergency rule, first partial in '85 and then full-blown in '86:

> I can't bear another funeral; we've been to, heard about, so many funerals. They are the battlefronts now. The clunk of a stone against an armoured vehicle is met with a 37-mm gas canister that lands on a shack. Defiant chanting crowds face rubber bullets. Then always, the screams of panicking people ... youth falling to the ground, and always the toyi-toyi through the streets, security forces, stones, petrol bombs, sharp ammunition, and more burials – a never-ending cycle of protest and death.

This passage is reminiscent of poet Don Mattera's observation that South Africa had become a 'nation of pallbearers', so habituated was the majority of its citizens to living from one funeral to the next.

Hilton-Barber was detained for three months. Despite being interrogated by the notorious Spyker van Wyk – 'and there behind the desk sits a freshly scrubbed psychopath' – her time in detention was relatively uneventful. Indeed, a major theme in her account is the special treatment she received: 'Without doubt, we are the luckiest detainees, white women who don't fear beatings or torture.' Hilton-Barber's ordeal was more psychological than physical. She writes of days 'filled with hopelessness and irritation and anxiety, the fighting of which consumes me. I can barely read, I can barely think.' She resented having to knit to pass the time. It reminded her of home economics classes at school, in which she and her classmates were trained to be good wives and mothers. 'Fuuuck!' she screamed one day, and hurled her knitting across the prison dining hall.

Hilton-Barber experienced depression on her release. Her personal suffering had no place, she felt, 'after what has happened – is happening – to hundreds if not thousands of people'. She bottled her emotions. The technical term for her condition, a psychologist later told her, was 'unprocessed trauma'. It didn't help her state of mind when she met up with her friend Ray Hartley, who was in hiding from the police (almost all her friends were 'in hiding, on the run, crossing the border, in exile, in detention, in jail'). Hartley told her that her arrest had been no accident: 'Olive was a spy for the Branch.'

Olivia Forsyth, a fellow student and activist, had been one of her closest friends. Yet all along, Agent 407 had been gathering intelligence for the security police. Soon after betraying Hilton-Barber – and many others – Forsyth set off for Harare. It's unclear whether she intended to infiltrate the ANC or, as she later claimed, join it as a double agent. Either way, the ANC was having none of it. Forsyth was interned in Camp Quatro in Angola. This 'self-assured girl who rode into Grahamstown on a motorbike, shook her hair out of her helmet, and started off on her own road to hell' had reached her destination. She endured horrific conditions in Quatro. One senior ANC man insisted on seeing her naked every time she reported to him. She was eventually moved to a safe house, from which she escaped to the British Embassy in Lusaka.

In 2015, Hilton-Barber contacted Forsyth, who was then living in Britain. Forsyth expressed excitement on the phone, saying that she and her husband Eric 'were finalists on a television game show, hoping to win an Italian villa for free'.

~

On 3 July, near Bushbuckridge in the eastern Transvaal, a nine-teen-year-old student activist named Lucky Mnisi was stabbed and burnt to death. Ten years later, his mother Jameya attended the TRC hearings held in Nelspruit and told his story.

Lucky had been involved in the struggle, said his mother, 'because he wanted to taste the new government that we have today'. He and his fellow comrades 'used to go for their meetings … at a place called Shangaan Hill'. The police often raided the Mnisi household and Lucky was detained a number of times. After not seeing Lucky for a few weeks, his mother testified, 'I heard from rumours that my son was moving in police vans and I was shocked.' People pointed at her in the street and said loudly to one another that her son was collaborating with the police. Friends warned her that her house would be burnt down, as would her mother's and her sister's houses. When Lucky was released from detention, his mother confronted him:

> I said to him, 'I heard rumours that you are involved with police.' He said, 'Yes mother, the police ended up arresting me, they took me to the cells and they assaulted me and after assaulting us we spent a week in jail and at the end of that the police gave us uniforms and they gave us guns.' And I said, 'Why did you take those?' and he said, 'Mother, I thought that they would leave me alone.'

The day after Lucky's release, his mother attended a church gath-ering. She pleaded with her son to stay home. 'I went to church. When you are inside the church you can still see my house. I saw him moving out of the gate.' The next morning, her sister told her that Lucky had been killed outside Mkalipani Secondary School. Mnisi inspected her son's body at the mortuary:

> I turned him and I looked at him, he was stabbed eighteen holes, I was brave enough to count those holes, and my

sister wanted to pull me from counting them. I said to her, 'Please stop it, I want to see him.' My son was burned. He was my first born and I was looking to him, he was my future.

~

On 10 July, *Finance Week* reported that Kilpatrick (Pty) Ltd, a firm of electrical contractors in Randburg, had been refused permission to register a subsidiary company in Venda. The homeland's registrar general observed that the Life President of the Republic of Venda was named Patrick Mpephu. People might think that a company of this name intended the president harm.

~

On 16 July, the South African Air Force unveiled its new fighter jet, the Cheetah. President Botha addressed workers at the Atlas Aircraft Corporation in Kempton Park near Johannesburg. The new aircraft, he said, proved South Africa's ability to overcome the United Nations arms embargo. 'This will always be our response to international boycotts and threats against us in every field of life. We will fight back with self-respect and determination.'

The Cheetah was a reconstruction of the aging French fighter, the Mirage III. Atlas, a subsidiary of Armscor, the state-owned arms manufacturer, had stripped the Mirage down to fifty per cent of its airframe. It had then fitted locally designed bodywork, weaponry and guidance systems. 'We believe it will match the MIG-23 class aircraft,' said the chief of the air force, General Dennis Earp. 'As far as its handling goes, it is in many respects comparable to the best in the world.'

The air force was in desperate need of an aircraft to match

the MIG. The Soviet fighter was controlling the airspace over Angola, which spelt disaster for South Africa's undeclared war in that country.

~

On 16 July, White House Chief of Staff Don Regan remarked in an interview that, if the United States instituted comprehensive sanctions against South Africa (a policy his administration opposed), American women would have to 'give up all their jewelry'.

~

On 24 July, the Commonwealth Games commenced in Edinburgh. Thirty-two nations boycotted the games in protest against Britain's refusal to impose sanctions on South Africa. It was practically a whites-only affair, with African, Asian and Caribbean nations staying away. (Pretoria's client states, Lesotho, Swaziland, Botswana and Malawi, were notable exceptions.)

Ten days before the games commenced, two South African-born athletes – middle-distance runner Zola Budd and swimmer Annette Cowley – were expelled from the English team. For months, anti-apartheid protesters had been pressurising the authorities to close what they called 'the passport-of-convenience loophole'. In the end, the protesters managed to get Budd and Cowley expelled for not having satisfied residency requirements. Budd, for example, had continued to live in Bloemfontein ever since receiving her British passport in a record ten days, just in time for the 1984 Olympics. She fell far short of the Commonwealth Games requirement that athletes spend six of the preceding twelve months in the country for which they compete.

Budd, who earlier in the year had won the World Cross

Country Championship for England, was the favourite to win gold over 3 000 metres. Cowley was the favourite to win gold in the 100-metres freestyle. The pair expressed their disappointment to the BBC. 'I am being used as a pawn,' said Budd, 'and I can see why.' Cowley, who had an English mother, said she was 'as British as the local pub'.

~

On 29 July, Piet Ntuli, minister of the interior for KwaNdebele and leader of the reviled vigilante group Mbokodo, was assassinated. He was driving along a road in Siyabuswa, the homeland's capital, when an explosion ripped through his vehicle. The people of Siyabuswa took to the streets to celebrate. They sang freedom songs and painted slogans: 'The Dog Ntuli is dead. Viva the ANC.'

The South African government duly blamed the ANC for Ntuli's death, and the liberation movement was happy to take the credit. This narrative, however, did not survive the inquest. In an affidavit, a witness claimed to have seen a South African security policeman lying under Ntuli's car shortly before the explosion. For a number of years, the identity of the killer or killers remained unknown. Brian Pottinger, for instance, discusses Ntuli's assassination in his 1988 biography of PW Botha:

A hit by elements within the SA police? Had Ntuli become too much even for his mentors? Or was he simply in the way of more ambitious actors? The answer will probably never be known.

But the answer is known. It was supplied – as is the case with so many of the dark deeds of the Seventies and Eighties – by the TRC. Brigadier Jack Cronjé, former commander of the Northern Transvaal Security Branch, together with a number of his men, applied for amnesty for Ntuli's killing. Special Forces, they said, had built the bomb. Cronjé testified that the South African government had been grooming Ntuli to succeed Simon Skosana as chief minister, 'however he went out of control … and the only way out was to get rid of him'.

For the first seven months of 1986, Ntuli presided over a reign of terror. Mbokodo attacked anyone who opposed either the incorporation of Moutse into KwaNdebele or the homeland's quest for independence. A resident told a reporter about Ntuli's motivation:

> He was a very cunning gentleman. You could call him a con man. He only believed in money. He only believed in capitalism. He was gunning for independence because he knew that he was going to benefit out of it.

Ntuli issued business and taxi licences to friends and cronies. The mercantile class was indebted to him and so supported Mbokodo.

In May, PW Botha announced that KwaNdebele would take independence in December. The homeland exploded. Journalist Phillip van Niekerk reports that 'armies of children, some as young as ten, roamed the shanty towns at night, attacking the shops of Mbokodo and executing suspected vigilantes by the necklace method'. The young comrades taunted Skosana, saying they would return to school when he passed Standard Four (only one member of Skosana's cabinet had completed junior school).[*]

---

[*] This lack of formal qualifications didn't dampen the cabinet's enthusiasm. In 1988, KwaNdebele's minister of education announced: 'If our youth maintain their high morale for education … it will neither be ambitious nor mythical to foresee the establishment of a space centre at KwaMhlanga from which Ndebele space crews can be launched to the uncharted side of the moon.'

The conflict fast became 'one of the bloodiest sideshows in the black rebellion', with estimates for lives lost ranging between 150 and 200. A journalist driving through the homeland in early July found a 'blasted, frightening landscape' littered with burnt-out cars and gutted shops.

Two weeks after Ntuli's assassination, the KwaNdebele Legislative Assembly reversed its earlier decision to take independence. This was not the result Pretoria had been hoping for. It cracked down hard, reports Van Niekerk, imposing 'the most severe emergency regulations in the entire country'. The battle moved to the South African courts, eventually escalating to the Appellate Division. Lawyers acting for the people of Moutse argued that incorporating Sotho people into a Ndebele homeland was inconsistent with the government's stated aim of ethnic consolidation. In essence, they used apartheid ideology to undermine apartheid. The Appeal Court agreed with the lawyers, ruling that the incorporation of Moutse had been illegal.

# AUGUST

SUN: Ever wondered about the secret fears and desires of the men who fly cropdusting airplanes? OM 'N VLIEGTUIG ANN TE TREK (TV1, 6.05pm) promises to reveal all, whether or not you wonder. Higher flyers may enjoy THE ENCHANTMENT OF OPERA (9.55pm), a documentary examing all aspects of a production of La Traviata.

UNDERGROUND, Chelsea Hotel, Catherine Avenue, Hillbrow. Every parent's nightmare of a disco ... too loud, too dark and too much strobe. Highly attractive for teenagers. Thurs nights, dance evening for singles over 30 (give or take) with Beatles, Rock 'n Roll and Twist. Ph: 642-4541.

*Weekly Mail*, 1 August 1986

ON 2 AUGUST, over 100 000 soccer fans crammed into Ellis Park Stadium in Johannesburg to watch the second leg of the JPS Knockout Cup final. The stadium's official capacity was 75 000. 'There's nothing we could do,' said Abdul Bhamjee, the public relations officer of the National Soccer League. 'We had to accommodate as many fans as we could. There's little doubt that had there been a stadium big enough to hold 150 000 we would have filled it easily.' The R5 40 000 taken at the gates was an all-time record for a South African sporting event.

Kaizer Chiefs came into the second leg with a 2–1 lead over Moroka Swallows. The Chiefs' strike force, featuring Absalom Thindwa, Marks Maponyane and Nelson 'Teenage' Dladla, was held in check by the Swallows' defence, while at the other end of the pitch there was likewise a stalemate. The goalless draw gave Chiefs the trophy.

~

On 3 August, in a speech to mark the fiftieth anniversary of the South African Broadcasting Corporation, PW Botha said: 'The SABC and every other member of the South African media must make a decision these days and show where they stand.'

~

On 5 August, the Commonwealth instituted a range of economic sanctions against South Africa. The announcement came after the leaders of seven Commonwealth countries had spent two days in Marlborough House, London, discussing the Eminent Persons Group report. The leaders of Australia, the Bahamas, Canada, India, Zambia and Zimbabwe all agreed that Pretoria was not making adequate progress towards its stated goal of abolishing apartheid. Only Margaret Thatcher of Britain dissented, which almost led to a split in the Commonwealth.

The leaders went ahead and introduced a range of punitive measures, including the withdrawal of consular facilities and air links. They banned new loans and investments, as well as agricultural imports and certain mineral imports.

'We are prepared to accept a lowering of our standards of living,' responded foreign minister Pik Botha. 'We are prepared to make sacrifices for what we believe in.'

The Commonwealth decision came just a few weeks after the European Economic Community had imposed its own set of sanctions. Every month seemed to bring a new boycott, embargo, excommunication or expulsion, whether economic, military, sporting, cultural, religious or diplomatic. Oliver Tambo considered sanctions the ANC's 'most important' weapon. It was 'the trump card with which we can mobilise international opinion and pull governments over to our side'.

While isolation hurt South Africa psychologically, it is unclear how much damage it did economically. Patti Waldmeir argues that growth was depressed not so much by sanctions as 'by apartheid itself'. She cites 'the uncontrolled spending of homeland governments and the huge triplicated bureaucracies introduced under the tricameral constitution', as well as 'the rising costs of internal unrest', which included millions of man-days lost to strikes and hundreds of millions of rands lost to township rent boycotts.

At a press conference called immediately after the Commonwealth announcement, Pik Botha observed that there were 'ways and means of circumventing sanctions'. Western governments had to keep their voters happy, but they also needed South Africa's strategic minerals, particularly uranium, platinum, manganese and vanadium. Sociologist Heribert Adam remarks that one of the major effects of sanctions was to change 'a formal marriage into an illicit affair'.

~

On 6 August, the *Cape Times* ran an article titled 'Children necklace puppy'. The incident had taken place the previous week in Kleinskool, a squatter camp outside Port Elizabeth. A volunteer worker for the Animal Anti-Cruelty League reported that a six-month-old dog had been brought to its clinic after a group of children had 'put a tyre around the animal and set it alight'.

~

On 12 August, President Botha addressed the National Party at its federal congress in Durban. The press dubbed the event 'Rubicon revisited', in reference to Botha's speech a year earlier. The rerun was similar to the original: again he delivered reformist content with defiance and aggression.

Botha abandoned the concept of homelands, promising citizenship to everyone and black political representation 'up to the highest level'. His successor, FW de Klerk, later reported that the congress 'constituted a 180 degree change in policy for ever away from apartheid, separate development and racial discrimination'. All that was left for him to do, said De Klerk, was to carry through the resolutions of the congress to their logical conclusions.

Botha used his address to attack the hypocrisy of 'manipulated world opinion': 'We are probably no better, but certainly no worse than the rest of the world.' As always, he revealed flashes of the iron fist under the velvet glove. 'Those who want to force us into negotiation with radical elements … should not underestimate us,' he warned. 'I'm not a jellyfish, we're not a nation of jellyfish.'

~

On 14 August, in the early hours of a cold and rainy morning, a team of Security Branch policemen broke into a jail in Swaziland and abducted Glory Sedibe, a senior member of MK. The raiding party was led by Eugene de Kock, and included some of his Vlakplaas men, along with others from Ermelo and Piet Retief, two towns in the eastern Transvaal.

Sedibe, better known by his nom de guerre Comrade September, had been arrested in Manzini two days earlier for being in the country illegally. The Swazi police passed him on to the South African police, receiving R150 000 in exchange for moving him to a small jail close to the border. The plan was for the guards to be unarmed, but somehow the message didn't get through and De Kock had to relieve one of them of an automatic weapon. Sedibe was in a cell with two stock thieves, who were less than happy at being ejected into the cold night. Sedibe fought like a man possessed, and it took six policemen to subdue him. They eventually choked him with a scarf. He regained consciousness in the vehicle and took up the fight. One of the policemen hit him so hard in the face with a Makarov pistol that the silencer bent. Sedibe would carry the scar for the rest of his days.

The raiding party used Eastern Bloc weapons to make it look as if the jailbreak was an ANC job. So successful were they that the liberation movement itself was fooled. A spokesperson told *Swazi News*: 'The ANC does not usually free its men like that in independent countries. What we usually do is talk to the authorities responsible or make it official if we want any of our men held by the police to be freed.'

Sedibe was taken to a farm outside Piet Retief where he was interrogated and tortured. Almond Nofomela, a policeman who took part in the raid and whose job it was to guard the prisoner, describes one of the methods the torturers used: 'They would take one hand to squeeze his testicles into a bubble and then smash them with the other. There was no way he could have resisted.' Nofomela reports that Sedibe started 'telling them stories' almost immediately. Siphiwe Nyanda, one of Sedibe's MK comrades, later said that 'within hours of the abduction' South African agents attacked the homes of ANC members in Swaziland.

The mood on the farm was festive, recalls Nofomela. His colleagues slaughtered a sheep and braaied it on a spit. They stood around drinking as they took turns to torture Sedibe.

Jacob Dlamini, in his book *Askari*, describes how Sedibe was turned by his interrogators. From being someone who had talked under torture, he became someone who had changed sides. He moved from resister to collaborator, revolutionary to counter-revolutionary, insurgent to askari. Sedibe's defection, remarks Dlamini, 'goes down as the biggest in the history of the ANC'. Within a year of him defecting, South African agents had carried out eleven cross-border assassinations. Sedibe's information all but wiped out MK in Swaziland, and crippled it in the Transvaal.

*Askari* is partly a biography of Sedibe and partly, to quote its subtitle, *A Story of Collaboration and Betrayal in the Anti-Apartheid Struggle*. Dlamini is interested in the choices Sedibe made: to cooperate with the enemy; to turn against his former comrades; to hunt them down with relish. He's also interested in the broader issue of collaboration as an endemic feature of apartheid:

One needs only to compare the numbers of people slaughtered by the Argentine and Guatemalan juntas, for example, with those killed by successive apartheid governments over forty years to realise that, as criminal as apartheid was, as a killing machine it was no match for the murderous

189

regimes found in Latin America. The truth is that, as in Eastern Europe, apartheid depended far more on collaboration to work.

For most South Africans, 'the face of apartheid was black':

> From the clerks who staffed government offices, the teachers who taught Bantu Education, the 'elected' and non-elected officials who ran townships, to the policemen and -women who enforced apartheid laws, the average bureaucrat was black. These black faces were not isolated apparatchiks. They lived in the same communities they 'served'.

Dlamini suggests that much of this inconvenient history has been swept under the carpet. We would do well as a nation, he says, 'to examine the taboos, the secrets and the disavowals at the core of our collective memories'.

Glory Sedibe was born in Pilgrim's Rest in 1953. He was one of nine siblings, all of whom had names starting with the letter 'G'. He did well at school, and dreamed of pursuing a Bachelor of Administration degree. This would have set him up for a career in public service in Lebowa. Had his family had the financial means, remarks Dlamini, Sedibe would in all likelihood have gone to university and become a 'bantustan bureaucrat'. Like many youths of his generation, he became politicised only when his dreams were denied him.

Sedibe joined the flood of young people who left the country following the Soweto uprising. He had hoped to further his studies in exile, but instead chose the military route after listening to a compelling lecture by Jacob Zuma, then a prominent member of MK. Sedibe spent time in Mozambique, Tanzania and Angola, before receiving specialised intelligence training in Teterow, East Germany. He joined the ANC's Transvaal Machinery, as it was known, and was flown to Moscow for additional training. In 1984, he was appointed head of military intelligence for the Transvaal. He was good at his job. According to De Kock, 'MK September was well-known to the security police as an excellent and successful operative: wily, crafty and keeping to all the basic rules of security and counter-surveillance, and hard to catch.'

After his defection, Sedibe became one of De Kock's askaris at Vlakplaas. The word 'askari' is Arabic for 'soldier'. It migrated to Swahili and came to mean a local who fought for a colonial army. In South Africa it took on a new inflection, something along the lines of 'a rehabilitated terrorist who is now working for the police'. Security policeman Rudolph Liebenberg told the TRC that his unit 'did not use … the word "askari", we called them "rehabilitateds"'.

The Security Branch set up its askari programme in 1979. The idea was to use enemy fighters to fight the enemy. This was not a new idea. Collaboration had long been a feature of counter-insurgency warfare. Dlamini provides several examples: the British in Malaya and Kenya; the French in Indochina and Algeria; the US in Vietnam. As one former askari observes, 'Not everyone could become an askari. One needed to have been a trained insurgent before one could become a counter-insurgent.' Though there's a hint of pride in this statement, askaris were generally shunned. Almond Nofomela, for one, would become very angry when people took him for an askari. He was a black policeman, he would say, not a traitor.

In addition to their core function of identifying former comrades – usually at taxi ranks, train stations and border posts – askaris were used as state witnesses, double agents and assassins. They were also sent out into black communities to act as agents provocateurs. They typically launched 'false-flag' operations, whereby unsuspecting youths were supplied with booby-trapped weapons. The government's propaganda machine would use the resultant mayhem to showcase both the ANC's murderous intent and its incompetence. When the Security Branch later tried to explain away Vlakplaas as 'a rehabilitation centre for former terrorists', the TRC observed: 'There is no sign that any rehabilitation took place.'

Sedibe's main tasks at Vlakplaas were to hunt down ANC operatives and to testify against his former comrades. He was an enthusiastic employee and got on well with De Kock. 'September was actually given a kombi and guys under his command,' notes a former askari. 'That was not normal at the farm because such a position was normally a preserve of black cops who'd trained at Hammanskraal and were given the task to oversee us.' An ANC intelligence operative reports that Sedibe 'was particularly active in pursuing us. He was particularly vicious in torturing some of our comrades.'

In 1988, Sedibe was the star witness at a major show trial. As the mysterious Mr X1, he testified for six weeks against Ebrahim Ebrahim, Simon Dladla and Acton Maseko, who were facing charges of terrorism and treason. 'He was quite arrogant,' Ebrahim would later remark. 'He appeared to be quite confident. He was not shy about giving evidence against us.' Dlamini tries to make sense of Sedibe's dedication to his new job. He concludes that it was less 'fanatical devotion to a cause' than an attempt to prove his loyalty to new masters. He surmises that the job offered Sedibe 'a sense of self that compensated for the shame of his collaboration'.

In 1987, De Kock insisted that all the askaris at Vlakplaas move to Letlhabile, a new settlement bordering on Bophuthatswana. Letlhabile had been built for people forcibly removed from Oukasie near Brits and, as such, lacked both history and a sense of community. It was ideal for those seeking to make a fresh start. Sedibe lived there with his family until 1990, at which point he left the police and joined Military Intelligence. By then, the Group Areas Act was no longer enforced, so he bought a home in the formerly white suburb of Verwoerdburg. It was here, under mysterious circumstances, that Sedibe died in March 1994.

De Kock claims that a former Military Intelligence officer poisoned Sedibe as a way of protecting the identities of MI agents within the ANC. In return, these agents, who were assured of senior jobs in the post-apartheid dispensation, would shield their former handler from prosecution. Dlamini concurs with this assessment: 'Sedibe had fought for so long on both sides of the political divide that it could safely be said that he knew too much about the skeletons in both closets.' An informant told Dlamini that his biggest surprise on becoming an askari was 'finding out just who in the ANC was in the pay of the South African police and spy agencies'.

Sedibe was chronically depressed at the time of his death. A former colleague reports that he was drinking 'about three 750 ml bottles of vodka' a day. 'He would have killed himself if they had not killed him first ... He was going down. He would not eat, he would not sleep, he would not get out of bed or wash himself.' Sedibe's widow Ção tells a similar story: 'Ele não comia – he would not eat. Only drink. It was whiskey. It was wine. It was beer. It was gin.'

~

On 23 August, the *Weekend Argus* published an article about a twelve-year-old boy who had been detained a number of times. Activist Mavis Smallberg saw the article and was inspired to write a poem:

First the face, and then
the caption caught my eye:
Small Boy Seen As
Threat To State Security

Smallberg's poem is an elegy to the children of the Eighties, many of whom became activists at an early age. They considered their parents' generation to be ineffectual and took it upon themselves to protect their communities.

Smallberg turns her attention to the photograph that accompanies the article:

> A small boy should not have such eyes
> eyes which glower, two black coals
> smouldering on the page

The boy's name is Gilly Nyathele. He lived in Tumahole township near Parys in the Orange Free State. The poem charts his life: the R60 a month his mother earned doing domestic work for a white family; the 'salt and porridge' on which he and his siblings subsisted; his deepest wish, which was to 'eat and eat and eat'. Nyathele belonged to the Fourteens, a gang of a hundred or so children aged fourteen and under. (A fellow member was Stompie Seipei, whose name became well known a few years later when he was killed by one of Winnie Mandela's bodyguards.)

The Fourteens effectively ran Tumahole, protecting it from The A-Team, a group of vigilantes supported by the local authority. The Fourteens were particularly militant, hence Nyathele's four spells in detention.

> A small boy should not be
> detained

~

On 25 August, Warner Bros. Records released Paul Simon's album *Graceland*. It started out as a cross-cultural experiment, but became a smash hit, winning the Grammy for best American album of the year and selling fifteen million copies worldwide.

*Graceland* is a fusion of American pop and South African township jive. Simon collaborated with a number of musicians, including choral group Ladysmith Black Mambazo, guitarist Ray Phiri of Stimela, and bassist Bakithi Kumalo. He acknowledged the influence of Johnny Clegg and Sipho Mchunu of Juluka, and was joined on tour by Miriam Makeba and Hugh Masekela.

The album's signature tracks include 'The Boy in the Bubble', 'Homeless', and 'Diamonds on the Soles of Her Shoes'. In Simon's view, the collaboration was best realised – 'the DNA most intertwined' – in the title track, 'Graceland', with its distinctively American lyrics ('The Mississippi Delta / Was shining like a National guitar') and Phiri's soulful bassline. The *Weekly Mail* suggested the song was 'a cross between Nashville and Soweto', with 'Simon's whimsy saved by South African roots'.

*Graceland* was controversial on two fronts: Simon was accused of exploiting local musicians, and of violating the cultural boycott. He dismissed the first charge out of hand. Whenever 'a white collaborates with a black', he said, there was always the assumption that 'the white is taking advantage'. But this wasn't the case with *Graceland*: 'We shared credit, we shared royalties, there's never been any complaint about that.'

The second charge was more serious, particularly as it came at a time of heightened awareness regarding the cultural boycott. In October 1985, Artists United Against Apartheid released the protest song 'Sun City'. Over fifty musicians – including Bob Dylan, Bruce Springsteen, Miles Davis, Keith Richards and U2 – sang the words:

I, I, I, I, I, I
I ain't gonna play Sun City

Many other musicians – including Elton John, Dolly Parton, Rod Stewart, Ray Charles and Queen – had already played at the venue. (Paul Simon had twice turned down million-dollar offers.)

In February 1985, Simon visited Johannesburg to record material for *Graceland*. He had been invited by black musicians, he said, who 'felt very strongly that they wanted to get their music out'. Simon was heavily criticised by the Anti-Apartheid Movement for not asking permission from the ANC, and for thinking 'he knew better than Mandela'. Dali Tambo, son of the ANC president, noted that white South Africans were 'desperate for things like European pop records which make them feel that their way of life is normal'. He implored artists not to 'help them keep their morale up'.

The musicians who collaborated with Simon took a different view. Masekela said 'it was great to see South Africa's music get to so many people that would never otherwise have listened to it'. Phiri felt that music, 'if utilised in the right way', could bring people closer – 'And *Graceland* did that.' Clegg pointed out that there was 'a difference between the culture of the oppressed masses and the culture of the ruling elite': playing Sun City was one thing, popularising black music was another thing entirely.

When the musician and activist Steven Van Zandt met with the Azanian People's Organisation, he saw Simon's name at the top of their hit list. 'Do me a favour,' he reportedly told them: 'The war I'm about to fight is a tricky one in the media. It's a modern way of fighting the war. It's not going to help if you assassinate Paul Simon, okay?'

~

On 31 August, Mangosuthu Buthelezi addressed the annual conference of the Inkatha Youth Brigade. He spoke about the school boycotts, which were then in their third year. 'Liberation Now, Education Later' was an 'insane slogan', he said. It had been coined by the ANC mission in exile, and could only have been devised by people whose children were attending private schools abroad.

Black South Africans, said Buthelezi, needed to seize every opportunity for betterment, while the ANC's slogan would lead to 'a generation of illiterates'.

# SEPTEMBER

*Sowetan*, 1 September 1986

ON 1 SEPTEMBER, the South African Police launched its new Special Constables programme. The recruits were mostly unemployed black men, many of them former members of right-wing vigilante groups. Others had backgrounds in crime. Their training was conducted at the SAP's Koeberg base near Cape Town, and lasted just six weeks. As a result, they became known as kitskonstabels (instant constables).

The SAP saw the programme as a quick and easy way to increase its presence in townships. The objective, as explained in a position paper, was to establish an 'effective physical counter to the tyranny of the "comrades" ... from the ranks of the blacks themselves'. Critics were quick to label the programme 'black-on-black policing'.

The first kitskonstabels were deployed to unrest areas in October 1986. They had been trained to view the UDF and the ANC as the enemy, and fast developed a reputation for brutality and lawlessness. Township residents considered them 'the dogs of the South African Police, doing all their hunting and watching'. Kitskonstabels were 'the biggest nonsense', a policeman later told the TRC, 'They shot people unnecessarily. They were drunk on duty and rude most of the time. The problem was that they had not received enough training ... they were wild.'

When a group of former Witdoek vigilantes returned to New Crossroads as kitskonstabels, they were immediately attacked, and within a week had been dispossessed of eighteen guns.

~

On 7 September, Desmond Tutu was enthroned as Archbishop of Cape Town. He had previously been Bishop of Johannesburg. The ceremony, held in St George's Cathedral, was attended by over a hundred and fifty bishops from every corner of the globe.

In his enthronement sermon, the new archbishop said, 'Whether I like it or not, whether he likes it or not … PW Botha is my brother and I must desire and pray for the best for him.'

~

On 9 September, Andrew Zondo, an MK operative, was executed by the state. The previous December, he had placed a limpet mine in a shopping centre in Amanzimtoti on the Natal South Coast. Five people had died in the ensuing blast.

Sociologist Fatima Meer tells Zondo's story in *The Trial of Andrew Zondo*. He was born in the Transkei in 1966. When he was three, his family moved to KwaMashu, a township outside Durban. Zondo's father was a priest. As a child, he was struck by how poor their family was, while the white priest they visited was so rich. Not that Zondo wanted a lot of money: 'Rich people for me were people with shops. I saw rich Africans looking down on poor Africans. I didn't want to be like that.'

In 1980, the police tear-gassed Zondo's school after a group from another school had urged pupils to join a boycott. The following day, Zondo attended his first political meeting. He read the Freedom Charter and other banned literature, thereby receiving answers to all the questions his parents had brushed off over the years. He came to the conclusion, reports Meer, that his parents were too worried about the next life to notice what was happening in this one.

In 1981, Zondo joined the ANC. He formed a discussion group and distributed pamphlets. The following year, the ANC summoned him to Swaziland. Zondo thought the organisation was worried that he was about to be arrested, but in fact the leadership wanted to assess his credibility and commitment. They sent him home with instructions to carry on as before.

In 1983, Zondo was arrested. The Swazi police had found a biography he'd written for the ANC, and had passed it on to their South African counterparts. Zondo was held for a night and then released into his parents' care on the understanding that he would inform on his comrades. Meer describes the 'unbearable tension' the sixteen-year-old felt at the prospect of either letting down his parents or letting down his organisation. He took flight, first going into hiding and then crossing the border into Mozambique.

Zondo had been planning to further his studies in exile. Soon after his arrival in Maputo, however, the South African Air Force conducted a bombing raid, killing and wounding a number of ANC members, as well as Mozambican civilians. 'It was then that I told a woman comrade who knew the people high up in the ANC command that I didn't want to study. I had changed my mind. I wanted to go for military training.' Zondo trained in Angola for a year before re-entering South Africa.

On 20 December 1985, a Vlakplaas death squad raided two houses in Maseru. It killed nine people, including two senior MK operatives. Zondo's handler, Tallman Lulama, contacted him. The 'high authorities', said Lulama, had determined that a retaliatory attack should take place within three days. Zondo knew a comrade who had a limpet mine in his cache. He approached him and they decided to conduct an operation together. They reconnoitred 'government targets' in Amanzimtoti, but found that the police station and the post office were well guarded. They eventually settled on what appeared to be a South African Airways office in the Sanlam Centre (it was in fact a travel agency with prominent SAA branding).

On 23 December, at 10.30 in the morning, Zondo and his accomplice stood eating fast food next to a refuse bin in one of the centre's arcades. Christmas shopping was in full swing. They finished their food and disposed of the wrappers in a Checkers bag which contained an activated limpet mine. Zondo deposited the bag into the side opening of the bin. Half an hour later, an explosion ripped through the centre, blasting shop windows and propelling thousands of shards of glass. A baby, two young children and two women died. Almost fifty people were injured. Judging by their names and addresses, notes Meer, most were Afrikaners on holiday from the Transvaal.

Zondo was arrested six days later, when the police raided a friend's house. They weren't specifically looking for Zondo. He later said in court that he'd been feeling bad that five people had died, and so told the police that he was responsible for the 'Toti bombing'. His parents visited him in prison – it was the first time they had seen him in three years. Zondo rummaged through his mother's handbag, looking for sweets, and then sat with his head on her bosom. Who rubbed her back when she had cramps, he asked, now that he wasn't there to do it? His father, she said.

In pre-trial hearings, Zondo refused legal counsel: 'I don't want them because they are offered by the government and I did harm to the government.' He pleaded not guilty to murder on the grounds that 'I had not the intent to kill'. The magistrate encouraged him to make a fuller statement, and he said: 'I did not go there with the aim of killing these deceased people. I went to the offices of the South African Airways. My intention was to blow up these offices and not to kill the people who might have been there.'

Since Zondo freely admitted to placing the limpet mine, the state's case centred on proving that he had intended to kill people. Its star witness was Zondo's accomplice, who had been granted indemnity to testify against him. The accomplice was referred to as Mr X, and was allowed to testify in camera. He told the court that their intention had been to avenge the deaths of the nine people killed in Maseru. Zondo had been unhappy, he said, when they only managed to kill five.

The state tried to show that Mr X acted on Zondo's every word. It emerged under cross-examination, however, that Mr X was almost twice Zondo's age and was already a seasoned activist. 'A man and a boy detonated a mine,' comments Meer. 'The court exonerated the man and pinned it on the boy.' She observes that the court had no qualms about accepting the testimony of a 'Judas' who stood to gain 'not simply thirty pieces of silver, but life itself'.

Extenuation was always going to play a key role in the trial. When asked why he had joined the ANC at age fifteen, Zondo said the movement offered 'something far better than what I could see around me'. The judge interrupted, asking in what ways it was better. 'The Freedom Charter says South Africa belongs to all who live in it,' replied Zondo. 'To me that was much better than what was happening where South Africa belongs to whites.'

Zondo told the court that he had planned to phone in a warning. After placing the bomb, he parted ways with his accomplice and walked to the post office. All five payphones were occupied, however, and there was a queue. He waited ten minutes, but then had to go. He would have drawn undue attention to himself, he said, had he begged to jump the queue.

Fatima Meer presented evidence in mitigation. Zondo's life, she said, was based on contradictions: his childhood versus those of the white priest's children; his parents' Christianity versus the ANC's sense of justice; the subservience inculcated by Bantu Education versus the goals and aspirations propagated by western media. Zondo's situation was not exceptional, she said, but rather the norm for thousands of young Africans. Ultimately, the responsibility for his act lay with society.

The prosecutor argued that only someone with 'inherente boosheid' (inherent evil) could have committed such an act. 'What sort of person,' he asked, 'would walk into a shopping centre carrying death in a bag?'

Judge Ramon Leon and his assessors found Zondo guilty of murder. They argued that there were no extenuating circumstances. The telephone story was 'preposterous', said Leon. And why, he asked, would you pick that particular place at that particular time of day if you didn't wish to kill people?

In his speech before sentencing, Leon spoke of 'a divided and deeply troubled society' in which 'the monopoly of political power and its fruits is in the hands of the white section of the population'. He acknowledged that Zondo considered himself to be a soldier fighting an unjust system – yet this was precisely what made his crime 'so appalling'. A soldier had chosen to launch 'a deliberate, indiscriminate attack on the civilian population'.

Judge Leon (whose son Tony would later become leader of the opposition in Parliament) was known to oppose the death penalty. In the case of Andrew Zondo, however, he felt that his hands were tied:

> On count one you are sentenced to death.
> On count two you are sentenced to death.
> On count three you are sentenced to death.
> On count four you are sentenced to death.
> On count five you are sentenced to death.
> May the Lord have mercy on your soul.

Zondo gave a clenched-fist salute, shouted 'Amandla!' and marched from the dock. Judge Leon called him back for count six: ten years for endangering lives.

~

On 12 September, the *Weekly Mail* reported that 'a large slice of the Groot Marico district, immortalised by author Herman Charles Bosman', was to be incorporated into Bophuthatswana.

'This includes the farms around Abjaterskop, where Willem Prinsloo made his famous peach brandy.'

~

On 13 September, in Soshanguve, a township north of Pretoria, the security police arrested three members of an MK assassination unit. Ting Ting Masango, Neo Potsane and Joseph Makhura were driving past a filling station, when several cars pulled out of the forecourt and slotted in behind them. It was clear to the assassins that they were being followed. The car behind them accelerated and drew level. Men with R4 rifles leaned from the windows. Masango pulled over. All was not yet lost: they weren't carrying identification, nor did they have with them any weapons or other incriminating evidence. The police, however, knew exactly who they were. The following day, their commander, Jabu Masina, was also arrested. Collectively, they became known as the Delmas Four, after the town where they eventually stood trial.

Peter Harris, who defended the Delmas Four, tells their story in his book *In a Different Time*. The unit came into being as a direct result of the ANC's National Consultative Conference held in Kabwe, Zambia, in June 1985. At the conference, the liberation movement had resolved to shift its focus from sabotage and bombings to direct attacks on the personnel (particularly black personnel) who helped run the apartheid state. Chris Hani ordered the formation of the unit in February 1986. Technically, it was one of several MK Special Operations units. Practically, however, it was an assassination or 'icing' unit (i.e. it put people 'on ice' at the morgue). The unit reported directly to Hani. Masina, Masango, Potsane and Makhura had each left South Africa a decade earlier, in the wake of the Soweto uprising. Having variously received military training in Angola, Mozambique, Tanzania and East Germany, they were eager to return to the land of their birth and put their skills to use.

The Delmas Four were responsible for a number of assassinations. Among their victims were Constable Senki 'Seun' Vuma, a ruthless policeman from Mamelodi, and David Lukhele, a right-wing politician from the self-governing homeland of KaNgwane. Their highest profile killing was that of Brigadier Andrew Molope, the Bophuthatswana policeman who had presided over the Winterveld massacre in March 1986. The unit also planted a number of landmines in townships (targeting military vehicles), and placed a limpet mine in a dustbin near a bus stop in Silverton, a suburb of Pretoria. The Silverton attack represented a conscious decision to take the war to white areas, in retaliation for PW Botha's bombing of neighbouring capitals in May.

After their arrest, each member of the Delmas Four was held at a separate police station. They were all tortured. Masango's kneecaps were smashed with the bottom end of a Coke bottle. Masina, as commander of the unit, had a particularly hard time of it. Two policemen took turns in assaulting him. His head swelled up, and he passed in and out of consciousness. A tall policeman with a black moustache intervened. He introduced himself as Captain Hendrik Prinsloo and asked the detainee whether he wished to eat anything. Masina requested fish. Prinsloo adopted a fatherly tone:

> You have two choices, Jabu. We will make you talk, everyone talks, you know, they really do, trust me on this. …
> You can have the pain and the jail or you can join us. We have a special unit for people like you. We will keep you safe and give you money and food. Of course, you must help us in our work, but you will not be in jail or dead. And you know what, if you are worried about selling out your former comrades, let me tell you, you are going to betray them anyway. You will betray them once my men start to work on you. In the next few hours or maybe in

a day if you are strong, but I promise you, you will break and tell us everything.

Masina had no intention of becoming an askari, but he decided to buy time by telling Prinsloo about a solo mission he'd undertaken some years earlier. He confessed to the 1978 shooting and killing of Orphan Chapi, a notorious Soweto policeman. No sooner had he completed his account, though, than Prinsloo asked him about his recent missions 'with Ting Ting and the others'. Masina denied that there had been any such missions. The beating started again, and it was wilder than before. Great chunks of his hair were pulled out. He was blindfolded and electrocuted. Prinsloo remained calm throughout: 'Jabu, we must both accept that this is a long and slow process ... We have all the time in the world, there is no rush.' Eventually, when electrodes were attached to his testicles, Masina gave up the fight. He made a full confession in front of a magistrate. Under threat of further torture, he stated that his confession was free and voluntary. The magistrate seemed unperturbed by the fact that his face was bruised and swollen.

Masina's ordeal pales in comparison to the fates of the fifth and sixth members of the unit. Moss Morudu was abducted by the security police a month after the arrest of the initial four. He was taken to a farm named Kaallaagte, where he was interrogated, tortured, and then strangled to death. His body was tied to a telephone pole and destroyed with limpet mines. Justice Mbizana was abducted three months after Morudu. He was taken to a farm named Klipdrift, where he was interrogated, tortured, singed with burning logs, drugged, and finally hacked to death with a spade. His body was likewise destroyed with limpet mines.

In April 1987, the ANC appointed Harris to represent the Delmas Four. Harris notes that their arrests had remained secret for six months 'so that the police could run their "investigation" without the irritation of lawyers wanting to see their clients'. The Four faced a number of charges, including treason, murder, attempted murder, sabotage and possession of weapons. Like many of Harris's political clients, the Delmas Four weren't interested in denying the charges. 'Murderers holding a smoking gun proclaim their innocence,' he remarks. But ask his clients whether they intended to overthrow the state 'and you will get a strong yes'.

After much deliberation, which involved Harris consulting with both Govan Mbeki in Port Elizabeth and Chris Hani in Lusaka, the accused decided not to participate in their trial. They planned to refuse counsel and take no part in the proceedings. Harris explained their decision to Judge Marius de Klerk in a pre-trial meeting:

> They see themselves as soldiers fighting a just war and not as criminals to be tried in a criminal court. They believe they are prisoners of war and do not accept the legitimacy or jurisdiction of the court.

De Klerk asked Harris whether his clients understood that they would be 'severely prejudiced' if they took this route. They wouldn't be able to contest the police's version (they couldn't, for instance, argue that their confessions had been obtained through torture). And, if found guilty, they wouldn't be able to present mitigating circumstances. In absence of mitigation, the judge was obliged to impose the harshest penalty – in this case, the death sentence.

Yes, said Harris, his clients understood.

The trial was set down for Delmas, a small town an hour's drive from Johannesburg. The state preferred to use small rural towns for big trials. The distance from urban centres discouraged large crowds from attending, and made life difficult for the press. Access could be controlled with roadblocks, and the courtrooms were small. Delmas was particularly well suited for a trial, as it was close to Modder B prison. From 1985 to 1987, it hosted to the Delmas Treason Trial, in which twenty-two UDF members, including Popo Molefe and Mosiuoa 'Terror' Lekota, were charged with treason, terrorism and furthering the objectives of an unlawful organisation.

Harris notes that political trials were 'public contests between the government and the resistance organisations', with each side fighting for 'the moral high ground':

> The government, caught between its urge to deal violently with all opposition and its strange desperate pursuit of international credibility and legitimacy, has left the legal door ajar. It's a door into a small room. But people use the opportunity. As you do when you have nothing else.

The non-participation of the accused was a mixed blessing for the state. It wouldn't have to deal with the usual 'trial within a trial', in which the accused challenged the admissibility of their confessions. Typically, such testimony hinged on brutality and torture, and embarrassed the police. On the other hand, the state faced the problem of evidence that hadn't been tested by the defence, and so carried less weight than it might otherwise have done.

Unexpectedly, Judge De Klerk took it upon himself to ask tough questions of the state's witnesses. He was effectively intervening on behalf of the defence. Whenever a witness contended that the accused had given up information 'freely and voluntarily', or that there had existed between captor and captive a relationship of 'mutual understanding' and 'spontaneous warmth', the judge would interrupt and ask just how likely this was. At one point, Captain Prinsloo argued that 'a terrorist is a cowardly person' who, once arrested, would tell you whatever you wished to know. 'It does not appear to me,' muttered the judge, 'that it is the action of a coward to admit deeds that he knows will very possibly lead to the death sentence.'

In the event, De Klerk found the Delmas Four guilty on all the major charges, with the exception of Makhura, whom he found not guilty of murder. He warned the other three that, if they failed to submit arguments in mitigation, they would face the gallows. When Harris next met with his clients in Modder B, they made it clear that they had no intention of forsaking their principles at this late stage. Harris applied to the court for the families of the accused to present extenuation on their behalf. It was a long shot, but De Klerk allowed it, thereby setting a legal precedent. The families called on three people to provide a context for the actions of the Delmas Four: an historian of the urban rebellion, Potsane's father, and a Catholic priest who had been based in Soweto at the time of the uprising.

On the day of their sentencing, the accused arrived in court in full MK combat uniform, including black berets with gold stars. The gallery erupted. The police tried to clamber up the walls of the dock, only for the accused to push them back down again. Even the lawyers got involved. In the midst of this me-lee, an orderly shouted, 'Stand in court!' and De Klerk walked in. Everyone fell silent. The accused shook themselves free of the policemen's hands and straightened their berets. De Klerk proceeded as if nothing was amiss. He presented the merits of the case, and then announced that he had found there to be extenuating circumstances. The defence was about to celebrate, when De Klerk added that his two assessors (one of whom happened to be the father of Eugene de Kock) did not agree with him. The court was bound, he said, by the majority view, 'and consequently I am compelled to impose the death sentence in respect of the convictions of murder'.

The fact that there was disagreement between the judge and the assessors allowed for the possibility of an appeal. Again, the accused declined to participate. At Harris's urging, Lusaka ordered them to appeal. While the move was sure to fail, it would buy the accused a year or more. Time was a valuable commodity, particularly with the first glimmerings of a negotiated settlement coming into view.

While on death row, Masina, Masango and Potsane played a pivotal role in one of the biggest news stories of the apartheid era. They became friendly with a fellow prisoner, Almond Nofomela, who was due to be hanged for killing a farmer in the course of a botched robbery. Nofomela told them that he had been a member of a police hit squad. His specific job, he said, had been to hunt down MK guerrillas such as themselves. There had long been rumours that death squads existed, but there had never been any proof. No one had yet heard of Vlakplaas.

Nofomela boasted that his former commander wouldn't let anything happen to him, because he knew so much. He grew increasingly nervous, though, as his execution date approached. He smuggled out a message to his commander, but heard nothing in response. Masina, Masango and Potsane did their best to convince Nofomela that the police had abandoned him. They urged him to get a lawyer and tell his story.

The final straw for Nofomela came when Eugene de Kock finally replied to his message. He instructed Nofomela to 'take the pain'. Nofomela contacted Lawyers for Human Rights and, with just hours to go to his execution, gave a detailed affidavit. So explosive was his testimony, the minister of justice had little choice but to grant him a stay of execution. Harris visited his clients a few days later. Now that Nofomela had broken his silence, complained Masina, he wouldn't stop talking about what he had done. 'I have heard the same story about twenty times and it's driving me mad. Maybe we made a big mistake in saving him.'

Nofomela's story ran in the *Weekly Mail*, but no one paid much attention to it. Death row prisoners often made outrageous allegations in a bid to escape the noose. A month later,

Max du Preez and Jacques Pauw of *Vrye Weekblad* scored a major coup. The two journalists secured a confession from De Kock's predecessor, Captain Dirk Coetzee: 'I was the commander of the South African Police death squad. I was in the heart of the whore.'\* Coetzee had been named in Nofomela's affidavit, and had decided to save himself. He not only corroborated Nofomela's version, but gave a much fuller account of the goings-on at Vlakplaas, including kidnapping, torture, killing and the often grisly disposal of bodies. Coetzee's confession proved beyond doubt the existence of state-sponsored hit squads – and caused an international uproar. The TRC later granted amnesty to Coetzee and Nofomela, while De Kock received two life sentences and 212 years (in part, it could be said, for the supreme arrogance of telling Nofomela to 'take the pain').

The Delmas Four were released from prison in 1991. With the advent of democracy, each of the former assassins found employment in a state institution: Neo Potsane in national government, Jabu Masina in national intelligence, Joseph Makhura in provincial crime intelligence, and Ting Ting Masango in broadcasting.

~

On 16 September, 177 miners died in a gold mine at Kinross, a small town east of Johannesburg. A welding team had been repairing a damaged track in a tunnel 1 600 metres underground, when their acetylene cylinder sparked and flared. It set fire to insulated wiring, which then ignited the polyurethane foam

---

\* De Kock would later have the following to say about Coetzee's 'heart of the whore' comment: 'This was not strictly true. For, if you want to pursue his metaphor, Coetzee was the kind of man who visits a brothel but stays in the parlour: he always had others do his dirty work for him. Furthermore, compared to me, he hadn't visited all that often. I doubt whether the whore would have recognised Coetzee in the street.'

used to seal the walls. As the fire spread down the tunnel, it gave off poisonous fumes. Those closest to the scene of the accident managed to evacuate, while those further away were caught unawares. The bodies of the dead were spread over an area three kilometres in diameter.

Mine management was slow to report the disaster. It took them five hours to contact the emergency services in the nearby town of Evander, and a further three hours to inform the press. Journalists were barred from the scene of the accident and weren't allowed to interview survivors. The *Weekly Mail* remarked that Gencor, which owned the mine, was 'even more adept than the South African government at controlling the flow of information'. The company released the names of the five white miners who had died, but not those of the 172 black miners, saying that their relatives hadn't yet been informed. In lieu of names, the company provided an ethnic breakdown: 45 Sothos, 29 Xhosas, 20 Pondo, and so on for Tswanas, Venda, Pedi, Hlubi, as well as for foreign nationals from Mozambique, Malawi and Swaziland.

The National Union of Mineworkers announced in a statement that the disaster had taken the industry 'back to the dark ages'. NUM's general secretary, Cyril Ramaphosa, pointed to 'unacceptably low safety standards': the welders were not equipped with a fire extinguisher; the foam sealant was known to be hazardous (it had been banned in other countries); and there was no alarm system to warn workers of the approaching poison cloud.

South Africa's gold mines had always been dangerous places of work. Forty-six thousand miners had died in accidents since 1900 (a mortality rate second only to labourers working on the Panama Canal), and a further million had been crippled or injured. The authorities did not seem overly concerned. When sixty-eight miners died in a methane explosion at Hlobane colliery in 1983, the owners of the mine were fined just R400 for 'hair-raising' lapses in safety.

One of the 'cruel ironies' of Kinross, reported the *Weekly*

*Mail*, was that NUM had been due to launch a booklet on mine safety on 19 September, three days after the disaster. It was titled 'A Thousand Ways to Die'. The booklet made a number of allegations: experienced white miners didn't 'spend much time in the stopes anymore', and seldom did safety inspections; black miners received inadequate training as management was 'in a hurry to send them underground'; and workers who complained about safety standards were victimised and sometimes even fired.

NUM called for a day of mourning for the Kinross dead. The mining houses opposed it, proposing a five-minute silence instead. On 1 October, 325 000 miners downed their tools. The UDF released a statement of support: 'We accuse the mine bosses of preoccupation with the never-ending chase for super-profits at the expense of the well-being of those who toil to make this wealth possible.'

The Kinross disaster took place a hundred years after George Harrison first found gold on the Witwatersrand. His discovery kick-started not only a century of industrialisation, but also a century of legislation designed to force blacks to work on the mines – be it hut tax, poll tax, native reserves, influx control or the plethora of laws that governed the migrant labour system. As a result, argues economist Francis Wilson, black rural areas became 'less able to provide a means of livelihood for their inhabitants in 1986 than they were when gold was discovered in 1886'.

The city of Johannesburg had planned an elaborate hundredth birthday party, but the festivities were cut short by threats of mass action and boycotts. A range of organisations, including the ANC, the UDF and the Soweto Chamber of Commerce, campaigned under the slogan 'One hundred years of exploitation. We have nothing to celebrate'. There could be no party, they said, without the consent of 'the people who built this city'.

~

On 18 September, the *London Review of Books* published novelist Angela Carter's review of the anthology *A Land Apart: A South African Reader*. The book had been issued by Faber and Faber the previous month.

Co-editors André Brink and J M Coetzee explain in their introduction that the anthology represents 'a mere sample of the variety and quality of South African writing in English and Afrikaans of the past ten years or so'. Coetzee took primary responsibility for selecting the English-language works, while Brink did the same for works translated from Afrikaans. They approached their task, they state, 'as if the apparatus of censorship did not exist'. Carter spells out the inevitable result: 'This is an anthology for export only.'

There is a marked difference, observes Carter, between the two sections into which the book has been divided. The pieces translated from Afrikaans, she says, are 'almost entirely pervaded by a deep sense of dread', while in the English pieces, many of which are by black and coloured writers, 'there is less psychological violence ... and more of the ordinary, physical kind'. Brink and Coetzee remark that almost everything written in Afrikaans at the time carried 'an intimation of apocalypse'. This dark mood, they say, 'implies not just the death of the individual or the end of his hopes, but the destruction of the entire known world or a way of life'. This is not to suggest that the Afrikaans pieces are overtly political. Often, a sense of foreboding infiltrates personal experience – as with the female impersonator who kills himself in Hennie Aucamp's 'For Four Voices', or the child who pulls the wings off a butterfly in Ina Rousseau's 'Do You Remember Helena Lem?'

The English section of *A Land Apart* presents a more diverse set of viewpoints and experiences. It includes a number of iconic poems. There's Jeremy Cronin's 'Walking on Air', in which John Matthews is given permission by his wife Dulcie to spend fifteen years in prison rather than betray his comrades. (Poet Peter

Anderson has described 'Walking on Air' as 'not only our best poem of political resistance, but also our best love poem'.)

There's Motshile wa Nthodi's 'South African Dialogue':

...

Baas Ben's Baasboy says,
Baas Ben want to see
Baas Kleinbaas if
Baas don't use
Baas Kleinbaas,
Baas.

...

And Chris van Wyk's 'In Detention':

...

He hanged himself
He slipped on a piece of soap while washing
He fell from the ninth floor
He hanged himself while washing
He slipped from the ninth floor

...

Some of the prose punches as hard as the poetry. Here is the opening sentence of Mtutuzeli Matshoba's story 'Call Me Not a Man':

By dodging, lying, resisting where it is possible, bolting when I'm already cornered, parting with invaluable money, sometimes calling my sisters into the game to get amorous with my captors, allowing myself to be slapped on the mouth in front of my womenfolk and getting sworn at with my mother's private parts, that component of me which is man has died countless times in one lifetime.

Maria Tholo, in an excerpt from her diary, describes helping a friend find her son after an extended spell of rioting. Fearing the worst, they visit a mortuary. 'What happens,' says Tholo, 'is that they put all the unidentified bodies in one place and you have to search through them like a pile of old clothes to find yours.'

Carter makes the point that most fiction 'would pale in significance beside this kind of direct and unmediated recounting of experience'.

~

On 25 September, in the nominally independent homeland of Ciskei, a group of men armed with automatic weapons stormed a maximum-security prison and freed Charles Sebe, former head of state security, and brother of the president, Lennox Sebe. No shots were fired. It later emerged that the day of the raid had been carefully chosen: it was pay day and the warders were 'enjoying their paychecks'. The press made much of the fact that the raiders were white. It was alleged that they were former Selous Scouts from Rhodesia, now working for the neighbouring homeland of Transkei.

At approximately the same time as the jailbreak, the president's son, a major-general in the police force, was abducted from a hotel in Bisho, the capital city. Namba Sebe, brother to Lennox and Charles, claimed responsibility for both the jailbreak and the abduction. He had formerly been minister of transport and was now living in exile in Transkei. The family had for some years been engaged in an epic feud (sometimes referred to in the South African press as 'the Sebe circus'). In 1983, Lennox had jailed Charles, together with Charles's son and Namba's son, on suspicion that they had been plotting a coup. Namba managed to evade arrest. 'Sebe runs out of brothers', ran a *City Press* headline.

After the abduction, Namba offered to exchange Lennox's son for his and Charles's sons. He also demanded that the president resign, along with his entire cabinet: 'If Lennox goes, there will be democracy there, by that simple act. He has messed up that constitution. There are a lot of amendments that he has put there to protect himself.' The president didn't take much notice of his exiled brother. He blamed both the jailbreak and the abduction on George Matanzima, the prime minister of Transkei. For years, he said, both Matanzima and his brother Kaiser, the former president of Transkei, had been seeking to undermine Ciskei's sovereignty. It was all part of their grand plan to incorporate Ciskei into Transkei, thus uniting 'Greater Xhosaland'.

Lennox Sebe, a former school principal, became president of Ciskei on independence in 1981. He immediately consolidated his power, stacking Parliament with tribal chiefs. They outnumbered the elected officials and, in exchange for patronage, supported his every move. His security forces harassed political opponents and crushed any sign of dissent. In 1983, they broke a bus boycott by firing on commuters boarding a train; ninety people died in the attack. Ciskei fast became the most intolerant and repressive of the homelands. Two years into his reign, Sebe declared himself 'President for Life', and had a bronze bust of himself placed outside the legislative assembly.

Sebe had a close relationship with Israel. He visited the country several times and bought aircraft from Israeli firms, both for his personal use and for his fledgling air force. Ciskeian pilots were trained by Israeli instructors, and Bisho was twinned with Ariel, a settler community on the West Bank. It was not unusual for the independent homelands, whose only official diplomatic links were with each other and with South Africa, to reach out to pariah states. Bophuthatswana was likewise friendly with Israel, while Venda cultivated relations with Taiwan.*

Xhanti Charles Sebe was his brother's enforcer. He had

joined the South African Police in 1957, working first for the Special Branch in Port Elizabeth and later for the Bureau of State Security. In the Sixties, he participated in the arrest of Govan Mbeki and the mass roundup of Poqo, the armed wing of the Pan African Congress. In the Seventies, he tailed Steve Biko. In 1977, Sergeant Sebe left the SAP to establish the Ciskei Intelligence Service. Six years later, he was Lieutenant-General Sebe, in charge of state security and head of the armed services, including the defence force, the police, the traffic police and the prison service. He was the quintessential strongman, with almost unlimited power and a reputation for brutality.

Joseph Lelyveld devotes a chapter of *Move Your Shadow* to Charles Sebe. He describes him as a flamboyant generalissimo who 'wore a black Stetson with his smoked glasses and Christian Dior suits'. For a few brief years, Sebe 'wielded more power and accrued more notoriety within the South African system than any black man had before him'. He was, says Lelyveld, 'exactly what the system needed ... a dependable black ally who believed, more or less, in its purposes'.

Sebe liked to say that he was on a 'divine mission' to root out communism. He was crucial to Pretoria's internal defence system, not only because of the enthusiasm with which he took the fight to the comrades, but also because the eastern Cape was a hotbed of resistance. When Charles was imprisoned by his brother in 1983, the South Africans did what they could to get him released. But there was only so much pressure they

---

* South Africa itself was on good terms with Israel, Taiwan, Iran, Paraguay, Argentina, Chile, Bolivia and Nicaragua. As historian Bernard Porter has observed: 'Pariahs can't be choosers.' These countries were acutely aware of one another's shortcomings. Prime Minister John Vorster once asked his counterpart Alfredo Stroessner why Paraguay had a navy when it was landlocked. For the same reason, replied Stroessner, that South Africa had a minister of justice.

could exert. Ciskei was, after all, by their own proposition, an independent nation.

Historian James Sanders has revealed South Africa's hidden hand in the Sebe feud. In 1986, the SADF launched two 'programmes of action' to instigate violence in the homelands. One was Operation Marion, which involved two hundred Inkatha recruits receiving military training in the Caprivi Strip. The other was Operation Katzen. Katzen's ultimate goal was to merge Transkei and Ciskei into a Greater Xhosaland under the leadership of George Matanzima. Its intermediate goals involved the escape from prison of Charles Sebe, the creation of an invading force to be led by him, and the toppling of President Lennox Sebe. Many of the soldiers assigned to Katzen were former Selous Scouts, now in the employ of the SADF. Several of the intermediate goals were realised, but the invasion itself failed.

In 1990, Lennox Sebe was deposed by Brigadier-General Joshua 'Oupa' Gqozo. He died of natural causes a few years later. In 1991, Charles Sebe was lured back to the homeland in the belief that he was to lead a coup. Instead, he was ambushed by Ciskei security forces and shot in cold blood. Gqozo stood trial for the murder, but was acquitted. The TRC found that the fake coup had been orchestrated by South African military intelligence.

# OCTOBER

# Why can't I kiss fellow workers?

SIR — I work at a leading chain store.

My boss made me sign a final warning slip for kissing a female friend of mine. Is this worth a final warning?

I was told that I had breached the company standards and regulations. Now what puzzled me is tha we have books of rules and regulations of this shop but I've never came across such a clause (breach of company standards and regulations.

I'm not surprised, this shop, like the Government, is making laws and not informing us and is expecting us to accept them, be they good or bad.

So watch out gents, don't go around kissing friends.

**JAWS**

*Sowetan*, 1 October 1986

ON 1 OCTOBER, M-Net was launched. It was South Africa's first pay-television channel, and the first channel of any kind that wasn't controlled by the state. M-Net's major shareholder was the print-media company Nasionale Pers. In time, it would become the multi-media conglomerate Naspers.

M-Net's programming consisted of general entertainment, movies and sport. It was prohibited from broadcasting news programmes. Speaking on the day of M-Net's launch, P W Botha made it plain that the SABC was to retain its monopoly on the dissemination of information.

Television came late to South Africa. The government resisted calls in the Fifties and Sixties, deferring to the Dutch Reformed Church and the Broederbond. The Calvinist churchmen feared moral decay and corruption, while the Broederbond was wary of 'subversive' ideas from abroad. 'For the time being at least,' noted *The Times* of London in 1960, 'there is to be no television for fear that it might open unwanted windows on the world.' Dr Albert Hertzog, the minister of posts and telegraphs, was central to any decision. He considered television 'the devil's own box', and declared that it would only be introduced over his dead body. Friends of his had visited Britain, he explained. They had told him that 'one cannot see a program which does not show black and white living together, where they are not continually propagating a mixture of the two races'.

Calls for television grew louder in 1969, after the rest of the world got to see Neil Armstrong walk on the moon. Hertzog had resigned by then, so the government appointed a commission of inquiry. The commission came out in favour of television, provided that 'effective control' was exercised. In *Native Nostalgia*, Jacob Dlamini makes the point that the Nationalists could hardly claim to be the last defenders of 'Western civilisation' in Africa and yet be 'opposed to television'.

Full transmission commenced in January 1976. Many of the early shows featured the conservative values of the American west: *Shane, Bonanza, The Little House on the Prairie*. No sport could be broadcast on Sundays. In the early years, television was largely a whites-only affair, with broadcasting split evenly between Afrikaans and English. In 1982, two additional services were added: TV2 for speakers of Nguni languages and TV3 for Sotho languages. Government attitudes softened in the early Eighties. By the time of M-Net's launch, *The Cosby Show* was a favourite. Other popular programmes were *The A-Team, Airwolf, Knight Rider, Dallas, Derrick* and *Koöperasiestories*.

As the devil's box made its way into more and more households, it became integral to the government's propaganda campaign. Anxious white South Africans were assured that their nation was a bastion of Christian democracy and that their security forces held the upper hand against communist insurgents. The SABC tended not to show scenes of unrest. When their hand was forced, they unfailingly depicted township dwellers as a destructive and disorderly mob, while the security forces were models of restraint and order.

American journalist William Finnegan visited South Africa in 1986. He observed that the picture of daily life available on television and radio 'seems to bear only the most distant resemblance to what is actually happening in the country'. He found news reporting to be 'selective and tendentious, customarily presenting only the government's view of events while attacking or ignoring its opponents'. Finnegan's view is borne out by media expert Professor Johan van Zyl, who observes that the SABC's approach to the news was 'characterised by selection, omission and placement' and that these combined to give 'a weird picture of the world – a self-centred view of South Africa as a badly misunderstood and wrongly persecuted little nation'. White South Africans knew more about what was happening in Lebanon and Nicaragua than in their own country.

While local television may have been the government's friend, foreign television was not. By the mid-Eighties, nightly scenes of unrest were beamed into homes around the world. Images of children taking the fight to soldiers in armoured vehicles fuelled debate about South Africa's place in the world.

~

On 1 October, actors Robert Colman and Matthew Krouse went into hiding. Their satirical play, *Famous Dead Man*, had been banned the previous day and they'd received death threats.

The dead man in question was former prime minister Hendrik Verwoerd. In one scene, Verwoerd tells God to 'get out of my chair'. The show had been running at the Black Sun in Berea, Johannesburg, for eight weeks before anyone objected. The state apparatus then leapt into action. The Publications Control Board convened an urgent meeting and declared the show 'undesirable'. It acknowledged that the Publications Act did not protect political figures from ridicule. In this instance, however, it ruled that Verwoerd had been 'chosen as a symbol of a large section of the Republic in an attempt to insult and degrade them'.

The *Weekly Mail* traced the actors to a flat in Braamfontein, where they were lying low. They may have written the jokes, said Colman, 'but we didn't write the history'. Krouse was more circumspect: 'We aren't horny for the baton, we're horny for the stage.' He quoted a piece of advice from Breyten Breytenbach's *True Confessions of an Albino Terrorist*: 'Never go to jail.'

~

On 2 October, the US Senate overturned President Ronald Reagan's veto on sanctions against South Africa. As a result, the Comprehensive Anti-Apartheid Act came into force. It imposed the toughest penalties yet by an industrial nation. Immediate effects included the withdrawal of landing rights for South African Airways and a prohibition on all new US investments. Within three months, there was to be a complete ban on all imports of South African uranium, coal, iron ore, steel, textiles and agricultural products. South Africa's sugar quota was to be transferred to the Philippines.

While many had suspected the veto might be overturned, few had foreseen the 78–21 margin. The vote reflected outrage, suggested commentators, at last-ditch efforts by Pik Botha and Mangosuthu Buthelezi to intervene in support of the veto. Senator Ted Kennedy labelled Botha's threat to stop purchases of US grain 'one of the most notorious attempts by a foreign government to interfere in the foreign policy of the United States'. Botha, for his part, complained that the senators were being too 'emotional' and that their perception of what was actually happening in South Africa was 'twisted'.

The vote was Reagan's biggest foreign-policy defeat to date and sounded the death knell for his administration's policy of 'constructive engagement' with Pretoria. Where the Cold War warrior saw PW Botha beating back the communists, the Senate saw institutionalised racism, cross-border raids and martial law. American pension funds and university endowment funds had long been disinvesting from South Africa. Companies such as General Motors, General Electric, Johnson & Johnson and IBM now found that their small operations in the country weren't worth the 'flak factor' they faced back home. In 1986 alone, South Africa experienced a net capital outflow of over R6 billion.

Reagan's argument that sanctions would 'hurt blacks most of all' had been hotly contested. 'When the ladder falls over,' retorted Bishop Tutu, 'it is those at the top who get hurt most.'

During his visit to the US earlier that year, Tutu had shared the results of a survey which showed that seventy per cent of black South Africans welcomed sanctions. 'We are desperately poor already,' a resident of Oukasie township outside Brits told American journalist Richard Stengel. 'We are prepared to suffer. What more can sanctions do to us? We only eat pap here.'

While the passing of the Anti-Apartheid Act was a victory for the ANC, it wasn't all good news. The act singled out the 'abhorrent' practice of necklacing as an obstacle to political progress. It prohibited US assistance to any individual, group or organisation that supported 'execution by fire'.

~

On 17 October, the *Weekly Mail* ran an article about a recent phone-in show on Radio 702. Children had been invited to say what action they would take if they were South Africa's president. 'We have lots of troubles because blacks are rioting,' said thirteen-year-old Marco from Johannesburg. 'The Prime Minister should have a day when everybody can collect a gun and just kill one of them.'

The article noted that the show's host, John Berks, 'was audibly shaken by the deep conservatism of most of the callers'.

~

On 19 October, Samora Machel, the president of Mozambique, died in a plane crash. His Russian-made Tupolev was returning from Lusaka to Maputo when it hit the ground in mountainous terrain near Mbuzini, a small town in South Africa close to both the Mozambican and Swazi borders. There were forty-three people on board at the time, nine of whom survived.

Two investigations were conducted. The Margo Commission of Inquiry, appointed by the South African government, blamed 'pilot error'. A Soviet inquiry concluded that a 'decoy beacon' had been used to lure the Tupolev off course. Many suspected foul play, not least because of suspicious goings-on at the crash site. One of the survivors walked to a nearby house for help. On his return, he was surprised to find that South African security forces were already on the scene. Members of the public saw officers 'rummaging through the wreckage and confiscating documents'. The wounded were initially ignored, and a civilian nurse was shooed away. It took the South African authorities nine hours to inform their Mozambican counterparts about the crash.

The security forces seized the cockpit voice recorder – the black box – and for several weeks refused to hand it over to investigators. This allowed government spokesmen to muddy the waters without fear of contradiction. In one of their statements, they claimed the pilot 'mistook the lights of Komatipoort for Maputo'. In another, they suggested the pilot was drunk. They even resorted to verifiable falsehoods. Pik Botha referred to the Tupolev as 'dated and obsolete', when in fact the aircraft had been manufactured just six years earlier and was well maintained.

Speaking at a commemorative ceremony for Machel, Canadian academic John Saul warned against reading too much into either the suspicious circumstances surrounding the crash, or the campaign of disinformation that followed:

Accidents do happen, after all. Yet the fact that so many observers could immediately suspect the South Africans of having helped to engineer it is itself no accident. For such an act would be perfectly consistent with South Africa's brutal record of aggression, assassination and destabilization.

Samora Machel was painfully aware of this 'brutal record'. He had been president of Mozambique since independence in 1975. The country had been hoping for a new dawn after a decade of bitter fighting against the Portuguese. Instead, there followed a decade of equally bitter fighting against the South Africans – or, rather, against their proxy force, the Renamo rebels.

In March 1984, presidents Machel and Botha had signed the Nkomati Accord. Neither territory was to be used for attacks against the other. Mozambique was to expel the ANC and South Africa was to cease its support for Renamo. The South Africans had pressed hard for the accord. It was a key component of their strategy to replace the territorial buffer they had lost when the Portuguese colonies achieved independence.

Machel was a charismatic and much-loved leader. His obituaries speak of his energy, intelligence and deft sense of humour. He was a staunch opponent of apartheid and hated the idea of doing a deal with the South Africans. Chester Crocker, the American assistant secretary of state for African affairs, reports that reaction to the accord in 'Third World circles' was one of 'sullen shock'. But Mozambique, he says, 'had had enough'. After signing the Accord, Machel spoke publicly of how his country had been bludgeoned into submission by the South African-sponsored rebels:

> Our people had their property looted, their houses destroyed, their granaries raided, their crops pillaged and flattened, their cattle stolen and killed, their tools burnt and destroyed. … The systematic destruction of economic infrastructure, bridges and roads, shops and warehouses, sawmills, plantations, agricultural and industrial machinery, electricity supply lines, fuel tanks, lorries and buses, locomotives and carriages has prevented the implementation of economic development projects of the utmost importance for the well being of the Mozambican people.

Machel catalogued the kidnappings and murders of teachers and students, nuns and priests, civil servants and parliamentarians, journalists, shopkeepers and peasants. 'This is the enemy's cruel nature – kill everything, steal everything, burn everything.'

So popular was Machel, notes Saul, that the South Africans never really tried to present an alternative. 'Rather, theirs has been a scorched earth policy, one of destroying economic infra-structure, and terrorizing villagers, one of creating chaos and checkmating progress.' Renamo drew little distinction between military and civilian targets. Buses and trains were peppered with machine-gun fire, government supporters had their arms and breasts hacked off, crops were burnt, livestock killed, and carcasses dropped down wells to poison the water supply. In 1982 and 1983 alone, Renamo destroyed eight hundred schools and two hundred clinics.

The South African state hailed the Nkomati Accord as a major diplomatic success and proclaimed President Botha a peacemaker. He toured Europe on the back of it and, at Margaret Thatcher's invitation, became the first South African leader to visit Britain in twenty-five years. Machel, meanwhile, expelled the ANC from his country and waited for the mayhem to subside. The South Africans, however, had no intention of honouring the agreement and violated it from the outset. Crocker asks what purpose can possibly be served by actively destroying confidence in one's word. 'Perhaps it was an exaggeration,' he remarks, 'to speak of a "South African foreign policy" in the mid-1980s.'*

One of Pretoria's tactics was to cultivate its already cosy relations with Hastings Banda, Malawi's President for Life. In return for soft loans and other perks, Banda allowed Renamo to set up bases in his country. The aging dictator didn't need much convincing. He had long dreamed of a 'Greater Malawi', which would incorporate a chunk of Mozambique and so link

---

* In *The Imperial Presidency*, a study of PW Botha's first ten years in power, Brian Pottinger devotes a chapter to South Africa's foreign policy. The chapter is titled 'Talk and Thump'.

his landlocked country to the sea. Banda reportedly referred to Nacala, a coastal town in northern Mozambique, as 'my port'.

By the second half of 1986, Machel was on the warpath. In September, he travelled to Blantyre with Kenneth Kaunda and Robert Mugabe. The three presidents confronted Banda in a heated two-hour meeting. Machel warned him that, if he continued to support South African surrogates, Mozambique would close its borders with Malawi. This was a significant threat, as a large percentage of Malawi's exports were transported by road through Mozambique's Tete Corridor en route to South African ports. Machel was still fuming when he got back to Maputo. He called a press conference at the airport and told journalists: 'We will place missiles along the border with Malawi if support to the bandits is not ended.' He added that he would not hesitate to launch a pre-emptive strike.

In October, two weeks before the plane crash, six South African soldiers were injured in a landmine explosion on the Mozambican border. General Magnus Malan interpreted this as proof that Mozambique had reneged on the Nkomati Accord and had renewed its support for the ANC. He issued a direct threat: 'If President Machel chooses landmines, South Africa will react accordingly … If he chooses terrorism and revolution, he will clash head on with South Africa.'

A week before the crash, a journalist asked Machel whether he feared a South African assassination attempt. 'They've already tried,' he replied. Their most recent attempt, he said, had involved a plot to attack his motorcade with rocket launchers. On the night of the crash, Machel was returning from the Lusaka Summit. He and other Frontline leaders had been discussing how they might confront President Mobutu Sésé Seko regarding Zaire's support for Unita, South Africa's surrogate force in Angola.

In the late 1990s, South Africa's Truth and Reconciliation Commission investigated Machel's death. It collated all previous evidence and interviewed a number of new witnesses. The TRC found that a 'large number of South African Special Forces troops' had converged on 'Komatipoort/Mbuzini on the night of the crash', and that there had been 'a strong presence of police and military personnel in the area'. A former military intelligence officer testified that a number of high-ranking officials had descended on Skwamans, a secret police base near Mbuzini, the day before the crash. He named General Kat Liebenberg of the defence force, General Pieter van der Westhuizen of military intelligence, and Pik Botha of foreign affairs.

A flight sergeant in the South African Air Force told the TRC that he had seen a colleague building a mobile decoy beacon a month before the crash. The decoy had 'left the base with its builder during the weekend of the crash and was returned the following week'. The TRC heard that the only way 'a rogue beacon' would work was if an accomplice in the control tower at Maputo Airport switched off the real beacon. Witnesses testified that airport employees had been bribed to this end.

Investigative journalist Debora Patta probed Machel's death shortly before the TRC. She uncovered an intelligence document from a neighbouring country. It alleged that South African Military Intelligence had paid an airport official R1.5 million to switch off the Maputo beacon. Patta also spoke to a Renamo operative who had been sent a message by his South African military contact a few days before the crash: 'Pay attention to the news and stay near the telephone ... something big is going to happen.' Patta received a number of death threats while working on the story. Her principal source in Maputo survived two assassination attempts, on each occasion taking a number of bullets to the body.

Machel's wife Graça (who later married Nelson Mandela) told the TRC that she believed the plot to kill her husband had been instigated by Hastings Banda. She testified that the Malawian president had dispatched senior officers to South Africa for a meeting with PW Botha, and that Botha, in turn, had sent General Malan to meet with Banda. The two men had talked about enlisting 'senior Mozambican officials', and had even discussed 'the recruitment of an official at the Mozambican control tower'. Patta's intelligence document supports Graça Machel's version of events. It alleges that the plot to kill Samora Machel involved agents from three countries: Malawi, Mozambique and South Africa. Patta remarks that recruiting Mozambican officials would have been relatively easy, as Machel was about to fire a number of them for 'profiting from the war with Renamo'.

The TRC generated a mountain of circumstantial evidence, most of it pointing to the existence of a decoy beacon. Its investigation ran out of time and resources, however, and failed to produce a smoking gun. The commission concluded that the matter required 'further investigation by an appropriate structure'. It made a point of debunking the notion of pilot error, noting that it had reason to 'question the conclusions reached by the Margo Commission'.

Patta's take on Margo is somewhat less measured:

One has to ask why South Africa always hauled out Judge Cecil Margo whenever it needed to conduct a sensitive aviation inquiry.* At the time of the crash, the SADF was

---

\* Margo's cases included the Albertina crash of 1961, in which Dag Hammarskjöld, the secretary-general of the UN, died (most likely because South Africa, along with a handful of other countries, wanted to halt Congolese independence), and the Helderberg crash of 1987, in which 159 people died when a passenger aircraft caught fire (most likely because it was carrying a cargo of sanctions-busting armaments, including highly combustible missile propellant). Margo never failed to return a trite finding. 'The Republic of South Africa,' notes historian James Sanders, 'has a long and inglorious history of suspicious plane crashes.'

under suspicion. The mere fact that Judge Margo was an honorary colonel with ties to the old South African Air Force was reason enough for him to excuse himself from the inquiry into the Machel crash. But during the apartheid days it was customary for the accused to investigate themselves.

In the years following the Truth Commission, new stories continued to bubble to the surface. In 2002, a former operative for the Civil Cooperation Bureau confessed he'd been part of a 'back-up team' instructed to shoot down Machel's aeroplane with air-to-surface missiles 'if the first plan [the false beacon] failed'. The following year, General Tienie Groenewald alleged that senior members of Frelimo, including Joaquim Chissano, who succeeded Machel as president, were in on the plot and were instrumental in 'the shutting down of a Maputo Airport navigational beacon'.

The Tupolev crash has become Machel's crash, and little is heard of the thirty-three people who died alongside him. One such casualty was Aquino de Bragança, the director of Maputo's Centre for African Studies. In 1982, he lost his hearing in the parcel bomb that killed Ruth First. Four years later, he lost his life in the plane crash that killed Samora Machel.

~

On 21 October, the Nederduitse Gereformeerde Kerk – better known in Afrikaans as the NG Kerk and in English as the Dutch Reformed Church – opened its membership to all races. The church had erred, ruled its general synod, in offering a biblical justification for separate development. The NG Sendingkerk, a breakaway denomination for coloured members, went further, declaring apartheid a sin.

Andries Treurnicht, the leader of the Conservative Party, told a Durban audience that it was no longer unthinkable for the NGK to have a moderator sympathetic to the UDF. He referred to this hypothetical churchman as 'a second Tutu'.

~

On 21 October, David Goldblatt photographed a man named Lucas Kgatitsoe. The image, which first appeared in *Leadership* magazine, shows Kgatitsoe sitting on a pile of stones in the open veld. He is dressed in a three-piece suit, his hands resting on his knees. A spectacles case protrudes from the breast pocket of his jacket. His back is straight, but his face betrays bitterness and defeat. The photograph is shot in black and white. As Goldblatt later observed: 'During those years, colour seemed too sweet a medium to express the anger, disgust and fear that apartheid inspired.'

The pile of stones on which Kgatitsoe was sitting were the ruins of his family home. The government had bulldozed it two years earlier, during the forced removal of Mogopa, a black farming community in the western Transvaal. At the time of Goldblatt's photograph, Kgatitsoe was resident in Soweto. He was a member of The Reef Committee, a group of migrant workers who were fighting for the return of their ancestral land. A fellow member of the committee recalls that Kgatitsoe was dressed in a suit that day not because he was having his photograph taken, but rather because 'we were always smart back then'.

*Leadership* had commissioned Goldblatt to produce a photo essay on human structures, with particular emphasis on how these structures conveyed the contrasting values of the people who had built them. It was a theme that Goldblatt had been investigating for several years already, and that would culminate, a decade later, in his book *South Africa: The Structure of Things Then*. Goldblatt's central idea is that people's 'needs, imperatives and values' are embedded in 'the bricks, mud, stone, steel and concrete' of the structures they choose to build. The same is true of those they choose to destroy: 'When buildings cease to exist as coherent structures, their remains or footprints may yet be eloquent … of what ruined them.'

By the time of the removals, the Bakwena community had been living at Mogopa for several generations. Their forebears had originally been farm labourers in the Orange Free State. In 1911, a group of them had banded together and bought land in the western Transvaal. This was two years before the Natives Land Act would outlaw such acquisitions. Over the course of the next seventy years, the Bakwena baMogopa developed their land without subsidy or assistance. They sank boreholes, installed windpumps, erected fences, built roads and a reservoir. They raised livestock and grew maize, sorghum, beans and vegetables. By the 1970s, they had a church, a clinic and shops, as well as two schools constructed from cut stone. Their agricultural endeavours produced a surplus, which they sold to a co-op in Ventersdorp.

Mogopa was, however, a 'black spot', rural land owned by black people in an area that was subsequently declared white. Early in the 1980s, government officials told the community that they needed to move. They refused point blank. Had this been ten years earlier, bulldozers and trucks would have arrived, accompanied by men with guns. In the intervening decade, however, forced removals had become politically costly for the state. It had started to speak instead of 'voluntary' removals. The idea was to 'motivate' or 'persuade' people to move, rather than force them.

Towards the end of 1981, the community voted to depose their headman, Jacob More, accusing him of corruption and 'failing to adhere to democratic principles'. The local magistrate sensed an opportunity to undermine the community's cohesion. Invoking the Black Administration Act of 1927, he informed the community that the state president was the paramount chief of all blacks. Only the president could appoint a headman. In the absence of the president, the magistrate assumed the role: 'I as a white man and Magistrate of this whole area say Jacob More will rule until he dies.'

The following year, the magistrate called a 'resettlement meeting' and reiterated that the community needed to move. Land had been set aside for them at Pachsdraai, he said. Formerly a white-owned farm, it was a hundred kilometres to the north, and was earmarked for incorporation into Bophuthatswana. Again, the community refused. The magistrate then got to work on More, offering him a number of inducements, including the use of the main farmhouse at Pachsdraai. In the winter of 1983, More and his family left for Pachsdraai along with ten other families. The moment they left, bulldozers flattened their houses – and then, for good measure, demolished the clinic, the church and the schools. The government removed water pumps, withdrew bus services, and refused to renew the shopkeepers' licences. The elderly were informed that their pensions could only be drawn at Pachsdraai. A demolition team set up camp next to the village.

'Virtually we were left in an island,' recalls resident Andrew Pooe. 'We were totally cut out from the world.' From the government's perspective, it wasn't forcing people to leave, it was persuading them. Earlier that year, Piet Koornhof, the minister who signed the Mogopa removal order, had stated that the government approached resettlement with 'compassion and respect for human dignity after deep thought and careful consideration'.

Aninka Claassens of the Black Sash describes the state's strategy:

What does the state do once [it has] smashed the schools, stopped the transport, cut off the water, threatened force – and people still refuse to move? … It waits. There is a limit to how long people can live without schools, without pensions, without migrant labour contracts, and with daily uncertainty about their future. If it is a matter of who can sit it out, the state is the more likely winner.

Succumbing to the pressure, a further 170 families moved to Pachsdraai. But several remained. One day, while the men were at work, state officials showed up and said they needed to paint numbers on the houses. Most of the women refused, but a few agreed. Soon afterwards, trucks arrived to pick up those who had 'agreed' and their houses were demolished.

In November 1983, the magistrate issued an ultimatum: the remaining residents of Mogopa had ten days to move of their own accord, or else they would be forced to move. By then, the community was being assisted by a number of organisations, including the Black Sash and its offshoot, the Transvaal Rural Action Committee, which specialised in fighting forced removals. Lawyers from the Centre for Applied Legal Studies at the University of the Witwatersrand applied for an interdict to stop the removal. When this was denied, they lodged an appeal.

On the appointed day, a crowd gathered at Mogopa to hold a vigil in protest against the removal. In attendance were churchmen, leaders of the UDF, activists, students and members of the media. The government trucks arrived, but soon backed down. 'Publicity is what TRAC is all about,' noted one of its employees. 'The government hates publicity.'

Buoyed by this victory, the community rebuilt one of its schools. The government, however, was biding its time. Early one morning in February 1984, Mogopa was surrounded by armed police. Jacob More announced through a loudhailer that the people should load their possessions onto the waiting trucks and join him at Pachsdraai. Those who resisted were beaten and arrested. The media and the Black Sash were refused entry to Mogopa that day, but local white farmers were allowed in with their flat-bed lorries. They bought up the community's cattle and goats for a pittance. An old man who was bedridden was forcibly removed in an ambulance.

The Surplus People Project has estimated that between 1960 and 1983 the South African government forcibly moved 3 522 900 people. This was in line with one of the stated objectives of apartheid: to turn South Africa into a 'white' country. An unstated objective was to turn the homelands into reservoirs of cheap labour, as well as dumping grounds for those who were unfit for work. A government minister referred to the wives, children and parents of black workers as 'superfluous appendages'. Another minister called them 'surplus people'. Such phrases were used to justify uprooting people from the land on which their ancestors had lived for generations, and depositing them hundreds of kilometres away on tracts of barren veld with few, if any, amenities. Sheena Duncan, a long-time president of the Black Sash, considered forced removals apartheid's 'greatest evil'.

Mogopa was the last forced removal of a rural community. In part this was due to government reforms, and in part to the negative publicity generated by Mogopa itself. But credit must also go to those communities that were resisting removal at the same time as Mogopa. Driefontein and KwaNgema, neighbouring 'black spots' in the eastern Transvaal, each emerged victorious after lengthy struggles.

The people of Driefontein initially tried to negotiate. They met with minister Piet Koornhof, who said they had to move because they were squatters. They pointed out that they had owned the land since before 1913, but Koornhof rejected their claim: 'All black people in South Africa are squatters if you are outside your traditional lands.' When a policeman shot and killed their leader, the community took a more aggressive line, fighting the government every inch of the way. They won minor legal battle after minor legal battle – overturning, for instance, the local commissioner's decisions to withhold their pensions and to ban public meetings. These victories emboldened the community and galvanised them to keep up the fight. A group of women resisted by digging their own graves: 'We will stand beside our graves because we are not moving from here. You can shoot and we will lie in our land forever.'

The people of KwaNgema took a more politic approach. They wrote to Queen Elizabeth, asking: 'How can the South African government have the right to take away from us that which was given to us by your great grandfather?' (Never mind that they were playing fast and loose with their own history.) The Queen passed on their letter to Margaret Thatcher. The prime minister took up the issue with PW Botha, who was visiting the UK at the time – his pariah status temporarily lifted thanks to the signing of the Nkomati Accord. Botha gave a public assurance that the Ngema would be fairly treated.

The community also contacted the chief ministers of KwaZulu and KaNgwane, asking them to refuse entry to the Ngema. Mangosuthu Buthelezi rebuffed their approach, but Enos Mabuza, in an unprecedented step for a homeland leader, announced that he would ban from his territory 'any truck carrying displaced people or their possessions'. He had no interest, he said, in administering a resettlement camp for Pretoria.

For the people of Driefontein and KwaNgema, these were but the opening volleys in their respective fights. Each community faced countless acts of attrition, including the shared threat of flooding by a new dam. They held firm, however, and in 1985 each received a reprieve. That same year, the government announced that its policy of forced removals was to be suspended. Seemingly undeterred by this failure, the government came up with a new strategy: incorporation. Instead of physically moving people, it instructed the Government Printer's office in Pretoria to redraw homeland boundaries. People would fall asleep one evening in South Africa, only to wake up the next morning in

Gazankulu. 'How do you fight the drawings of a pen?' asked the leader of a community thus affected.

Six years after their removal, the Bakwena baMogopa returned to their ancestral lands. The story of their travails in Bophuthatswana is even more torturous than that of their removal. Suffice to say that the Appeal Court eventually ruled in their favour, and the government abandoned its obduracy once Nelson Mandela walked free.

~

On 31 October, the *Weekly Mail*'s Apartheid Barometer indicated a 'brain drain'. Almost 10 000 people had emigrated between January and August, the largest number on record for an eight-month period. The exodus included 328 engineers, 201 accountants, 195 educationists and 69 medical doctors.

# NOVEMBER

**By DIANE CASSERE**
**Environment Reporter**

"CRAYFISH for everyone!" is the message from the Minister of Environment Affairs, Mr John Wiley, at today's start of the 1986/87 rock lobster (crayfish) season.

Mr Wiley announced late yesterday afternoon that four outlets in the Western Cape will be able to sell whole crayfish at about R5 for an average-size whole crayfish "as soon as is reasonably practical".

This would be at least by the start of the December holiday season.

*Cape Times*, 1 November 1986

ON 4 NOVEMBER, in Moscow, the Soviet leader Mikhail Gorbachev met with Oliver Tambo, the president of the ANC. Gorbachev told Tambo that his government regarded the ANC as 'the spokesman for the genuine interests of the South African people'.

In a photograph of the meeting, shot in black and white, the camera looks down a long table lined with chairs. Only the four chairs closest to the camera are occupied. On the left are Gorbachev and a colleague, on the right, Tambo and a youthful Thabo Mbeki.

At one point during the meeting, Gorbachev mentioned that he had been watching news footage and was surprised to see elderly white women taking to the streets in protest against apartheid.

'Yes,' quipped Mbeki, 'we have our babushkas too.' Mbeki knew Russia well. For two years, he had studied revolutionary warfare at the Lenin Institute in Moscow, taking such courses as 'The History, Theory and Tactics of National Liberation'.

~

On 5 November, the government announced that Piet Koornhof would be South Africa's next ambassador to the United States. The appointment was a demotion for Koornhof, who had been in the cabinet for over a decade. As a long-time verligte, he was being punished by the ruling party's verkrampte faction (so went the story) for telling President Botha that the only way to achieve peace was to free Nelson Mandela.

Koornhof was a man of extraordinary contradictions. He was opposed to Mandela's imprisonment, and yet his twenty-seven years in service of the National Party coincided almost exactly with Mandela's twenty-seven years in prison. He claimed that he was opposed to apartheid per se, and yet in the late Seventies and early Eighties he was responsible for administering some of the government's most inhumane policies. In a 2007 obituary, *The Telegraph* suggested that Koornhof's contradictions were 'almost comic'.

Koornhof was born in 1925 in Leeudoringstad in the western Transvaal. He attended school in Bloemfontein. In his final year, he was head boy and his future wife Lulu was head girl. He studied theology at Stellenbosch and then won a Rhodes Scholarship to Oxford, where he spent five years working on a doctorate in social anthropology. As part of his field work, he lived for nine months in a Zulu kraal called Nkandla. He later described his time there as 'one of the happiest periods of my life'. His dissertation was titled 'The Drift from the Reserves among the South African Bantu'. It was highly critical of the migrant labour system, which had stripped Zulu society of its adult males. Koornhof argued that the government's attempts to push blacks into tribal homelands would ultimately fail. Urbanisation, he said, was inevitable.

Oxford wanted to publish the dissertation, but Koornhof declined. He felt it would count against him back in South Africa. He wasn't wrong. When he applied for a job at Rhodes University in Grahamstown, a supposedly progressive institution, there were fears that he was too liberal for the post. Instead, he worked as a researcher for Hendrik Verwoerd, who at the time was minister of Native Affairs. Koornhof quickly climbed the ladder of Afrikanerdom. By 1962, he was secretary of the Broederbond, and two years later he became a member of Parliament. In 1972, he joined John Vorster's cabinet as minister of energy.

In 1978, Koornhof was appointed minister of Native Affairs – except the department's name had changed twice since Verwoerd's tenure, first to Bantu Administration and then to Plural Relations and Development. Koornhof changed it again, this time to Cooperation and Development. The new name wasn't so much euphemistic as Orwellian. There was very little 'cooperation' involved in the bulldozing of shanties or the forced removal of 'black spots'. Helen Suzman remarked that Koornhof may have written a dissertation criticising the migrant labour system, yet as minister he carried out 'the opposite policy'. He played a leading role in the drafting of both the Tricameral Parliament and the 'Koornhof Bills' (which ushered in the Black Local Authorities). As we have seen, it was resistance to this new legislation that sparked the urban rebellion of 1984–86.

Apartheid was not an easy policy to defend. Its functionaries were prone to outlandish statements – and none more so than Piet Koornhof. In 1979, with P W Botha's reign still in its infancy, Koornhof announced that apartheid was dead. In 1984, when asked why television crews were no longer permitted to visit black areas, he replied: 'In the discretion of the relevant authorities it was deemed necessary in the interests of all concerned in view of prevailing circumstances.'

Utterances such as these make it clear why Koornhof was satirist Pieter-Dirk Uys's favourite character. His appearance added to the appeal. Koornhof was 'blessed', says Uys, 'with a face wonderfully made for lampoon: big ears, a long mournful nose set between twinkling eyes, and a constantly amused mouth'. Uys would slip on a latex mask 'with two hugely prominent ears and a nose to match' and adopt a nasal patter:

Thank you very much, thank you very much. I'm very glad you asked that question. Now – on behalf of my Department of Cooperation and Development – thank you very much, thank you very much – I'm glad you asked that question – I'll come to that question in a minute – on behalf of my Department of Cooperation and Development, we have always said most categorically and I repeat that again with conviction, we have said it: if they don't have bread, give them cake.

'Koornhof' would then whip out a *Kyk* magazine and open it over his head, demonstrating that it could be used to construct a shelter. 'But that's not all,' he continued, 'the inks is nutritious and delicious.' Malnourished babies could suck on the pages, he said.

Uys tells of an unnerving experience in the theatre one evening. When the curtain rose, he saw Koornhof and a fellow minister seated in the front row. The moment Uys lifted the big pink nose from the prop box, Koornhof's companion nudged him and said: 'Hei, Piet, hier kom jy nou!' ('Here you come!')

In 1993, two years after his retirement from public life, Koornhof shocked his former colleagues by leaving his wife Lulu and moving in with Marcelle Adams, a coloured woman forty-four years his junior. They had twin boys together. 'My relationship with Marcelle,' said Koornhof, 'is really the answer to apartheid, an answer by deed. I can honestly say I have risen above colour.' In 1997, Koornhof appeared before the TRC. He was one of very few National Party ministers to acknowledge the atrocities committed under his watch. In 2001, Koornhof joined the ANC. Four years later, Adams left him for a German aerobatics pilot. He returned to Lulu and spent the final two years of his life with her.

Koornhof left a conflicted legacy. His supporters saw his adaptability as a virtue, while critics said it pointed to opportunism and a lack of principle. Steve Biko once said of him: '[I]t seems there is quite a nice guy there trying to get out.' This accords with Pieter-Dirk Uys's assessment: 'One wonders whether his appointment over black affairs was a lesser evil than if any other minister had used it as his fiefdom. At least Piet Koornhof has a sense of humour.'

~

On 6 November, in the Rand Supreme Court in Johannesburg, Marion Sparg was sentenced to an effective twenty-five years in prison. Earlier in the week, Judge Pieter van der Walt had convicted her of treason and arson for petrol-bombing properties used by the Progressive Federal Party in 1981, and for placing limpet mines in three police stations in 1986. Sparg had pleaded guilty to all charges – only she had acted out of patriotism, she said, not treason. Throughout the proceedings, she wore the colours of the ANC – a black suit, a green shirt and a yellow ribbon.

In his judgment, Van der Walt described her as 'a dedicated Marxist and revolutionary' who had allowed herself to be 'misguided by persons like Joe Slovo'. He attributed her actions to obesity, quoting a defence witness who had testified that Sparg's weight had negatively influenced her ability to relate socially. The fact that she was white, said the judge, was an aggravating factor.

Van der Walt's judgment inspired activist Annemarie Hendrikz to write a poem:

How do you plead?

Guilty your Honour
Guilty
Guilty
Guilty and proud

20 years for you

Not for treason
Not for arson

Not for courage
Nor commitment

20 years for aggravating factors
Woman
White
Misguided
by Joe Slovo
A history
of obesity
inability
to relate socially
Very aggravating indeed

Viva woman
Beautiful, brave, fat, white, woman
Viva

Sparg had studied journalism at Rhodes University. A classmate, Janice Warman, remembers her as 'one of the quietest girls in the class'. She was 'tall, awkward, reserved' and 'seemed the least likely to become a freedom fighter … I had her down as a bluestocking, possibly bound for an academic career'. Warman notes that many of their cohort were planning to leave the country, 'neither happy to stay and enjoy a lifestyle based on the disenfranchisement of others, nor brave enough to stand up and fight'.

Sparg told Warman that her politicisation began with Steve Biko's death in 1977. 'It was not just the circumstances of his death that were shocking, but the reaction on Rhodes campus that really shocked me – the complete lack of concern from most students and the outright glee from many others. To most of them Steve was just "another terr" and his death was something to celebrate.'

While working at the *Sunday Times*, Sparg and two other journalists formed a unit called the 'South African Liberation Support Cadre'. In 1981, outraged at the PFP's failure to boycott Republic Day celebrations, they petrol-bombed three of the party's premises in Johannesburg. They then slipped out of the country. Sparg hitch-hiked to Gaborone to make contact with the ANC. She joined the organisation and remained in exile for the next five years. She completed six months of military training in the Angolan camps Caxito and Pango. At times, she was the only woman in camp. 'So unusual a sight was a white woman,' reports Warman, that when Slovo visited and saw her from a distance, he presumed she was a Soviet commander. Told she was South African, he summoned her to his office and took her under his wing. Speaking of her time in camp, Sparg says: 'I can honestly say that I have never felt more at home, more safe, than I did then. The most wonderful thing that happened – and I only realised this much later – was that I literally forgot that I was white. I know that will never happen in my life again.'

After her military training, Sparg worked in the ANC's Department of Communication for two years before joining MK's Special Operations division. Early in 1986, she and another operative entered South Africa from Lesotho. Hidden in the door panels of their car were eight limpet mines. In February, Sparg placed two of them in the toilet of a police station in East London. There were no fatalities. In March, she walked into John Vorster Square Police Station in Johannesburg. A black policeman stepped forward to search her. 'You can't search a white woman,' snapped his white colleague. Sparg placed a limpet mine on the stairwell between the second and third floors. The mine blew a five-metre hole in a wall and shattered windows on several floors. Four people were injured.

Three days later, the police raided Sparg's flat. She asked whether they had come about 'the Hillbrow bomb'. An alarmed policeman said no, and asked her where she'd placed it. In the toilets at Hillbrow Police Station, she replied. The police detonated the mine in a controlled explosion. A search of Sparg's flat uncovered three more limpet mines, as well as an unposted letter to her mother:

> I value the past four or five years more than you could know. The people I have met, the experiences I have gone through, I believe have made me a more complete person. My life has meaning now. I know where I am going and I know we will reach there – even if I don't personally make it. I have never been more fulfilled.

Sparg was released from prison in 1991. In the democratic era, she served the government in various capacities, including Chief Executive Officer of the National Prosecuting Authority.

~

On 14 November, the *Weekly Mail* reported that the ANC had a half-share in a Scandinavian racehorse. A Swedish 'computer expert' had donated the share after watching television footage of children suffering under the state of emergency. Half the horse's winnings were forwarded to Solomon Mahlangu Freedom College, the liberation movement's school in Tanzania.

The ANC's chief representative in Sweden, Lindiwe Mabuza, told the *Weekly Mail* that she had visited the track to watch the horse. 'I don't like gambling or racing, but I had to tell myself that this was a political act.'

'I never thought I could get so excited,' she added.

~

On 22 November, in the Sandton Clinic in Johannesburg, Oscar Pistorius was born with a rare disorder known as fibular hemimelia. Eleven months later, each of his legs was amputated below the knee. Pistorius overcame his disability, becoming a Paralympic sprinting legend known as Blade Runner. In 2012, he competed as an able-bodied athlete in the London Olympics. The following year, he shot and killed his girlfriend, Reeva Steenkamp, through a bathroom door. At his trial, the prosecution painted a picture of toxic masculinity. The defence played on fears of the black intruder in the home. Either way, the story of Pistorius's demise is acutely South African.

~

On 25 November, a columnist for the *Sowetan* wrote that he had been 'rummaging through some prized relics'. In among English primers and school setworks, he had discovered a twenty-year-old copy of the *Rand Daily Mail*. It was a December edition, providing a wrap of the year. The top newsmakers in 1966 had been Dimitri Tsafendas, who assassinated Prime Minister Hendrik Verwoerd, and Bram Fischer, who, after nine months on the run, received a life sentence for conspiracy to overthrow the government.

Leaping forward twenty years (instead of twenty years back), the top newsmaker was Jacob Zuma. In 2006, he was acquitted of rape charges, and saw the dismissal of corruption charges relating to the arms deal.

~

On 30 November, the *Sunday Times* reported that three Johannesburg bus routes would be 'open to passengers of all races from tomorrow'. Buses 1 (Parktown North), 78 (Craighall) and 79 (Parkhurst) would be desegregated for six months. The 'experiment' was economic rather than political, said an official for the city council. Buses carrying white workers into town in the mornings were returning to the suburbs empty, he explained, while many black workers who caught Putco buses into the city centre needed further transport to their places of work in the suburbs. 'Blacks who want to travel on white buses will have to pay the higher fares while whites will pay less if they travel on black buses.'

A week later, the *Sunday Times* followed up on the story. 'Apartheid began to crumble on Johannesburg buses this week,' reported Gwen Gill and Samkelo Kumalo, 'and nobody, neither black nor white, turned a hair.' A passenger on a white Craighall bus told the reporters that blacks had been using the service for some time: 'Our usual bus driver, a coloured man, lets anyone on.' The driver of a black Parkhurst bus handed the reporters their tickets 'seemingly without noticing the colour of our skin'. When questioned, the driver said, 'Whites, particularly young ones, have been coming on my bus for ages, without any problems.'

Gill commented that opening routes to 'the liberal north' was a case of preaching to the converted: 'The real crunch will come when open buses start on routes to the rather more conservative east, west and south of Johannesburg.' Kumalo worried that white passengers would be put off by the preaching and hymn-singing on black buses, as the daily commute often turned into 'a mobile church service'.

The open-bus experiment wasn't without its administrative challenges. 'Blacks can only ride on a white bus with a blue board on the front,' reported the *Sunday Times*. 'Whites can only get on a black bus with a yellow indicator board.' The 'blue' buses only stopped at white stops (a white sign with black lettering), while 'yellow' buses only stopped at black stops (a black sign with white lettering).

# DECEMBER

# On TV this week

## MONDAY
- Graffiti (TV1, 6.15): A-Ha special.
- Knight Rider (TV1, 7.05)
- You Again? (TV4, 9.03)
- Collage (TV1, 10.15)
- Starsky And Hutch (TV4, 10.22)

## TUESDAY
- Rieksie Rautenbach: Baasspeurder (TV1, 5.20)
- The Jackson Five (TV2, 5.34)
- Spenser For Hire (TV4, 6.03)
- Falcon Crest (TV1, 9pm)
- The War (TV4, 9.03)
- Laurika in België (TV1, 11pm)

## WEDNESDAY
- The Cosby Show (TV1, 5pm): repeat of first season.
- Who's The Boss? (TV1, 7.05)
- Kane And Abel (TV4, 9.03)
- Derrick (TV4, 9.55): repeat
- Night Court (TV4, 10.59)

## THURSDAY
- Cagney And Lacey (TV4, 6.03)
- Ingxubevange (TV2, 7.58)
- Shaka Zulu (TV1, 9pm)
- Kane And Abel (TV4, 9.03)

- St Elsewhere (TV1, 10.30)
- Spellbound: Behind The Scenes (TV4, 11.09)

## FRIDAY
- Solid Gold (TV4, 6.03)
- MacGyver (TV1, 7pm)
- Ziyaduma (TV2, 8.31)
- The Cat And The Canary (TV4, 9.03)
- McClain's Law (TV4, 10.45)
- M*A*S*H (TV4, 11.55)

## SATURDAY
- Happy Endings (TV4, 5.02)
- The Cosby Show (TV4, 6.30): new season.
- Fox 'en Vennote (TV1, 7pm)
- Shaka Zulu (TV2, 7.40)
- Hunter (TV1, 8.35)
- Moonlighting (TV4, 9.03)
- The Day Of The Dolphin (TV1, 9.35)

## SUNDAY
- For Love And Honour (TV1, 4.30)
- Kate And Allie (TV4, 9.03)
- Rich Man, Poor Man (TV4, 9.28)
- Web Of Persuasion (TV1, 9.30)

*The Argus*, 1 December 1986

ON 2 DECEMBER, Dr Oscar Dhlomo, the Inkatha representative at the KwaNatal Indaba, reacted angrily to criticism of the Indaba by Brendon Barry, the president of the National Union of South African Students. Barry had labelled the Indaba 'elitist and undemocratic'.

'We are sick and tired,' said Dhlomo, 'of the arrogance of white pseudo-liberals like Mr Barry who claim to be speaking on behalf of blacks during the day, but disappear into their elitist white suburbs at night.' During his university days, said Dhlomo, he had known a number of Nusas leaders, all of them white. 'When they completed their studies they either became capitalist fat cats or police informers.'

The Indaba was an initiative by centrist organisations to introduce a multi-racial legislature to KwaZulu and Natal. It fizzled out in December 1986, by which time it had become clear, after eight months of trying, that neither the government nor the UDF/ANC would have anything to do with it.

~

On 5 December, at Mpophomeni in the Natal Midlands, Inkatha members abducted and killed three shop stewards from Mawu, the Metal and Allied Workers' Union. A fourth managed to escape. The attack was related to a long-running strike at the British Tyre and Rubber Sarmcol factory outside Howick. Mawu supported the strike, while Inkatha and local chiefs opposed it. A further five people died the following day.

Micca Sibiya told the TRC that he had been travelling in a car together with his brother Phenias, Simon Ngubane and Florence Mnikathi. All four were prominent Mawu members. A group of armed men forced them to stop, ordered them from the vehicle, and took them to a local community hall. 'We were put in a room, although the woman was put in another room, and they kicked and hit us while asking us why we were not members of Inkatha. They continually asked us about Sarmcol and the strike.'

The four were then bundled into another car and driven in the direction of Lions River. When the car came to a stop, Sibiya made a run for it. He was hit by a bullet, but he kept going. He hid in the river and managed to get away. He told the TRC he didn't know what had happened to his brother or his comrades. TRC commissioner Ilan Lax informed him that they had been stabbed and then shot, and their car set alight. Nine people were found responsible, including Vela Mchunu, one of two hundred Inkatha recruits who'd been trained by the SADF in the Caprivi.

A month after the Mpophomeni incident, a group of Caprivi trainees killed thirteen civilians in KwaMakhuta on the Natal South Coast. A decade later, General Magnus Malan, formerly the minister of defence, along with other senior figures, including Mangosuthu Buthelezi's personal assistant MV Khumalo, stood trial for the KwaMakhutha massacre. In a heavily criticised judgment, the court found that the incident could not be linked to the SADF. The Caprivi trainees had indeed done the shooting, ruled the court, but they had been bored and had been indulging in 'private frolics'.

In 1995, the *Mail & Guardian* reported that these two incidents, Mpophomeni and KwaMakhutha, had been 'pivotal in transforming the Natal Midlands into South Africa's killing fields'. In addition, they represented 'the beginning of "third force" operations in South Africa'. Anthea Jeffery, in her book

*The Natal Story: Sixteen Years of Conflict*, reports that from 1980 to 1984 fewer than ten people per year were killed in political violence in KwaZulu and Natal. In 1985 and 1986, this figure rose to around a hundred as a result of the township rebellion. But then, just as the unrest was beginning to subside in the rest of the country, it erupted in KwaZulu and Natal. Starting in 1987, the number of political killings per year were: 451, 912, 1279, 1811, 1684, and so on. By 1994, over 10000 people had died.

This sharp escalation in political deaths coincides precisely with the return of the Caprivi trainees from South West Africa. In 1987, the first batch of trainees was incorporated into the KwaZulu Police. Many of them were assigned to protection units. Those who couldn't be placed, primarily due to financial constraints, continued to have their salaries paid by the SADF. In January 1988, 130 Caprivi trainees joined 170 other Inkatha recruits for six weeks of 'kitskonstabel' training at an SAP base near Cape Town. Part of this training entailed watching footage of Inkatha supporters (predominantly women and children) who had been killed in UDF raids. On completion of their training, the Inkatha kitskonstabels were deployed to those parts of KwaZulu and Natal where the comrades were in the ascendancy, particularly around Pietermaritzburg and in Mpumalanga township near Durban.

The political commissar of the Caprivi trainees, Daluxolo Wordsworth Luthuli,* later testified before the TRC:

---

* Luthuli has an unusual biography. Related to Nobel laureate and ANC leader Albert Luthuli, he went into exile at age fifteen, joined MK, and trained at the Odessa Military Academy in Ukraine. He was arrested in Botswana and spent ten years on Robben Island. On his release, he infiltrated Inkatha as a spy for the ANC, but defected, becoming a Caprivi commander. In the early 1990s, regretting his role in fanning black-on-black violence, he rejoined the ANC. After 1994, he served as a senior officer in the SADF.

During the day the Caprivians worked as police, go out of the police station, do their raids. However, in the evening they have to take off their uniform and get involved in the struggle. When I refer to 'struggle' I mean it's getting themselves to do what they were trained to do in Caprivi. ... During this period, there were literally hundreds of incidents where attacks were launched against UDF people, property or homes. It is impossible for me to record the extent of these attacks. The comrades responded by attacking us with equal vigour. A state of war existed between us.

The TRC reports that during the first year of their deployment in Pietermaritzburg 137 Inkatha kitskonstabels had their services terminated owing to 'acts of extreme criminal brutality'. Many of those who were dismissed either joined vigilante groups or were recruited into hit squads within the KwaZulu Police. They were involved in a number of high-profile incidents, including the Trust Feeds massacre of December 1988, in which eleven people attending an all-night vigil were killed, and the 1990 Seven Day War near Pietermaritzburg, in which almost a hundred people died.

In 1994, a Transitional Executive Council task group was mandated to look into the matter of hit squads within the KwaZulu Police. It found that hit-squad activity was 'rife', with much of it 'specifically associated with persons who underwent training in the Caprivi Strip in 1986' and thereafter joined the KZP. Furthermore, the training in the Caprivi had 'little to do with the stated purpose of VIP protection, but had in fact equipped the trainees with a deadly repertoire of skills in offensive military techniques and guerrilla warfare'.

The hidden hand of the Caprivi trainees was not confined to KwaZulu and Natal. When fighting broke out on the East Rand, pitting Inkatha hostel-dwellers against ANC 'self-defence units', many of the trainees were bussed to Johannesburg. They almost certainly played a role in the Sebokeng massacre of July 1990 (twenty-seven dead), the Boipatong massacre of June 1992 (forty-five dead), and the train violence on the Johannesburg–Soweto line (over five hundred dead) – to say nothing of the hundreds of smaller incidents that failed to make the news.

~

On 8 December, the French newspaper *Le Figaro* published an interview with PW Botha. South Africa had been 'badly repaid for her loyalty', the president said. '[T]he West has expelled her from the family circle while befriending the most dictatorial regimes on Earth.'

~

On 15 December, at ten o'clock at night, ANC member Ebrahim Ebrahim was abducted from a house in Mbabane, Swaziland. Two men dressed in overalls knocked at the door, asking for tools to fix their vehicle. When Ebrahim obliged, they pulled guns on him, bundled him into his car, and smuggled him into South Africa.

Ebrahim's abduction was part of a round-up of activists prior to 16 December, the twenty-fifth anniversary of Umkhonto we Sizwe, and thus also of the armed struggle. Three days earlier, in a televised speech, President Botha had warned that the ANC had 'plans to incite revolution' on the sixteenth 'by way of extensive acts of sabotage'.

Ebrahim had known he was in danger. Ever since Glory Sedibe's abduction by Eugene de Kock and his men in August, there had been a spate of cross-border raids and assassinations. Shortly before his own abduction, Ebrahim had urged the head of the anti-apartheid movement in Holland to spread the word that Sedibe was now working for the state. 'A lot of the comrades have already had to leave [Swaziland],' he wrote, 'and I'm holding the fort with a few others. We can't give up this post, but we won't last long if things go on like this.'

Born in 1937, Ebrahim had joined the Natal Indian Congress at an early age. As a fifteen-year-old, he helped with the preparations for the Defiance Campaign. He joined MK the year it was formed. In 1962, he was part of a sabotage squad that upended an electricity pylon in Montclair, Durban. The following day, in his capacity as a journalist for the *New Age*, he photographed his own handiwork. In 1964, Ebrahim was charged with three counts of sabotage, found guilty, and sentenced to fifteen years on Robben Island. For ten of those years, he shared a communal cell with Jacob Zuma. 'I was one of those who taught Zuma to read,' he later said in an interview. 'He had had no formal education. But I have to say that he was exceptional. I'm not kidding. He began by being illiterate and six months later was reading Tolstoy.'* Ebrahim completed his fifteen-year sentence in 1979. On attaining his freedom, he skipped the country and worked for the ANC as a senior organiser in Angola, Mozambique and Swaziland.

Following his abduction in 1986, Ebrahim was taken to the notorious John Vorster Square in Johannesburg. He was subjected to psychological torture as detailed in the CIA's 'KUBARK' manuals. He was held in a sealed cell, where he had to endure a piercing noise for twenty-four hours a day, with the light permanently on. 'I was completely cut off for days on end and never allowed to sleep. I have to tell you that I almost went mad, I really did.' Unusually for political prisoners, Ebrahim was not subjected to physical brutality. Jacob Dlamini, in his book *Askari*, suggests

---

* Ebrahim's account of Zuma's reading habits calls to mind what sixteenth-century scholar Richard Mulcaster once said about stories filtering back from a far-off war: 'I dare not saie lies, but verie incredible newes.'

that this was likely because of an observation in one of the CIA manuals: 'Persons of considerable moral or intellectual stature often find in pain inflicted by others confirmation of the belief that they are in the hands of inferiors, and their resolve not to submit is strengthened.'

Ebrahim's interrogators gave him the option of swopping sides, but he refused. He was eventually transferred to Pretoria Central Prison. 'I was detained for six months in terms of section 29, the "Terrorism Act", which I was glad about, because at least I was detained in terms of something. There was a record of me. A lot of my comrades who were abducted or detained simply disappeared.' Ebrahim discovered by shouting out of his cell window that members of Qibla, a Muslim organisation affiliated to the Pan African Congress, were detained on the floor below. Achmat Cassiem, a comrade from his years on Robben Island, was among them. Ebrahim made a length of string from a plastic bag, and Cassiem passed up pen and paper. Ebrahim wrote a note to his lawyer, Priscilla Jana, and passed it back down. Cassiem handed the note to Jana. In it, Ebrahim described his mental state. 'I do not think I shall be able to mentally survive this torture, and what is still to come. I can feel my spirit breaking. Do something!'

Ebrahim was charged with treason in 1987. He stood trial alongside Simon Dladla and Acton Maseko, both of whom had been involved in the ANC's rural landmine campaign. The state alleged that Ebrahim, as a leading MK organiser, had helped co-ordinate the campaign. All three faced the death penalty.

In June 1986, Dladla and Maseko had planted mines in the Volksrust district. One blast injured a boy driving himself to school in a bakkie, and another a farmworker driving a tractor. Dladla and Maseko retreated to Swaziland, but returned to South Africa a few weeks later. Dladla drove through the border, while Maseko and a comrade named Michael Molapo jumped the fence with a load of hand grenades, limpet mines and Kalashnikovs, as well as an RPG launcher and rockets. On their return to Swaziland,

Dladla and Maseko were arrested at a roadblock. In July, Molapo went on a killing spree on the East Rand, targeting policemen and township officials. In three separate AK-47 attacks, he killed six and injured thirteen before the police gunned him down.

At the subsequent trial, Sedibe – or Mr X1, as he was referred to throughout the proceedings – testified against his former comrades. 'They were scraping the barrel to find evidence against me,' reports Ebrahim. '[Sedibe] said I instructed him to plant landmines. Of course, that was a complete lie. I had absolutely nothing to do with landmines. I did not even know what they looked like.' Sedibe testified that Ebrahim was the head of the ANC's military structure in Swaziland. He claimed that Ebrahim and Ronnie Kasrils, the head of MK intelligence, were present at a meeting he'd attended in December 1984, and that Ebrahim had issued military orders. The defence was granted permission to obtain evidence directly from the ANC. The legal teams travelled to London, where Kasrils testified under commission that Ebrahim was not involved in military work. Kasrils produced his passport, which showed that he couldn't have been in Swaziland in December 1984.

Ebrahim was nevertheless found guilty of treason. In a statement prior to sentencing, he said, 'I wonder in future whether freedom fighters should bother to even stand trial ... the testimony of secret witnesses of despicable character, who would sell their own soul for sixpence, was preferred over the testimony of respected leaders of our people.' Ebrahim was sentenced to twenty years on Robben Island. He apparently saw the humour in the judge's comment that it had to be twenty years, since 'clearly your earlier fifteen years didn't do you much good'.

Ebrahim was released in 1991, after the Appellate Division ruled that the courts hadn't had jurisdiction, as he'd been abducted from another country.

~

On 18 December, the *Sowetan* ran a full-page article titled '1986: A year of terror'. In the first nine months of the year, there had been over six hundred terrorist attacks worldwide. A bomb in the passenger cabin of a TWA flight over Greece killed four; an attack on a bus in Punjab, India, killed fourteen; a car bomb in east Beirut killed thirty-two; a retaliatory car bomb in west Beirut killed twenty-five. Libya and Syria were responsible for a number of attacks.

The article made no mention of southern Africa.

Nor did it mention that the UN had designated 1986 International Year of Peace.

~

On 18 December, police commissioner General Johan Coetzee released the names of twenty-eight ANC members who had died at the hands of their own organisation. He had decided to release the names, said the general, in the hope that this would discourage young South Africans from being misled by 'false promises'. Youths were lured into exile by assurances of 'a better education and even university degrees', he explained, but conditions in exile were harsh. When 'these young misled freedom fighters' complained, it was treated as subversion and they were severely punished. Some paid with their lives.

The liberation movement denied Coetzee's report: 'We expect this tactic from the enemy in an attempt to discredit the ANC.' But the report was largely correct. Between 1981 and 1984, the ANC executed at least thirty-one people in its Angolan camps alone. These executions were not isolated incidents, but rather the inevitable consequence of a culture of intolerance. The movement came down hard on anyone who voiced dissent or fell foul of the leadership.

Coetzee's report was the first the world had heard of the executions. The ANC's denial was taken at face value, as the police had a reputation for disseminating unreliable information. The goings-on in ANC camps remained largely under wraps until the early 1990s, when former detainees started to speak out. Nelson Mandela, then president of the organisation, appointed the Motsuenyane Commission of Inquiry 'into certain allegations of cruelty and human-rights abuse against ANC prisoners and detainees by ANC members'. The commission's report is one of the more damning documents to emerge from the apartheid era.

In the late Sixties already, there had been disaffection in the Angolan camps, with defectors accusing their commanders of 'extravagant living' and 'ethnic favouritism'. Frustration ramped up in the late Seventies, notes the report, as 'a torrent of young men and women' joined the ANC in exile in the aftermath of the Soweto uprising and 'placed heavy demands on the organisation for military, educational and welfare needs'. Numbers exploded, and there was a shortage of fresh food and medical care in the camps, to say nothing of recreational facilities and educational materials. The situation was exacerbated by the brutal conduct of Mbokodo, as the ANC's department of security and information was known. (This Mbokodo should not be confused with the band of vigilantes in KwaNdebele, which was fighting on the opposite side of the struggle.)

The ANC's Mbokodo was responsible for security in the Angolan camps. The wave of newcomers from South Africa posed a serious risk of infiltration. So concerned was the leadership in Lusaka, it gave Mbokodo carte blanche to root out spies. The organisation soon became a law unto itself. As one commentator observes, it devolved 'from its proper role as "the eyes and ears" of the ANC into an arbitrary and violent disciplinary arm'.

In the early Eighties, a new grievance started to spread through the camps. While MK had grown rapidly in size, there had been no corresponding increase in the number of cadres being infiltrated back into South Africa. Many foot soldiers began to feel that they were wasting their time – not to mention risking their lives – fighting Unita in Angola, when the real enemy was the government back home. Disillusionment set in and the rate of desertions grew, along with the number of suicides. Those who tried to voice their concerns were either silenced by Mbokodo or brushed aside by the leadership.

Matters eventually boiled over in January 1984. Fifty or so cadres based in Cangandala expressed their frustrations by discharging their Kalashnikovs into the air. An ANC delegation came to listen to their complaints, but the moment the leaders left they started firing again. They were moved to Viana transit camp, along with other disaffected cadres. The camp commander ordered them to surrender their weapons, but most refused. If they complied, they said, Mbokodo would beat them up.

The Viana mutineers, as they became known, called for a national consultative conference to air grievances and to elect a new leadership. The current leadership, they said, was more interested in embezzling funds and dealing in stolen motor vehicles than in intensifying the armed struggle. Lusaka panicked and asked the Angolan government to send in troops. After a tense stand-off in which two people died, the mutineers surrendered. Many were dispatched to a camp called Pango, ostensibly for 'reorientation', but in fact for punishment. After a few months at Pango, they staged another mutiny, this time disarming their guards and killing six of them. An assault force stormed the camp and sixteen people died. Once the uprising had been quelled, a further seven mutineers were executed. One of them was Xola Ernest Magqwashe. His name was on the list of twenty-eight released by General Coetzee in December 1986. The *Cape Times* tracked down Magqwashe's sister Sheila, a scullery worker, for comment. It was the first she'd heard of her brother's death, two and a half years after the fact.

The ANC leadership showed little interest in the mutineers' grievances. Instead, it declared them enemy agents and treated them harshly. Thirty were arrested and sent to a prison camp called Quatro. The Motsuenyane Report observes that Quatro had 'a widespread reputation as a hell-hole where persons were sent to rot'. Previously a banana-ripening centre, it had, in 1979, been converted into five isolation cells and seven communal ones. Ventilation was poor, there were no beds, and blankets were infected with lice. The communal cells were so crowded 'that a mere turn of a sleeping position by a single prisoner would awaken the whole cell'. The food was irregular and often spoilt, malaria was rife, and medical facilities were poor. Many inmates died.

The report notes that several of these problems – particularly those relating to food and medical supplies – stemmed from the fact that Angola was in the grip of a civil war. The difficult conditions were exacerbated, however, by Mbokodo's ill-treatment of inmates. In 1990, five mutineers published an account of their experiences. They recalled that the clinic at Quatro 'was one of the most horrible places to visit. Usually manned by half-baked and very brutal personnel, a visit to the clinic usually resulted in beatings of sick people.' Inmates needed to be careful how they framed requests for medical attention. Their injuries, they were obliged to say, were the result of 'correction' by the guards. If they used a word like 'beaten', they would face further 'correction'.

The Motsuenyane Commission compiled a list of the abuses at Quatro: being flogged while naked and prone ('Beirut'); being beaten on the soles of the feet with guava-tree sticks ('guava juice'); having one's face covered with the skin of a scooped-out pawpaw and then being punched ('pawpaw'); being made to roll naked in hairy beans that caused intense itching ('napalm'); having red ants put into one's clothing; being tied to a tree and left in public view for days on end; being interrogated non-stop for forty-eight hours or more; undergoing lengthy spells of solitary confinement. 'What I've seen there,' said one former detainee, 'is frightening and incredible.'

Several commentators have pointed to similarities between the ANC's prisons and those of the South African government. Even the names were recycled. Camp 32 was nicknamed Quatro (Portuguese for 'four') after No. 4, the notorious black section of Johannesburg's Old Fort Prison. The ANC's prison in Lusaka was called Sun City after another Joburg prison (itself nicknamed for the luxury resort in Bophuthatswana). The five mutineers who spoke out in 1990 accused Mbokodo of using 'the methods of the Boers':

Quatro became worse than any prison [that] even the apartheid regime – itself considered a crime against humanity – had ever had. However bitter the above statement, however disagreeable to the fighters against the monstrous apartheid system, it is a truth that needs bold examination by our people.

One of the tragedies of Quatro is that all inmates were treated with equal brutality, no matter whether they were common criminals, deserters, spies, or loyal members under investigation. The ANC had originally envisioned Quatro as a rehabilitation centre. It recognised that very few of its prisoners were in fact enemies in the strict sense of the word. Even the self-confessed spies had generally not volunteered to work for the South African government. Many of them, observes the Motsuenyane Report, 'came from among the under-employed, under-educated youth of the ghetto' and were motivated 'by the promise of pecuniary reward or, sometimes, assistance with a pending court case'. Some were paid as little as R20 for their services. Many abandoned their sponsor the moment they crossed the border, freely admitting to the ANC that they had been paid to infiltrate. Others were anti-apartheid activists who had been coerced into collaborating as a trade-off against lengthy terms of imprisonment.

The commission could not find any reason, it said, 'which satisfactorily explains why Camp 32, the rehabilitation centre, turned into Quatro, the dumping pit'. All it could suggest was that the good work Mbokodo had done in safeguarding the organisation from spies had blinded the leadership to the manifest abuses. This assessment seems generous. More likely, the leadership was playing it safe. Benjamin Franklin took the view that it is better for a hundred guilty persons to go free than for one innocent person to suffer. It would appear that Lusaka took the opposite view.

The Motsuenyane Report presents the testimonies of nineteen complainants. These testimonies make for difficult reading. Luthando Nicholas Dyasop, for instance, left South Africa in 1980, aged twenty-two. He trained in anti-missile weaponry and was subsequently stationed at a number of Angolan camps. He took part in the Viana mutiny and was detained in Quatro for four years. Dyasop had joined the mutiny, he said, because he felt that 'democratic practice was in jeopardy within MK, and that the rank and file could not freely state their views about the leadership without risking sanction'. His time in Quatro did nothing to disabuse him of his views. On arrival, he was badly beaten by the warders and then locked in isolation for two months. On his release, he was beaten almost daily for his entire first year in camp. As a result, he had difficulty walking and became prone to epileptic seizures. Along with other mutineers in camp, Dyasop was assigned the hardest and most hazardous tasks. One of their jobs was hauling a thousand-litre water tank from the river up steep, rough terrain (there was no running water in camp). In addition to his other ailments, Dyasop had been weakened by malaria. He regularly fell behind, which resulted in further beatings. After one such beating, he lost consciousness for several hours. He was sent to the clinic, where a medical officer named Stalin subjected him to further beating.

The commission asked Dyasop whether he had suffered any losses during his four years of confinement. He replied that he had possessed little of value during his time in MK, but he did ask that consideration be given to 'the pain and suffering' he'd endured. The commission found that a number of individuals had violated Dyasop's rights:

1. Dan Mashigo: excessive force (Quatro)
2. Kingsley: excessive force (Quatro)
3. Dexter Mbona: excessive force (Quatro)
4. Fortunate: excessive force (Quatro)
5. Donald: excessive force (Quatro)
6. Stalin: excessive force (Quatro)
7. Mayibuye: excessive force (Quatro)
8. Johnson: as Camp Commander failed to stop use of excessive force by his subordinates (Quatro).

In addition to the nineteen complainants, the commission heard from eleven defendants, many of them former members of Mbokodo. The commission remarked on how young they had been (the first commander of Quatro was just nineteen). It summarised the testimonies of the defendants as 'the bitter voices of young men, who were thrown into the wilderness and told to guard the enemies of their people – only now to be scolded for abiding by a code of brutality that nearly all deemed to be the order of the day'. As one defendant testified:

[A]t a very young age, we had to sacrifice our lives as security officers. Whenever there was a problem that cropped up in Angola, it would always be the security of the ANC who should be in the forefront. We were not different to most of these complainants. We were all human beings, and the impression is created as if, you know, the security of the ANC was a bunch of kindergarten security officers who had no understanding, no human values.

In 1985, at its conference in Kabwe, the ANC adopted a code of conduct and duly appointed Dr Zola Skweyiya as its first officer of justice. Such was the impunity, however, with which Mbokodo was operating by then that this amounted to little more than a gesture. Skweyiya told the Motsuenyane Commission that Mbokodo threatened to imprison him and his team for 'poking our noses in matters that did not concern us' – when, in fact, the running of the camps was precisely the concern of the officer of justice: it was the reason his post had been created. The five mutineers remark that discouraging people from speaking out is a trait common to liberation movements everywhere: no matter how wrong one's leaders might be, the imperialists are always worse.

The commission heard a number of cases that centred on the stifling of dissent. When Samuel Mngqibisa complained that cadres were receiving insufficient food, he was told it was all the ANC could afford. Mngqibisa disputed this, observing that the bulk of the organisation's resources was being skimmed off by corrupt officials. A security officer told him that the way he complained was 'the way enemy agents are taught to operate within the ANC'. Mngqibisa was arrested the following day and detained for two years. In another complaint, Dumisani Khosa was attending an ANC meeting in Lusaka when the discussion turned to problems within the organisation. He 'candidly expressed his views' on nepotism and the morality of the leadership, some of whom were sexually harassing young women. Khosa was arrested and spent three years in Quatro. Cases such as these ensured that atrocities in the camps took a long time to emerge. The five mutineers contend that those who survived the prison camps 'did so knowing that to reveal what they had been through meant re-arrest, renewed tortures and, in all probability, death'.

In August 1993, the National Executive Committee of the ANC issued a six-page response to the Motsuenyane Report. The report had been 'painful' to read, said the NEC. It accepted the findings and apologised for the human-rights violations in its camps. It noted, however, that, as had been the case in countries such as Chile and El Salvador, 'violations committed by the liberation forces have comprised only a minute proportion of the number of total transgressions by illegitimate and authoritarian regimes'. The NEC called for a 'broad national truth commission'. Such an institution, it argued, would reveal the true proportions of the transgressions committed by each side.

~

On 24 December, shortly after breakfast, Gawie Marx, deputy commander of Pollsmoor, visited the cell of its best-known inmate and casually asked, 'Mandela, would you like to see the city?'

Together, they negotiated fifteen locked metal doors, climbed into Marx's car, and drove out of the prison gates. They took the coastal road, passing through Hout Bay, Llandudno, Camps Bay and Sea Point. Marx had no destination in mind, and they meandered around the city. 'It was absolutely riveting,' reports Mandela in his autobiography, 'to watch the simple activities of people out in the world: old men sitting in the sun, women doing their shopping, people walking their dogs. It is precisely those mundane activities of daily life that one misses most in prison.' It was the first time Mandela had observed civilian life in twenty-two years.

Marx parked in front of a small shop and went in to buy two cans of Coca-Cola. Mandela was left alone in an unlocked car in a quiet street. He became extremely agitated at the prospect of escape, and was greatly relieved to see Marx returning with their drinks.

In the months that followed, Mandela was taken on many excursions. It was clear that the government was preparing him for life after prison. He was allowed to choose his own destinations. Some were hours away, deep in the hinterland. He sat in cafés and walked on beaches. There was little chance of the famous prisoner being recognised, as the most recent photo of him had been taken in the early Sixties.

Mandela was struck by the 'wealth and ease' that whites enjoyed: 'Though the country was in upheaval and the townships were on the brink of open warfare, white life went on placidly and undisturbed.'

Dress shop window. Johannesburg. 1986. © Lesley Lawson

# Author's note

IN 2017, I read Rian Malan's memoir *My Traitor's Heart* for the first time. Midway through the book, Malan identifies 1986 as a watershed year in South African politics. This took me by surprise. I knew that the Eighties in general had been pivotal – it was the decade apartheid crumbled – but why didn't I know that 1986 was a year of particular significance?

I was midway through high school at the time, at a private institution in Cape Town. The school did a good job of shielding its pupils from politics. I do, however, remember a speech the headmaster, an Etonian named John Peake, delivered at prize-giving towards the end of 1985. He remarked that the school was 'rightly content' with itself for achieving much in many fields. 'Yet only a few kilometres from our gates, there is to be found a scene of nightmare, of burning, looting, murdering. A negation of education.' Peake's tendency to speak political truths didn't endear him to the school community – the staff, the parents, the old boys – and he was pushed out.

Only a handful of my memories from that time are in any way 'political'. I remember doing cadet training in the chocolate-brown fatigues of the defence force. I remember the casual racism. Anyone who did something questionable was 'a waste of white skin'. I remember playing rugby with Thobile Ndzube, who was on a scholarship and was one of the few black boys in the school. I was in the centre and he was on the wing. Often, I'd make the final pass and watch Thobile fly forty metres or more to the try line. Thobile lived in Gugulethu. On weekends, he'd have to change into civvies before catching a taxi home. Had he shown up in Gugs in blazer and boater he'd have been attacked.

In June 1986, we as a family took an overseas holiday for the first time. In London, we stayed with my father's uncle. The World Cup was on, and everyone was football crazy. I remember France versus Brazil, Joël Bats's save against Socrates. My brother and I arranged an impromptu game with the two boys living next door. Their mother brought out refreshments at half-time. The moment she heard we were South African, that was the end of that. BBC television news was a revelation. Nightly, we watched soldiers in Casspirs engage in battle with groups of children on the streets of Athlone, Nyanga, Gugulethu. As our headmaster had observed, this 'scene of nightmare' was just a few kilometres from the gates of our school. We'd never seen footage like this before. We sat in shock, our eyes fixed on the screen.

In 2017, I started to toy with the idea of an essay about Thobile and me, our different experiences of school and society in 1986, our different worlds. I met up with him at a restaurant in the N1 City Mall (Gugulethu was in flames at the time, with backyarders demanding land). Thobile liked the idea. I started to read up on the history. It was raw and elemental. Nineteen eighty-six was the year of the vigilante, the year of the necklace. Malan was right about it being a watershed: it was the last year in which civil war seemed at least as likely as a negotiated settlement. The more I immersed myself in the history, the more inappropriate it seemed to introduce my own story, or even Thobile's story, into this world of drama writ large, of heroism and endurance and sacrifice. It felt disrespectful, somehow, and thin on scruple.

History happened at a furious rate in the mid-Eighties. Stories that in a different time might have dominated the headlines for days on end had a shelf-life of just a few hours. Many of these stories aren't well documented. Some of them feature in the histories that came out in the late Eighties and early Nineties, but the details are often patchy. The problem with these histories is that they were published too close to the event horizon. Crucially, they missed out on the flood of information released by the Truth Commission. Jacob Dlamini speaks for many South African writers when he says that his book *Askari* 'owes its existence in a general sense to the TRC'.

Little in the way of general history concerning the 1980s has been published since the fall of apartheid. David Goldblatt's book *The Transported of KwaNdebele* sold poorly, he says, because it 'came out just before FW de Klerk's speech in 1990, which killed off an interest in apartheid from the publishing trade'. This tendency to shy away from a dark chapter in our history – to supersede the madness of the Eighties with the miracle of the Nineties – is understandable. Yet it is also dangerous. Any nation that loses touch with its past – with its 'real-real story' – paves the way for populists and other revisionists.

Many memoirs and local histories pertaining to the Eighties have been published in the intervening years. The written record is now vast in scope. Focusing on a single year has helped narrow the canvas. It has allowed me to investigate the lives of ordinary people, to supplement the broad sweep of history, as it were, with intimate details. I should perhaps make the obvious point that I'm not an historian and this book is not a history. Comprehensiveness was never an objective, and my account leaves out far more than it includes. Consider Solzhenitsyn: he required just one day in the life of Ivan Denisovich to capture the spirit of the Gulag.

~

Thank you to Terry and Barbara Bell, Fourie Botha, Michiel Botha, Breyten Breytenbach, Saul Burman, Aninka Claassens, Bertie Cloete, Lynda Gilfillan, Lily Goldblatt and Brenda Goldblatt, De Villiers Graaff, Fahiema Hallam, Annemarie Hendrikz, Lesley Lawson, Ismail Mahomed, Philip More, Palesa Morudu, Thobile Ndzube, Catriona Ross, Colette Stott, Hedley Twidle, Annari van der Merwe, Lindy and Francis Wilson, and Hannah Young.

Thank you also to the librarians in the reading room of the National Library of South Africa, Cape Town; the librarians in the Jagger Reading Room of the Chancellor Oppenheimer Library,

University of Cape Town; and the researchers who compiled the newspaper clippings collection for SALDRU, the South African Labour and Development Research Unit.

And thank you to those authors whose books have helped inform multiple entries in my book: Gavin Cawthra (*Brutal Force*); Jacob Dlamini (*Askari*); William Finnegan (*Dateline Soweto*); Peter Harris (*In a Different Time*); Joseph Lelyveld (*Move Your Shadow*); Ben Maclennan (*Apartheid: The Lighter Side*); Roger Omond (*The Apartheid Handbook*); Brian Pottinger (*The Imperial Presidency*); James Sanders (*Apartheid's Friends*); Thula Simpson (*Umkhonto we Sizwe*); Allister Sparks (*The Mind of South Africa*); and Patti Waldmeir (*Anatomy of a Miracle*).

# Sources

*(Abbreviated sources refer to entries in the bibliography overleaf.)*

1 January: Goldblatt 1989, pp.8, 55-9, 63, 70-2, 76; Lelyveld, pp.122-131; Finnegan, p.7; Claassens, Aninka, 'Rural Land Struggles in the Transvaal in the 1980s' in Murray & O'Regan, p.32; *Goldblatt: a documentary* (film), dir. Daniel Zimbler, 2017, A4 Arts Foundation, Cape Town; *Cape Times*, 4 & 6 January 1986

3 January: *Cape Times*, 4 January 1986

8 January: The ANC January 8th statements collected at South African History Online (http://www.sahistory.org.za/topic/anc-january-8th-statements); Cawthra, p.256

12 January: *Cape Times*, 13 January 1986; *Die Burger*, 13 January 1986

19 January: O'Meara, Dan, 'The Coup d'État in Lesotho', *Southern Africa Report*, Toronto, vol. 1, no. 5, April 1986; Cawthra, pp.141-3, 168, 175; Pauw, pp.71-2, 253; Maclennan, p.48; Macmillan, p.212; Sanders, p.205; *Illustrated*, p.482; Second Carnegie Inquiry, p.12

21 January: *Cape Times*, 22 January 1986; The Basil D'Oliveira page at South African History Online (http://www.sahistory.org.za/people/basil-lewis-dolly-doliveira); Hartman, pp.126, 144, 179; *Illustrated*, p.450; Maclennan, p.158; 'Prime Minister Hawke Called Us Traitors', *The Cricket Monthly* (ESPN Cricinfo online magazine), 12 January 2016

24 January: Dommisse, pp.284-5; De Villiers, pp.9-10; Du Preez 2003, pp.12-3, 111; Saul & Gelb, pp.219, 226-7, 253; Bell 2003, p.65; Hachten & Giffard, pp.59, 230; Sparks 1994, p.229; Butler, pp.93, 273; Adam & Moodley, pp.22, 117; Waldmeir, p.29; Cohen, p.38; Finnegan, p.108; Nixon, p.64

26 January: Crapanzano, pp.viii, 27, 45-7; *New York Times*, 14 April 1985

27 January: *Weekend Argus*, 25 January 1986; *Sowetan*, 27 January 1986; *Business Day*, 28 January 1986

31 January (1): Pottinger, pp.x, xii, 177, 352; Thompson, pp.217-8; Sparks 1994, pp.49-50; Bell 2003, pp.25, 215; Crocker, pp.307-8; Mandela, p.509; Moosage, p.25; Cawthra, p.122; Sanders, p.235; Suzman, p.157; Saul & Gelb, p.220; *Illustrated*, p.477; *Mission*, p.72;

Adam & Moodley, p.267; *House of Assembly Debates (Hansard)*, 1986, entry for 31 January; Coetzee, J M, 'Waiting for Mandela', *The New York Review of Books*, 8 May 1986

31 January (2): Jaffer, pp.10-11, 14, 18-22, 32, 37-8, 46, 61, 64, 128-133, 161; Hachten & Giffard, p.136; Hilton-Barber, pp.127-30; Warman, Janice, 'We lived on the edge for 10 years ... you could die any minute', *The Guardian*, 1 November 2009; The Zubeida Jaffer and John Issel pages at South African History Online (http://www.sahistory.org.za/people/zubeida-jaffer; http://www.sahistory.org.za/people/john-james-issel)

2 February: *Sunday Times*, 2 February 1986

7 February: Giliomee, pp.204, 213, 219-21, 228, 251, 293; LaMaitre & Savage, pp.45-7, 61, 120-2, 134, 141-2, 199; Slabbert, pp.47-8; Owen, pp.67-9; Waldmeir, pp.24, 34, 110; Du Preez 2003, pp.144-5; Hachten & Giffard, pp.97, 105, 212; Suzman, p.254; Barnard, p.146; Sanders, p.56; Mouton, F A, '"Had it too easy?" Frederik Van Zyl Slabbert's resignation as leader of the official parliamentary opposition, 7 February 1986', *Historia*, vol. 60, no. 2, November 2015; *The Guardian*, 16 May 2010; *Sunday Times*, 16 February 1986

11 February: Sanders, pp.256-69; Jeffery 1997, pp.1, 32-3, 43, 127, 691-2, 721; TRC *Final Report*, vol. 3, ch. 3, par. 31; Pauw, pp.127-8; Saul & Gelb, pp.41, 238; Macmillan, p.108; Ellis, p.222; Giliomee, p.254

13 February: Cawthra, pp.138-43, 178; Hanlon, pp.1-4; Saul & Gelb, pp.10, 220; UNSC Resolution 581 page on Wikipedia; O'Meara, op. cit. (19 January above); Sanders, p.161; Thompson, p.229

15 February: Bonner & Nieftagodien, pp.286-99; Bozzoli, pp.1-2, 66-9, 126-7; Seekings, pp.172, 175; Bell 2009, p.62; Finnegan, p.42; Owen, p.124; *Mission*, p.60; Pottinger, p.319; *Die Suid-Afrikaan*, Autumn 1986; The testimonies of Obed Bapela and Bennet Lekalakala at the TRC hearings held in Alexandra, 29 October 1996; *The Diocesan College Magazine*, vol. 70, no. 3, September 1986, pp.78-9 (which quotes from an undated article from the *Financial Mail*: 'Applying band-aid'); Unpublished pamphlet issued by Alexandra Crisis Centre, 1986; *Weekly Mail*, 21 & 28 February 1986

20 February: De Klerk 1998, pp.102-4; Sparks 1991, pp.349-51, 369-70; Sanders, pp.235-6; Bell 2003, p.254; Gevisser 2007, p.567; Butler, p.242; Slabbert, p.52; Owen, p.37; Pottinger, p.405; Krog 1988, p.267; *Cape Times*, 11 January & 21 February 1986; *The Star*, 11, 14 & 27 January 1986; *The Argus*, 20 February 1986

24 February: *The Star*, 24 February 1986

25 February: Sparks 1991, p.363; Waldmeir, p.71; Bell 2003, p.257; Terreblanche, p.7; Pauw, p.191

27 February: Maclennan, p.52

28 February (1): *Mission*, pp.12, 19-22, 65-6, 73, 101-4; Mandela, pp.512-3, 516-7; Bizos, pp.418-9; Gevisser 2007, pp.492-3, 497, 527; Waldmeir, pp.91, 94-6; Sparks 1991, p.352; Sparks 1994, pp.27-30, 33-4; Bell 2003, pp.250, 255-6; Macmillan, pp.204, 217; Sanders, p.237; Giliomee, p.295; Barnard, p.150

28 February (2): Bell 2003, pp.93, 116, 304-11; Personal communication with Terry Bell, January & August 2018; Sanders, pp.189, 215-8; McMillan, pp.71, 100-1, 170-1, 205; Gevisser 2007, pp.412, 478; Ancer, pp.126, 159, 192, 195; Assassination of Olof Palme page on Wikipedia; *TRC Final Report*, vol. 2, p.99; *The Observer*, 2 March 1986; *The New York Times*, 29 September 1996

1 March: Modisane, pp. 16, 34, 41, 58, 66, 70, 90, 189-203, 218, 250, 285; Tyson, pp.47-8; Gevisser 2014, p.101; Sampson, pp.229-31; Finnegan, p.99; *Illustrated*, p.427; Bonner & Nieftagodien, p.4; Twidle, p.154

2 March: *The Observer*, 2 March 1986; Gevisser 2007, p.500

3 March: *The Guguletu Seven* (film), dir. Lindy Wilson, 2000, Lindy Wilson Productions, Cape Town; *TRC Final Report*, vol. 2, ch. 3, par. 399-405; Nomvuyo Cynthia Ngewu's testimony before the TRC, 27 November 1996; Tikapela Johannes Mbelo's testimony before the TRC, 18 November 1997; Krog, Mpolweni & Ratele, pp.5-12, 175; Dlamini 2014, pp.52-3, 197; Edelstein, pp.143-4; Krog 1998, p.109; *The Argus*, 17 July 1986; *Cape Times*, 4 March 1986 & 29 November 1996

4 March: Dlamini 2009, pp.13, 28-31; Braithwaite, pp.15-7; *Cape Times*, 5 March 1986

7 March (1): Pottinger, pp.120, 255, 311, 323; Sparks 1991, pp.329-41; *Mission*, pp.40, 53-5, 62-4; Simpson, pp.335-7, 373; Cawthra, pp.219, 243, 247-9; *Illustrated*, pp.474-5, 480; Owen, pp.44, 47; Waldmeir, pp.45-6; Jeffery 2019, pp.74-5; Sanders, p.227; Saul & Gelb, p.212; Smuts, p.36; *Hansard*, op. cit. (31 January above), entry for 4 March; Second Carnegie Inquiry, p.160

7 March (2): Mashinini, pp.20, 21, 24, 110, 120; *Mission*, p.154

15 March: Malan, pp.139-42; *The Guguletu Seven*, op. cit. (3 March above)

17 March: Sanders, pp.238-9; Du Preez 2003, p.141

24 March: Gevisser 2007, p.537; *Sechaba*, June 1986, p.19

26 March: Harris, pp.28-30, 32-4; Second Carnegie Inquiry, pp.30-3; Sparks 1991, p.340; Johnson, p.27; Cawthra, p.127; Omond, p.104; Centre for Development and Enterprise, 'Pretoria – from apartheid's model city to an African rising star?', July 1998; BBC1 television news, 29 June 1986, 9.15 p.m.; *Weekly Mail*, 6 June 1986; *The Washington Post*, 7 & 23 June 1986

1 April: The Genius song lyrics page for 'I've Never Met a Nice South African (https://genius.com/Spitting-image-ive-never-met-a-nice-south-african-lyrics)

13 April: Myburgh, James, 'How the necklace was hung around Winnie's neck', article posted on Politicsweb, 17 April 2018 (http://www.politicsweb.co.za/opinion/how-the-necklace-was-hung-around-winnies-neck); Ball, Joanna, 'The Ritual of the Necklace', research report written for the Centre for the Study of Violence and Reconciliation, March 1994; Donaldson, Andrew, '"Mother of the nation" Madikizela-Mandela was a law unto herself', News24 website, 2 April 2018; Gumede, William, 'Winnie had to "fall" for South Africa to rise', News24 website, 11 April 2018; *TRC Final Report*, vol. 5, p.364; Moosage, pp.4, 6, 10, 34, 41, 60, 91, 145; Owen, pp.17, 26; Steyn-Barlow, pp.73-4, 78, 87; Hilton-Barber, pp.86-8, 209; Butler, pp.212-3; Edelstein, pp.163-4; Barnard, pp.145, 168; Beresford, pp.77-81; Dlamini 2014, pp.12-3; Macmillan, pp.212, 283; *Talking*, pp.24-6; Giliomee, p.316; *Illustrated*, p.480; Pauw, p.47; Sparks 1991, p.340; Bell 2003, p.182; Finnegan, p.44-5; Jeffery 2019, p.78; Sanders, p.290; Ramphele, p.163; Crawford-Browne, p.123; Ancer, p.197; *Cape Times*, 16 April 1986; *The New York Times*, 29 June 1986 & 8 March 1991; *Evening Post*, 17 October 1986; *The Guardian*, 27 January 1989; *Sowetan*, 28 September 1987; *Sunday Times*, 18 November 2018

14 April: Van Kessel, pp.87, 92, 99-105, 125-33; Ball, op. cit. (13 April above); Ritchken, Edwin, 'The Meaning of Rural Political Violence: The Meaning of the Anti-Witchcraft Attacks', paper presented at the Centre for the Study of Violence and Reconciliation, June 1989; *Leadership*, vol. 6, no. 1, 1987; Lodge & Nasson, pp.117, 121-2; Seekings, pp.181-2; Finnegan, p.205; *Illustrated*, p.480; *The Star*, 15, 16, 17 & 21 April 1986; *Business Day*, 15 & 17 April 1986;

*The Argus*, 15 April 1986; *Sowetan*, 18 April 1986; *Weekly Mail*, 18 April 1986

18 April: Simpson, p.375; SAPA, 'Instant amnesty for MK bombers', 28 April 1999 (http://www.justice.gov.za/trc/media%5C1999%-5C9904/s990428.htm); *TRC Final Report*, vol. 2, ch. 5, par. 182; The Pumzile Mayapi page at South African History Online (https://www.sahistory.org.za/people/pumzile-mayapi); *Daily Dispatch*, 11 April 2016

19 April: Carter, Angela, 'The End', *London Review of Books*, 18 September 1986; Trewhela, Paul, 'State Espionage and the ANC London Office', *Searchlight South Africa*, vol. 3, no. 4, June 1995; The Ian David Kitson page at South African History Online (https://www.sahistory.org.za/people/ian-david-kitson); Several pages on the 'Non-Stop Against Apartheid' blog (https://nonstopagainstapartheid.wordpress.com)

23 April: Uys 1987, p.86; *House of Delegates Debates (Hansard)*, 1986, entry for 23 April

24 April: *Sowetan*, 24 April 1986

26 April: Bell 2003, pp.63-5, 230-5; Du Preez 2001, p.44; Sanders, p.109; Gevisser 2007, p.515; *Mission*, p.44; *The Scotsman*, 1 May 2016; *The Glasgow Herald*, 23 April 1986

30 April: *TRC Final Report*, vol. 3, ch. 5, par. 301 (& summary for subsection 47); *The Argus*, 1 May 1986; *Cape Times*, 2 May 1986

1 May: Hill & Harris, p.65; Bonner & Nieftagodien, p.302; Saul & Gelb, p.236; Pottinger, p.233; Thompson, p.218; Green, Pippa, 'The Real Inkatha', *Southern Africa Report*, Toronto, vol. 2 no. 4, February 1987; *Cape Times*, 2 May 1986; *Mail & Guardian*, 23 October 1997

14 May: *Cape Times*, 14 May 1986

17 May: Cole, pp.1-2, 11-2, 20-3, 35-6, 43, 69, 83-9, 108, 113-22, 126-8, 131-4, 142-4; Lelyveld, pp.103-5; Haysom, pp.1-2, 7, 122; Pottinger, pp.187, 327-8, 342; Russell, pp.16-7; Saunders, pp.173-4; Moosage, p.5; Finnegan, p.137; *Illustrated*, p.47; Omond, p.126; *Talking*, p.28; Thompson, p.220; Hill & Harris, p.78; Drury, p.301; Slabbert, p.156; *Mission*, p.25; Second Carnegie Inquiry, pp.18, 110; *TRC Final Report*, vol. 1, ch. 2, par. 67 & vol. 3, ch. 5, par. 260-3; *Leadership*, vol. 5, no. 3, 1986; *Southern Africa Report*, Toronto, vol. 2 no. 1, June & vol. 2 no. 2, October 1986; *Grassroots*, vol. 7, no. 4, June 1986; *Cape Times*, 1, 3 & 4 January 1986; *Los Angeles Times*, 30 March 1986; *Sowetan*,

24 April & 26 May 1986; *The New York Times*, 11 June 1986 & 10 January 1988; *Weekly Mail*, 13 June 1986

19 May: *Mission*, pp.14, 23, 27, 39, 42-4, 79-82, 99-101, 120, 132-3, 140, 148; Sparks 1991, pp.353-4; Sparks 1994, p.26; Mandela, pp.518-9; Omond, pp.9, 166, 175; Pottinger, pp.96, 399; Bell 2003, pp.63, 259; Waldmeir, p.96; Macmillan, p.208; Giliomee, p.259; Cohen, p.6; Second Carnegie Inquiry, p.16; Pauw, p.18; Du Preez 2003, p.124; Maclennan, p.151; Magona, p.73

21 May: *Talking*, pp.21-2; *Hansard*, op. cit. (31 January above), entry for 17 April; *Weekly Mail*, 13 June 1986

22 May: Sparks 1991, pp.324-5; *Cape Times*, 23 May 1986

24 May: *Cape Times*, 24 May 1986

25 May: TRC *Final Report*, vol. 3, ch. 5, par. 288; Moosage, pp.58, 63; Seekings, pp.194-5; *Cape Times*, 27 May 1986; *The Argus*, 28 May 1986;

28 May: Cloete, pp.29, 91-9, 115-6; Personal communication with Bertie Cloete, May 2019; Unpublished voice recording made by Sacky Shanghala (in preparation for the publication of Bertie Cloete's book *Pionne*); Barnard, p.89; Cawthra, pp.192, 226; Stiff, p.36

31 May: *Sunday Times*, 1 June 1986; *Cape Times*, 2 June 1986

1 June: Waldmeir, pp.52-3, 63-4, 67-9; Sparks 1994, pp.72-5; Gevisser 2007, pp.506-8, 513; Pottinger, p.402; *The New York Times*, 16 June 1986

2 June: *Talking*, pp.iii, 1, 6, 24-7, 42; Moosage, pp.44-5; Pottinger, pp.332-3; Trabold, Bryan, '"Hiding our snickers": *Weekly Mail* Journalists' Indirect resistance in Apartheid South Africa', *College English*, Urbana, vol. 68, no. 4, March 2006, pp.382-406; Merrett, Christopher, 'In a State of Emergency: Libraries and Government Control in South Africa', *The Library Quarterly: Information, Community, Policy*, Chicago, vol. 60, no. 1, January 1990, pp.1-22; *Weekly Mail*, 6 & 13 June 1986

3 June: Finnegan, p.34

6 June: Moosage, pp.1, 61, 66; Finnegan, pp.14-6; *The Argus*, 17 July 1986; *Cape Times*, 5 May 1987; *Sowetan*, 29 May 1989

7 June: Maclennan, p.127; *Weekly Mail*, 13 June 1986

10 June: Finnegan, p.138; TRC *Final Report*, vol. 3, ch. 5, par. 264; *The New York Times*, 11 & 15 June 1986; *Weekly Mail*, 13 June 1986

11 June (1): *Hansard*, op. cit. (31 January above), entries for 2, 4 & 11 June; Finnegan, p.182

11 June (2): Pallister, Stewart & Lepper, pp.156-7; Butler, p.184; *Weekly Mail*, 6 & 13 June 1986

12 June (1): *Hansard*, op. cit. (31 January above), entry for 12 June; Finnegan, pp. 170-5, 179-80; Waldmeir, pp.69-70; Simpson, p.385; Bell 2003, pp.260, 274; De Klerk 1998, pp.120-1; Lodge & Nasson, p.91; Bozzoli, p.2; Tyson, p.264; Sparks 1991, p.358; Cohen, p.87; Cawthra, p.14, 23; Pottinger, p.316; Johnson, p.4; Foster, p.193; *Southern Africa Report*, Toronto, vol. 2 no. 2, October 1986; TRC *Final Report*, vol. 2, ch. 4, par. 280; *Weekly Mail*, 13 June 1986; *Cape Times*, 13 & 14 June 1986; *Business Day*, 16 & 20 June 1986; *Sowetan*, 18, 20 & 25 June 1986; *Sun-Sentinel*, 17 July 1986

12 June (2): Joubert, pp.342-5; Personal communication with Annari van der Merwe, June 2019; Twidle, p.222

14 June (1): Simpson, pp.377-80, 384-7; Rostron, pp.146-54, 198-202; Sanders, pp.350-1; Ancer, p.210; Edelstein, p.133; Steinberg, p.73; *Talking*, p.9; *Cape Times*, 16 June 1986; *The Citizen*, 13 February 2014; *Sunday Times*, 17 March 2019

14 June (2): Van Vuuren, pp.30, 258-69, 317

14 June (3): *The New York Times*, 15 June 1986; *The Washington Post*, 15 June 1986

15 June (1): Breytenbach, pp.17-9, 69-71; LaMaitre & Savage, pp.7-9; Personal communication with Breyten Breytenbach, November 2018; Du Preez 2003, pp.148-162; Hirson 2006, pp.77-8; Sparks 1991, p.326; *I Am Not Your Negro* (film), dir. Raoul Peck, 2016, Velvet Film, Berlin; *Business Day*, 20 June 1986

15 June (2): Pottinger, pp.344-5

16 June (1): Finnegan, pp.191-2

16 June (2): Tyson, p.314; Finnegan, p.225

20 June (1): Trabold, op. cit. (2 June above), pp.389, 396-7, 400-1; *Weekly Mail*, 20 June 1986

22 June: Finnegan, p.82

26 June: Finnegan, pp.199-201, 225; Merrett, p.127; Tyson, p.412; *Mail & Guardian*, 13 November 1987

27 June: Maclennan, pp.146-7

28 June: Bell 2009, pp.32, 39-40, 42-4, 60-1, 74, 77, 83, 87; Bonner & Nieftagodien, pp.267-8, 299, 320; Bozzoli, p.118; The biography of Moses Mayekiso at South African History Online (http://www.sahistory.org.za/people/moses-jongizizwe-mayekiso); Unpublished pamphlet issued by Alexandra Crisis Centre, 1986; *Illustrated*, p.479

29 June: BBC1 television news, 29 June 1986, 9.15 p.m.; Jeffery 1997, p.155; *Cape Times*, 30 June & 26 August 1986; *The Argus*, 26 August 1986

1 July: Pottinger, pp.168, 173-5, 190, 233; Stengel, pp.68, 182; Thompson, pp.220-1; Suzman, pp.252-3; Steinberg, p.63-4; Russell, p.322-3; Crapanzano, p.40; Wilson, p.102; *Hansard*, op. cit. (31 January above), entry for 23 April; *Mission*, p.36; *Sowetan*, 24 April & 1 July 1986; *Financial Mail*, 25 April & 8 August 1986; *Cape Times*, 1 May 1986; *The Argus*, 1 May 1986

3 July (1): Hilton-Barber, pp.72-3, 90-1, 108-10, 127, 132-4, 138, 141-3, 168, 177-8; Jaffer, p.60

3 July (2): TRC *Final Report*, vol. 3, ch. 6, par. 521; The testimony of Jameya Mnisi at the TRC hearings held in Nelspruit, 3 September 1996

10 July: Maclennan, p.127

16 July (1): Finnegan, p.110; *Los Angeles Times*, 16 July 1986; *Sun-Sentinel*, 17 July 1986

16 July (2): Crocker, p.321; *The New York Times*, 18 July 1986

24 July: *Southern Africa Report*, Toronto, vol. 2 no. 1, June 1986; *Cape Times*, 14, 15 & 25 July 1986

29 July: TRC *Final Report*, vol. 2, ch. 5, par. 336-41 & vol. 3, ch. 6, par. 470-7; *Truth Commission Special Report*, SABC, 4 December 1996; Goldblatt 1989, pp.51, 68, 70, 72-3; Finnegan, pp.3, 5; Pottinger, pp.268-9, 314; Pauw, p.237; Maclennan, p.127; Claassens, Aninka, 'Rural Land Struggles in the Transvaal in the 1980s' in Murray & O'Regan, pp.42-3; *Cape Times*, 31 July 1986; *The Mercury*, 13 August 1986; *Weekly Mail*, 12 September 1986

2 August: *Sowetan*, 4 August 1986

3 August: Pottinger, p.431

5 August: Waldmeir, pp.57, 133; Sparks 1994, p.65; Hachten & Giffard, p.234; *Illustrated*, p.483; Adam, Heribert, 'Pretoria Gets Ready', *London Review of Books*, 9 July 1987; *Weekly Mail*, 1 August 1986; *Cape Times*, 6 August 1986

6 August: *Cape Times*, 6 August 1986

12 August: De Klerk 1998, p.109; Waldmeir, pp.45, 112; Crocker, p.326; *Cape Times*, 13 August 1986; *The Washington Post*, 17 August 1986

14 August: Dlamini 2014, pp.11-3, 19-39, 41, 57, 60-75, 89-95, 126-134, 147-8, 155, 189-91, 213, 239, 260; TRC *Final Report*, vol. 2, p.129; Pauw, 73-4; Jansen, pp.187-8; Sanders, p.206; Twidle, p.80; *Cape Times*, 29 November 1996

23 August: *Women*, pp.400-2; Lodge & Nasson, p.102; Personal communication with Annemarie Hendrikz, January 2020; *Weekend Argus*, 23 August 1986

25 August: Drewett & Cloonan, pp.27-8; Baron, Terry, 'Sol's Dorp', *Frontline*, September 1983; Galbraith, David, 'States of Grace', *Southern Africa Report*, Toronto, vol. 2, no. 3, December 1986; Fricke, David, 'Paul Simon's Amazing Graceland Tour', *Rolling Stone*, 2 July 1987; Solomon, Dan, 'Steven Van Zandt Tells The Story Of "Sun City" And Fighting Apartheid In South Africa', *Fast Company*, 13 December 2013; *Under African Skies* (film), dir. Joe Berlinger, 2012, RadicalMedia, New York; *Weekly Mail*, 12 September 1986; *The Guardian*, 19 April 2012

31 August: Jeffery 1997, p.155; Saunders, p.171; *Cape Times*, 1 September 1986

1 September: Cole, p.154; Stemmet, Jan-Ad, 'Reflections on the Conduct of the South African Police (SAP) and Violent Political Conflict, ca. 1984-1989', *Journal for Contemporary History*, vol. 42, no. 2, 2017, pp.143-158; Fine, Derrick, 'Kitskonstabels: A Case Study in Black on Black Policing', *Acta Juridica*, 1989, pp.44-85

9 September: Meer, pp.3, 6, 11-2, 15-32, 37, 41-5, 51, 58-9, 94-7, 101-12, 126-8, 134-7, 144-5; 161-2; Pauw, pp.71-2; *Talking*, p.10; Cawthra, p.163; *Sowetan*, 10 September 1986; *Weekly Mail*, 12 September 1986; *Mail & Guardian*, 28 April 2018

12 September: *Weekly Mail*, 12 September 1986

13 September: Harris, pp.8-11, 21, 34-5, 60, 88-95, 103-8, 117-20,

123-9, 135-9, 144-56, 160-5, 176, 182, 206-11, 226-36, 320; Simpson, pp.371, 373, 383-4, 390; Dlamini 2014, pp.55, 79; Pauw, pp.150, 160; Macmillan, p.194; Bell 2003, p.11; Gordin, p.40; Bizos, p.442; Hill & Harris, p.26; Rousseau, Nicky, 'The Farm, the River and the Picnic Spot: Topographies of Terror', *African Studies*, vol. 68, no. 3, December 2009, p.357-9; *The New York Times*, 2 February 1989

16 September: Butler, p.146; UDF, 'Statement of support for National Union of Mineworkers on day of mourning for Kinross dead', 30 September 1986 (unpublished); Second Carnegie Inquiry, p.12; Russell, p.320; *Weekend Argus*, 1 February 1886; *Weekly Mail*, 21 February, 7 March, 19 September & 3 October 1986; *Cape Times*, 17 September 1986; *Time* (magazine), 29 September 1986

18 September: Brink & Coetzee, pp.7, 13, 23, 35, 50, 94, 154, 195, 205; Carter, op. cit. (19 April above); Anderson, p.6

25 September: Lelyveld, pp.155-68, 175, 182; Sanders, pp.265-6; Cawthra, pp.129, 235; Omond, pp.103-4; Pottinger, pp.117-8, 370; Van Vuuren, p.11; Dlamini, p.15; Porter, Bernard, 'Pariahs Can't Be Choosers,' *London Review of Books*, 24 June 2010; *TRC Final Report*, vol. 3, ch. 2, par. 338-42 & vol. 6, sec. 3, ch. 1, par. 278-80; *Evening Post*, 26, 29 & 30 September 1986; *The Natal Mercury*, 27 September 1986; *Weekend Argus*, 27 September 1986; *Cape Times*, 30 September 1986; *Daily Dispatch*, 30 September 1986; *Weekly Mail*, 3 & 24 October 1986

1 October (1): Hachten & Giffard, pp.5, 207,213, 225-8; Fourie, p.14; Finnegan, pp.26-7; Moosage, 38-9; Dlamini 2009, p.27; Omond, p.199; Bell 2003, p.157; Stengel, p.50; Second Carnegie Inquiry, p.5; *Cape Times*, 2 October 1986

1 October (2): *Weekly Mail*, 3 & 9 October 1986

2 October: Stengel, pp.164, 169; Crocker, p.317; *Illustrated*, p.483; Sanders, p.254; Myburgh, op. cit. (13 April above); *Weekend Argus*, 25 January 1986; *Cape Times*, 3 October 1986; *Mail & Guardian*, 10 July 1998

17 October: *Weekly Mail*, 17 October 1986

19 October: Sanders, pp.218-21, 439; Hanlon, pp.139-46; *TRC Final Report*, vol. 2, ch. 6, par. 1-48; *Southern Africa Report*, Toronto, vol. 2 no. 3, December 1986; Cawthra, pp.164-5; Dlamini 2014, pp.30-1; Crocker, pp.245-6; Slabbert, pp.46-7; Saul & Gelb, p.36; Pottinger, p.200; Harris, p.237; *Mission*, p.127; *Cape Times*, 21 October 1986; *Mail & Guardian*, 10 July 1998

21 October (1): *Sowetan*, 22 October 1986; *Cape Times*, 23 & 25 October 1986; *Patriot*, 7 November 1986

21 October (2): Personal communication with Aninka Claassens, February 2019; Personal communication with Philip More, March 2019; Omond, pp.114, 117-8; Hendrikz, pp.122-5; Russell, pp.318-21, 354; *Mission*, pp.49,51; Pottinger, p.198; Stengel, p.123; Claassens, Aninka, 'For whites only – land ownership in South Africa' in De Klerk 1991, pp.43-61; Claassens, Aninka, 'Rural Land Struggles in the Transvaal in the 1980s' in Murray & O'Regan, pp.27-65; Second Carnegie Inquiry, p.16; *Leadership*, vol. 6, no. 4, 1987

31 October: *Weekly Mail*, 19 September & 31 October 1986

4 November: Gevisser 2007, pp.286, 484; *Cape Times*, 5 November 1986; *The New York Times*, 6 November 1986

5 November: Maclennan, pp.39, 46, 52; Uys 1986, pp.35, 42-5; Hachten & Giffard, p.281; Hartman, p.144; Twidle, p.10; *Cape Times*, 6 November 1986; *The Washington Post*, 27 January 1991; *Mail & Guardian*, 15 November 2007; *The Telegraph*, 20 November 2007

6 November: Warman, op. cit. (31 January above); Simpson, pp. 279, 325, 370, 373; The Marion Sparg page at South African History Online (http://www.sahistory.org.za/people/marion-monica-sparg); Personal communication with Annemarie Hendrikz, January 2020; *Cape Times*, 4 & 7 November 1986; *Los Angeles Times*, 4 November 1986; *New York Times*, 6 November 1986; *Business Day*, 27 March 2015

14 November: *Weekly Mail*, 14 November 1986

22 November: Oscar Pistorius page on Wikipedia

25 November: *Sowetan*, 25 November 1986

30 November: Maclennan, pp.40-1; Giliomee, p.251; *Sunday Times*, 30 November & 7 December 1986

2 December: *Cape Times*, 1 & 3 December 1986

5 December: Jeffery 1997, pp.1, 692, 721; Sanders, pp.269-76; Green, op. cit. (1 May above); Dlamini 2014, pp.218-9; Pauw, pp.128, 318; Pottinger, p.393; TRC *Final Report*, vol. 3, ch. 3, par. 106, 124, 127, 187-8, 208, SAPA, 'Inkatha and Police Attacked Strikers, Truth Commission Told', 24 July 1996 (http://www.justice.gov.za/trc/media/1996/9607/s960724i.htm); *Mail & Guardian*, 8 December 1995

8 December: Uys 1987, p.41

15 December: Simpson, pp.385-8, 395; Dlamini 2014, pp.85-7, 89; Braam, pp.65, 76; Donaldson, Andrew, 'Glory Sedibe and the Boers', article posted on Politicsweb, 3 December 2014 (http://politicsweb. co.za/documents/glory-sedibe-and-the-boers); *Sechaba*, March 1989, p.2; *Sunday Independent*, 23 June 2007

18 December (1): *Sowetan*, 18 December 1986

18 December (2): Motsuenyane Commission Report, 1993 (included in the ANC's submission to the TRC); Stuart Commission Report, 1984 (included in the ANC's submission to the TRC); 'Mutiny in the ANC, 1984, as told by five of the mutineers', 1990, pamphlet jointly issued by Justice for Southern Africa and Solidarity with ex-Swapo Detainees, London; Simpson, pp.320-2, 329-30; Macmillan, pp.162-5, 313; Ellis, pp.187-93; *Cape Times*, 19 December 1986

24 December: Mandela, pp.520-1

Author's note: *The Diocesan College Magazine*, vol. 70, no. 1, March 1986, p.7; Personal communication with Thobile Ndzube, September 2017; Lodge & Nasson, pp.3-4; Dlamini 2014, p.16; Goldblatt 2006, p.18; Twidle, p.83

# Bibliography

Adam, Heribert & Kogila Moodley, *South Africa Without Apartheid*, 1987 (1986), Maskew Miller Longman, Cape Town

Ancer, Jonathan, *Spy: Uncovering Craig Williamson*, 2017, Jacana, Johannesburg

Anderson, Peter, *In the Country of the Heart*, 2004, Jacana, Johannesburg

Åsbrink, Elisabeth, *1947: When Now Begins*, 2018, Scribe, London

Baker, Nicholson, *Human Smoke*, 2008, Simon & Schuster, London

Barnard, Niël, *Secret Revolution*, 2015, Tafelberg, Cape Town

Bell, Terry (with Dumisa Buhle Ntsebeza), *Unfinished Business: South Africa, Apartheid and Truth*, 2003, Verso, London

Bell, Terry, *Comrade Moss*, 2009, RedWorks, Cape Town

Beresford, David, *Truth is a Strange Fruit: A Personal Journey Through the Apartheid War*, 2010, Jacana, Johannesburg

Bizos, George, *Odyssey to Freedom*, 2007, Umuzi, Cape Town

Bonner, Philip & Noor Nieftagodien, *Alexandra: A History*, 2008, Witwatersrand University Press, Johannesburg

Bozzoli, Belinda, *Theatres of Struggle and the End of Apartheid*, 2004, Witwatersrand University Press, Johannesburg

Braam, Conny, *Operation Vula*, 2004, Jacana, Johannesburg

Braithwaite, E R, *Honorary White*, 1977 (1975), New English Library, London

Breytenbach, Breyten, *Return to Paradise*, 1993, David Philip, Cape Town

Brink, André & J M Coetzee (Eds), *A Land Apart: A South African Reader*, 1986, Faber and Faber, London

Butler, Anthony, *Cyril Ramaphosa*, 2008, Jacana, Cape Town

Cawthra, Gavin, *Brutal Force: The Apartheid War Machine*, 1986, IDAF, London

Cloete, Bertie, *Pionne*, 2009, Hemel & See, Hermanus

Cohen, Robin, *Endgame in South Africa?*, 1986, James Currey, London

Cole, Josette, *Crossroads: The Politics of Reform and Repression 1976–1986*, 1987, Ravan Press, Johannesburg

Crapanzano, Vincent, *Waiting: The Whites of South Africa*, 1986 (1985), Paladin, London

Crawford-Browne, Lavinia (Ed.), *Tutu as I Know Him*, 2006, Umuzi, Cape Town

Crocker, Chester, *High Noon in Southern Africa: Making Peace in a Rough Neighbourhood*, 1993 (1992), Jonathan Ball, Johannesburg

De Klerk, FW, *The Last Trek – A New Beginning*, 1998, Macmillan, London

De Klerk, Michael (Ed.), *A Harvest of Discontent: The Land Question in South Africa*, 1991, Idasa, Cape Town

De Villiers, Les, *South Africa: A Skunk Among Nations*, 1975, International Books, London

Dlamini, Jacob, *Native Nostalgia*, 2009, Jacana, Johannesburg

Dlamini, Jacob, *Askari: A Story of Collaboration and Betrayal in the Anti-Apartheid Struggle*, 2014, Jacana, Johannesburg

Dommisse, Ebbe, *Anton Rupert*, 2005, Tafelberg, Cape Town

Drewett, Michael & Martin Cloonan (Eds), *Popular Music Censorship in Africa*, 2006, Ashgate, Farnham

Drury, Allen, *A Very Strange Society*, 1968, Michael Joseph, London

Du Preez, Max, *Louis Luyt: Unauthorised*, 2001, Zebra, Cape Town

Du Preez, Max, *Pale Native*, 2003, Zebra, Cape Town

Edelstein, Jillian, *Truth & Lies: Stories from the Truth and Reconciliation Commission in South Africa*, 2001, M&G books, Johannesburg

Ellis, Stephen, *External Mission: The ANC in Exile, 1960–1990*, 2012, Jonathan Ball, Johannesburg

Finnegan, William, *Dateline Soweto: Travels with Black South African Reporters*, 1988, Harper & Row, New York

Foster, Don, *Detention and Torture in South Africa*, 1987, David Philip, Cape Town

Fourie, Pieter (Ed.), *Media Studies: Institutions, Theories and Issues*, 2001, Juta, Cape Town

Gevisser, Mark, *Thabo Mbeki: The Dream Deferred*, 2007, Jonathan Ball, Johannesburg

Gevisser, Mark, *Lost and Found in Johannesburg*, 2014, Jonathan Ball, Johannesburg

Giliomee, Hermann, *The Last Afrikaner Leaders*, 2012, Tafelberg, Cape Town

Goldblatt, David et al., *The Transported of KwaNdebele*, 1989, Aperture, New York

Goldblatt, David, *Photographs*, 2006, Contrasto, Rome

Goldblatt, David & Nadine Gordimer, *On the Mines*, 2012 (1973), Steidl, Göttingen

Gordin, Jeremy (as told by Eugene de Kock), *A Long Night's Damage*, 1998, Contra, Johannesburg

Hachten, William & Anthony Giffard, *Total Onslaught: The South African Press Under Attack*, 1984, Macmillan, Johannesburg

Hanlon, Joseph, *Beggar Your Neighbours: Apartheid Power in Southern Africa*, 1986, Catholic Institute for International Relations, London

Harris, Peter, *In a Different Time: The Inside Story of the Delmas Four*, 2008, Umuzi, Cape Town

Hartman, Rodney, *Ali: The Life of Ali Bacher*, 2004, Viking, London

Haysom, Nicholas, *Mabangalala: The Rise of Right-Wing Vigilantes in South Africa*, 1986, Centre for Applied Legal Studies, University of the Witwatersrand, Johannesburg

Hendrikz, Annemarie, *Sheena Duncan*, 2015, Tiber Tree, Cape Town

Hill, Iris & Alex Harris (Eds), *Beyond the Barricades: Popular Resistance in South Africa in the 1980's*, 1989, Kliptown Books, London

Hilton-Barber, Bridget, *Student Comrade Prisoner Spy*, 2016, Zebra, Cape Town

Hirson, Denis, *I Remember King Kong (The Boxer)*, 2004, Jacana, Johannesburg

Hirson, Denis, *White Scars*, 2006, Jacana, Johannesburg

*Illustrated History of South Africa* (no author identified), 1988, The Reader's Digest, New York

Jaffer, Zubeida, *Our Generation*, 2003, Kwela, Cape Town

Jansen, Anemari, *Eugene de Kock: sluipmoordenaar van die staat*, 2015, Tafelberg, Cape Town

Jeffery, Anthea, *The Natal Story: Sixteen Years of Conflict*, 1997, SAIRR, Johannesburg

Jeffery, Anthea, *People's War: New Light on the Struggle for South Africa*, 2019 (2009), Jonathan Ball, Johannesburg

Johnson, Shaun, *Strange Days Indeed*, 1993, Bantam, Johannesburg

Joubert, Elsa, *Reisiger*, 2009, Tafelberg, Cape Town

Krog, Antjie, *Country of My Skull*, 1998, Random House, Johannesburg

Krog, Antjie, Nosisi Mpolweni & Kopano Ratele, *There Was This Goat: Investigating the Truth Commission Testimony of Notrose Nobomvu Konile*, 2009, University of KwaZulu-Natal Press, Pietermaritzburg

Lelyveld, Joseph, *Move Your Shadow*, 1985, Times Books, New York

LeMaitre, Alfred & Michael Savage (Eds) *Van Zyl Slabbert – The Passion for Reason*, 2010, Jonathan Ball, Johannesburg

Lewsen, Phyllis, *Voices of Protest: From Segregation to Apartheid, 1938–1948*, 1988, Ad Donker, Johannesburg

Lodge, Tom & Bill Nasson (Eds), *All, Here, and Now: Black Politics in South Africa in the 1980s*, 1991, David Philip, Cape Town

Maclennan, Ben, *Apartheid: The Lighter Side*, 1990, Chameleon, Cape Town

Macmillan, Hugh, *The Lusaka Years: The ANC in Exile in Zambia 1963–1994*, 2013, Jacana, Johannesburg

Magona, Sindiwe, *To My Children's Children*, 1990, David Philip, Cape Town

Malan, Rian, *My Traitor's Heart*, 1990, Grove, New York

Mandela, Nelson, *Long Walk to Freedom*, 1994, Macdonald Purnell, Randburg

Mashinini, Emma, *Strikes Have Followed Me All My Life*, 1989, Women's Press, London

Meer, Fatima, *The Trial of Andrew Zondo*, 1987, Skotaville, Johannesburg

Merrett, Christopher, *A Culture of Censorship: Secrecy and Intellectual Repression in South Africa*, 1994, David Philip, Cape Town

*Mission to South Africa – The Commonwealth Report: The Findings of the Commonwealth Eminent Persons Group on Southern Africa*, (no author identified), 1986, Penguin, Harmondsworth

Modisane, Bloke, *Blame Me on History*, 1986 (1963), Ad Donker, Johannesburg

Moosage, Riedwaan, 'The Impasse of Violence: Writing Necklacing into a History of Liberation Struggle in South Africa', 2010, unpublished MA thesis, University of the Western Cape

Murray, Christina & Catherine O'Regan (Eds), *No Place to Rest: Forced Removals and the Law in South Africa*, 1990, OUP, Cape Town

Ngcaba, Connie, *May I Have This Dance*, 2014, Face2Face, Cape Town

Nixon, Ron, *Selling Apartheid: South Africa's Global Propaganda War*, 2015, Jacana, Johannesburg

Nkosi, Lewis, *Home and Exile*, 1965, Longmans, London

Ntantala, Phyllis, *A Life's Mosaic*, 1993 (1992), University of California Press, Berkeley

Nunn, Cedric, *Call and Response*, 2012, Fourthwall, Johannesburg

O'Malley, Padraig, *Shades of Difference: Mac Maharaj and the Struggle for South Africa*, 2007, Viking, New York

Omond, Roger, *The Apartheid Handbook: A Guide to South Africa's Everyday Racial Policies*, 1985, Penguin, Harmondsworth

Owen, Ken, *These Times: A Decade of South African Politics*, 1992, Jonathan Ball, Johannesburg

Pallister, David, Sarah Stewart & Ian Lepper, *South Africa Inc: The Oppenheimer Empire*, 1987, Media House, Johannesburg

Pauw, Jacques, *Into the Heart of Darkness: Confessions of Apartheid's Assassins*, 1997, Jonathan Ball, Johannesburg

Pottinger, Brian, *The Imperial Presidency*, 1988, Southern Book, Johannesburg

Ramphele, Mamphela, *A Life*, 1995, David Philip, Cape Town

Rostron, Bryan, *Robert McBride: The Struggle Continues*, 2019, Tafelberg, Cape Town

Russell, Diana, *Lives of Courage: Women for a New South Africa*, 1990, Virago, London

Sampson, Anthony, *Drum: The Making of a Magazine*, 2005 (1956), Jonathan Ball, Johannesburg

Sanders, James, *Apartheid's Friends: The Rise and Fall of South Africa's Secret Service*, 2006, John Murray, London

Saul, John & Stephen Gelb, *The Crisis in South Africa*, 1986, Zed Books, London

Saunders, Stuart, *Vice-Chancellor on a Tightrope: A Personal Account of Climactic Years in South Africa*, 2000, David Philip, Cape Town

Second Carnegie Inquiry, *South Africa: The Cordoned Heart*, 1986, Second Carnegie Inquiry into Poverty and Development in Southern Africa, Cape Town

Seekings, Jeremy, *The UDF: A History of the United Democratic Front in South Africa, 1983–1991*, 2000, David Philip, Cape Town

Simpson, Thula, *Umkhonto we Sizwe*, 2016, Penguin, Cape Town

Slabbert, Frederik Van Zyl, *The Other Side of History*, 2006, Jonathan Ball, Johannesburg

Slovo, Gillian, *Every Secret Thing*, 1997, Little, Brown, London

Smuts, Dene, *Patriots and Parasites: South Africa and the Struggle to Evade History*, 2016, Quivertree, Cape Town

Sparks, Allister, *The Mind of South Africa*, 1991 (1990), Mandarin, London

Sparks, Allister, *Tomorrow Is Another Country*, 1994, Struik, Johannesburg

Steinberg, Jonny, *One Day in Bethlehem*, 2019, Jonathan Ball, Johannesburg

Stengel, Richard, *January Sun: One Day, Three Lives, A South African Town*, 1990, Simon & Schuster, New York

Steyn-Barlow, Chris, *Publish and Be Damned*, 2006, Galago, Johannesburg

Stiff, Peter, *The Silent War*, 1998, Galago, Johannesburg

Suzman, Helen, *In No Uncertain Terms*, 1993, Jonathan Ball, Johannesburg

*Talking with the ANC*, (no author identified), 1986, Bureau for Information, Pretoria

Terreblanche, Sampie, *Lost in Transformation: South Africa's Search for a New Future Since 1986*, 2012, KMM Review Publishing, Johannesburg

Thompson, Leonard, *A History of South Africa*, 2006 (2001), Jonathan Ball, Johannesburg

Twidle, Hedley, *Experiments with Truth: Narrative Non-fiction and the Coming of Democracy in South Africa*, 2019, James Currey, Woodbridge

Tyson, Harvey, *Editors Under Fire*, 1993, Random House, Johannesburg

Uys, Pieter-Dirk, *No One's Died Laughing*, 1986, Penguin, Harmondsworth

Uys, Pieter-Dirk, *PW Botha in His Own Words*, 1987, Penguin, Harmondsworth

Van Kessel, Ineke, *'Beyond Our Wildest Dreams': The United Democratic Front and the Transformation of South Africa*, 2000, University of Virginia Press, Charlottesville

Van Niekerk, Marlene, *Triomf*, 1994, Jonathan Ball, Johannesburg

Van Vuuren, Hennie, *Apartheid Guns and Money*, 2017, Jacana, Johannesburg

Waldmeir, Patti, *Anatomy of a Miracle*, 1998 (1997), Penguin, London

Wilson, Francis, *Dinosaurs, Diamonds and Democracy*, 2009, Umuzi, Cape Town

*Women Writing Africa: The Southern Region* (no author identified), 2003, The Feminist Press, New York

# Index of Select People, Places and Institutions

*(The index includes all acronyms used in the text.)*

NOTE: The African National Congress (ANC) and the South African government (also referred to as 'the state' and 'Pretoria') are mentioned too often to be usefully indexed.